BIOMIMICRY

Taking Inspiration from Nature,
from Leonardo da Vinci to the Present Day

EXHIBITION

Exhibition Curators
Pascal Brioist, Professor of Modern History at the University of Tours and member of the Centre d'études supérieures de la Renaissance (CESR)
Andrea Bernardoni, Professor of History of Science and Technology at the University of L'Aquila, and Consultant at the Galileo Museum in Florence

Advisory Committee
Pascal Brioist, Professor of Modern History at the University of Tours and member of the Centre d'études supérieures de la Renaissance (CESR)
Andrea Bernardoni, Professor of History of Science and Technology at the University of L'Aquila, and Consultant at the Galileo Museum in Florence
François Saint Bris, President of the Château du Clos Lucé – Parc Leonardo da Vinci

Château du Clos Lucé
François Saint Bris, President
Jacques de Tarragon, General Manager
Diane Junqua, Director of Communications and Sponsorship
Sandra Chupin, Exhibition Coordinator
Nina Germain, Communications Officer
Léna Desplans, intern, Exhibition and Communication
Stéphane Darras, Head of the Technical Department, and Franck Besse, technician

Exhibition Design
Agence NC, Nathalie Crinière, Jiebing Zhang and Élisa Laristan, scenographers
C Album, Thomas Mathis and Anna Radecka, graphic designers
Gelatic, Francesco Dal Molin, lighting designer

Institutions Loaning Exhibits
Amboise, château du Clos Lucé
Amsterdam, Iris Van Herpen
Aix-Marseille Université, Institut des sciences du mouvement Étienne-Jules Marey
Bry-sur-Marne, Festo
Lausanne, École polytechnique fédérale, Biorobotics Laboratory (BioRob)
Milan, Veneranda Biblioteca Ambrosiana – Pinacoteca
Milan, Polytechnic School
Montevarchi, Artes Mechanicae
Nantes, François Delaroziere
Paris, galerie Martinez D.
Paris, Jacques Rougerie
Paris, musée de l'Armée
Paris, musée de la Marine
Paris, Muséum national d'Histoire naturelle
Poitiers, private collection
Rombas, private collection
Toulouse, LAAS-CNRS, département robotique
Tours, bibliothèque municipale
Tours, Centre d'études supérieures de la Renaissance
Université de Tours, Institut de recherche sur la biologie de l'insecte

CATALOGUE

Project Management
François Saint Bris, President of the Château du Clos Lucé – Parc Leonardo da Vinci
Diane Junqua, Director of Communications and Sponsorship

Foreword
François Saint Bris

Contributors
Andrea Bernardoni
Pascal Brioist
François Delaroziere
Domenico Laurenza
Dominique Le Nen
Alexander Neuwahl
Enrica Pagella
Emmanuelle Pouydebat
Jacques Rougerie
Vinod Kumar Saranathan
Julien Serres
Philippe Souères
Thomas Steinmann

Château du Clos Lucé
François Saint Bris, President
Diane Junqua, Director of Communications and Sponsorship

With the financial support of the Centre-Val de Loire Region

Cover illustration:
Leonardo da Vinci, *Drawing of the structure of the wings*, Paris, bibliothèque de l'Institut de France, Manuscript B © GrandPalaisRmn / Agence Bulloz

BIOMIMICRY

Taking Inspiration from Nature, from Leonardo da Vinci to the Present Day

CHÂTEAU DU CLOS LUCÉ
Parc Leonardo da Vinci

SKIRA

CONTENTS

Essay Writers

François Saint Bris, President of Château du Clos-Lucé – Parc Leonardo da Vinci

Andrea Bernardoni, Professor of History of Science and Technology at the University of L'Aquila, and Consultant at the Galileo Museum in Florence

Pascal Brioist, Professor of Modern History at the University of Tours and member of the Centre d'études supérieures de la Renaissance

Emmanuelle Pouydebat, CNRS Research Director at the Museum national d'Histoire naturelle in Paris

Domenico Laurenza, Professor of the History of Science at the University of Padua

Dominique Le Nen, university lecturer and Surgeon at the Regional University Hospital in Brest

Philippe Souères, Director of Research at LAAS-CNRS, University of Toulouse

Alexander Neuwahl, architect and engineer, collaborator at the Leonardo da Vinci Museum in Vinci, expert in 3D reconstructions

Thomas Steinmann, researcher at the Institut de recherche sur la biologie de l'insecte (IRBI), University of Tours

Jacques Rougerie, French architect and oceanographer, Academician and member of the Académie des Beaux-Arts

Enrica Pagella, teacher and former Director of the Royal Museums of Turin

Julien Serres, researcher at the Institut des sciences du mouvement, CNRS-Aix-Marseille University

Vinod Kumar Saranathan, researcher at the Institut de recherche sur la biologie de l'insecte (IRBI), University of Tours

François Delaroziere, Production and Artistic Director of Compagnie La Machine, founder of Les Machines de l'Ile de Nantes

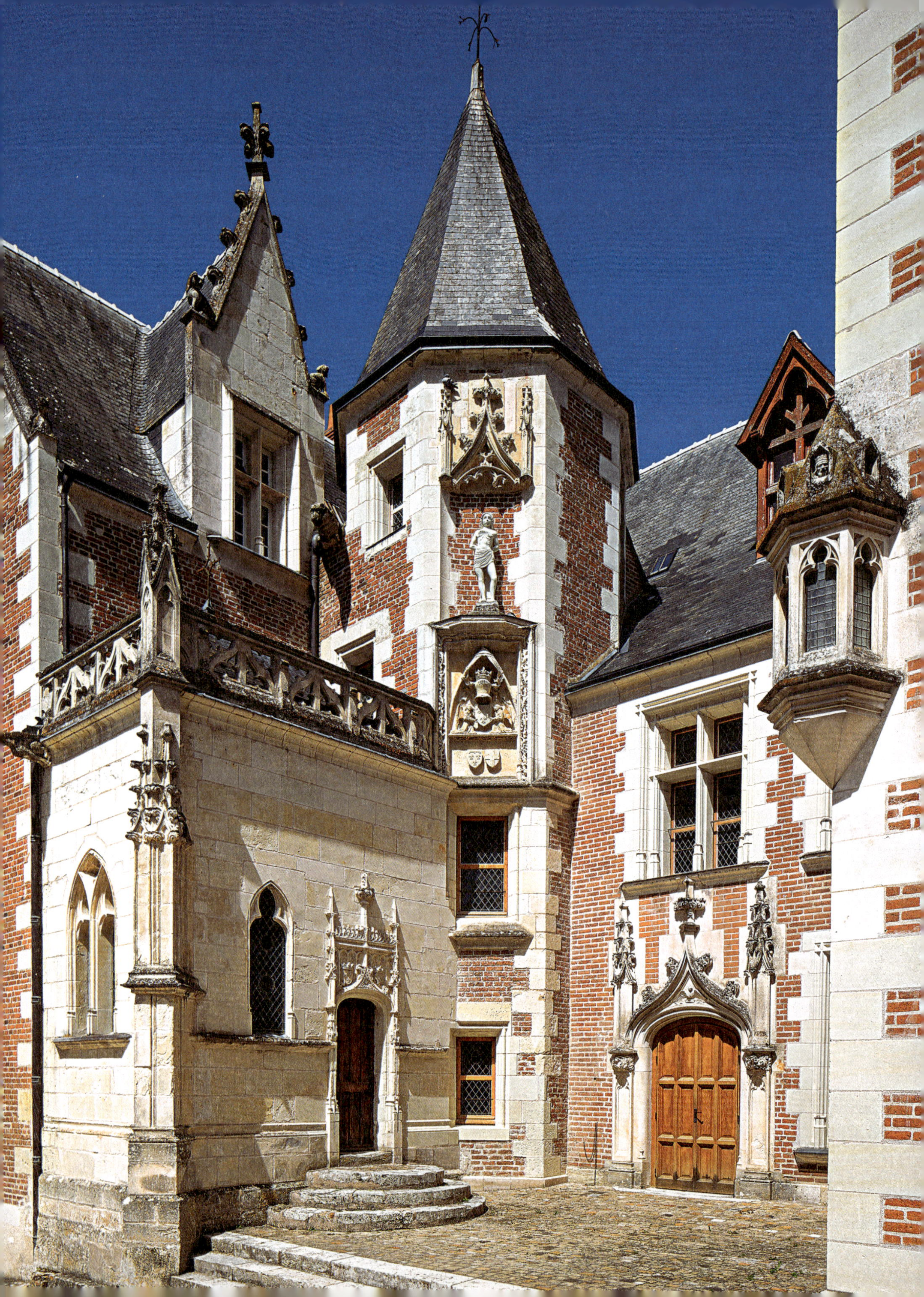

FOREWORD

François Saint Bris

The term 'biomimicry' is derived from two Greek words: 'bios' (life) and 'mimesis' (imitation), and literally means the imitation of life.

The scientific exhibition *Biomimicry: Taking Inspiration from Nature, from Leonardo da Vinci to the Present Day*, presented by the Château du Clos Lucé in Amboise from 7 June to 10 September 2025, explores Leonardo da Vinci's profound passion for observing and studying nature as an engineer, inventor and pioneer of a forward-thinking, sustainable philosophy.

The exhibition highlights the groundbreaking ideas of Leonardo da Vinci and the engineers of the Renaissance, and provides a key to understanding the challenges of biomimicry and its scientific breakthroughs in the 21st century. The exhibition shows how the Renaissance, with its innovative vision and profound connection with nature, serves as a true source of inspiration for our technological future.

Observing nature and the technical solutions it provides should enable us today to tackle the challenges of tomorrow, using the planet's resources in a way that is not based on domination and subjugation, but rather on a collaborative approach that promotes the preservation of and deep respect for nature.

This educational exhibition invites us to reflect and collectively embrace the possibility of a new relationship with nature. It challenges us to see nature not as an unlimited resource to be exploited no matter the cost to the planet, but rather as a boundless wellspring of alternative and sustainable technical solutions.

The idea of imitating nature is not new; it dates back to prehistoric times. In Antiquity, Greek philosophers such as the atomist Democritus developed the concept later defined by Plato as mimesis, the imitation of nature through technique (weaving imitating a spider's web, for instance). Aristotle, meanwhile, focused on biomechanics, the study of the mechanical properties of living organisms. He wrote the first book on the subject, *De Motu Animalium* (*On the Motion of Animals*).

Leonardo da Vinci, with his free spirit and pioneering vision of nature, spearheaded the great technological revolutions of our time. Self-taught, he lived and grew up in close contact with

LEFT
The Clos Lucé

nature. Throughout his life, he made it the subject of his study in order to imitate it as closely as possible, in the arts as well as the sciences, hoping in this way to unlock the secrets of the universe. By observing and experimenting with materials and phenomena, he discovered the laws that govern them. Leonardo said: "Nature is the source of all true knowledge. She has her own logic, her own laws, she has no effect without cause nor invention without necessity".

Through his methodical and rigorous scientific approach and interdisciplinary perspective, he applied his keen sense of observation and experimentation to each of his studies and research, while giving free rein to his imagination. Long before the term 'biomimicry' existed, Leonardo da Vinci employed analogical reasoning. For him, the principles, properties, forms, materials, processes and functions of living organisms served as models for creation, invention and innovation. He explored futuristic scientific and technical applications in fields we would now call human biomechanics and robotics, marine biomimetics, and aeronautics. The subjects he studied reflect this diversity: plants, insects, fish, crustaceans, fossils, birds and bats are just a few examples.

Of all the scientific subjects he explored, flight was his greatest passion, one he pursued with unwavering dedication for thirty-three years. His observations on "the art of flight" are among his most visionary. As a child, he dreamed of flying. Later, he wrote: "Upon the ridge of Mount Ceceri, the great bird shall take its first flight, filling all writings with its glory. Eternal praise to the nest where it was born".

As old as the hills, the dream of Icarus remained a utopia until Leonardo drew his numerous flying machines, imitating the flight of birds. "First study the anatomy of the wing, then the featherless quills, then the quills with their feathers", he instructed. In 1505, he compiled his knowledge on the subject in the *Codice sul volo degli uccelli* (*Codex on the Flight of Birds*), a work of 160 pages and 500 sketches, now held in the Royal Library in Turin [fig. 1]. There, he notes: "I have divided the treatise on birds into four books: the first deals with flight by beating wings (flapping flight); the second with flight aided by the wind (gliding flight); the third with flight in general – of bats, fish [i.e., flying fish], and insects; the fourth with artificial flight".

Leonardo da Vinci named his flying machines 'ornithopters'. Their wings were powered solely by the strength of human arms and legs. To this end, he studied aerodynamics, lift and materials. In the *Codex Atlanticus*, he sketched designs for rigid wings used for gliding and articulated wings for flapping flight, as well as all manner of other flying machines: vertical take-off aircraft, launch platforms and landing systems, an aerial screw that applied Archimedes' principle to human flight, a parachute, hygroscopes and anemometers.

These studies on flight remained largely unknown and thus could not contribute to the history of aeronautical development. His inventions related to flight were only pursued and refined five centuries later, in the late 19th and early 20th centuries. The Industrial Revolution and the discovery of new energy sources, such as steam and electricity, provided a springboard for biomimetic innovation. For instance, at the 1889 Universal Exposition, engineer Gustave Eiffel based his design of the 300-metre-high Eiffel Tower on the remarkable mechanical properties of the bone structure of a human femur.

It was not until 1950 that the American biophysicist and professor Otto Schmitt coined and theorised the term 'biomimetics'. This new discipline gained prominence in 1997, driven by American biologist Janine Benyus and her book *Biomimicry: Innovation Inspired by Nature*, which

Leonardo da Vinci, *Manuscript B.*, "Flying Wing", c. 1487-1489, parchment, 24.3 × 18.7 cm, f. 74r, Bibliothèque de l'Institut de France, Ms 2173

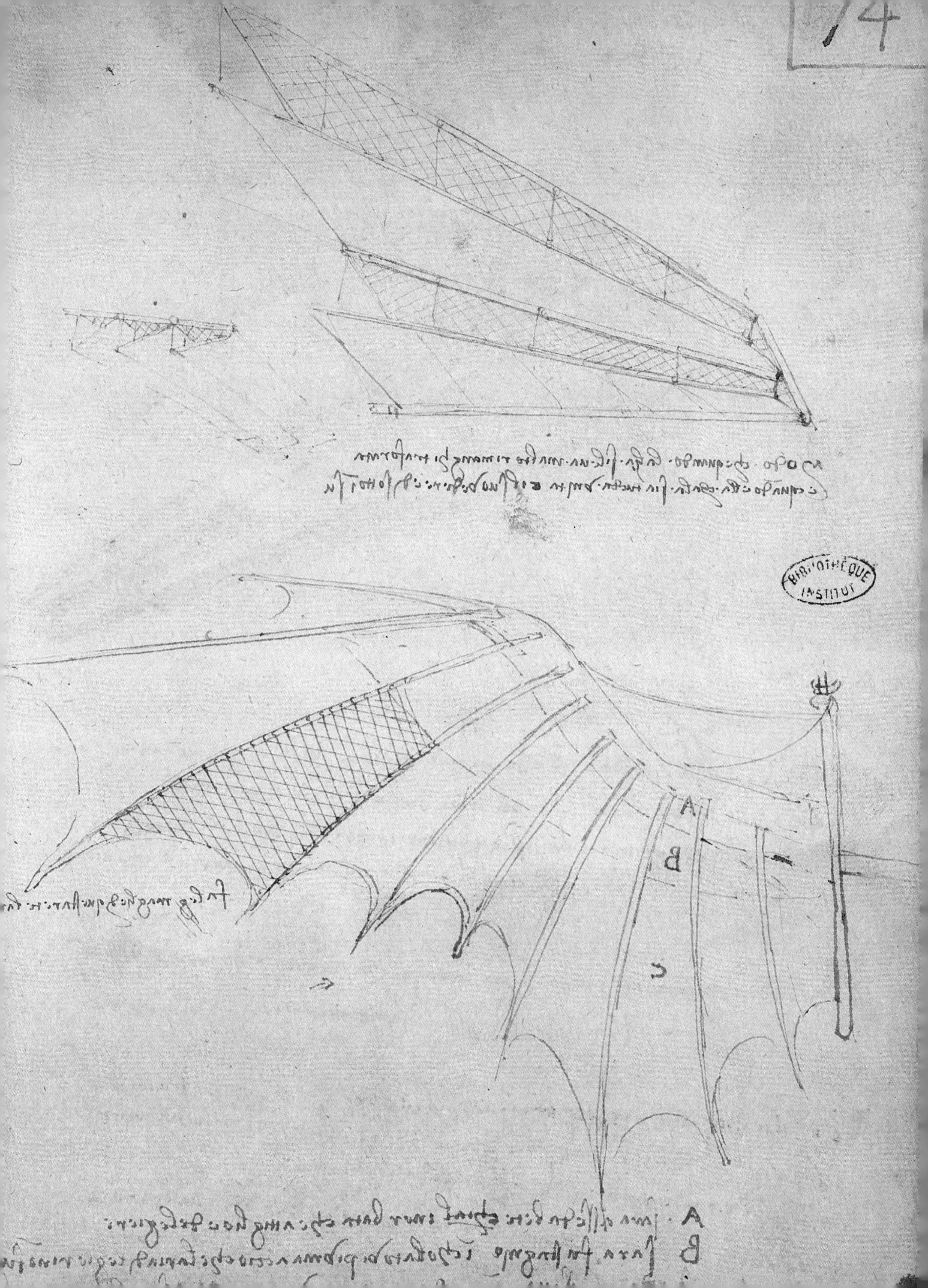
14
BIBLIOTHÈQUE INSTITUT
A
B
C
A
B

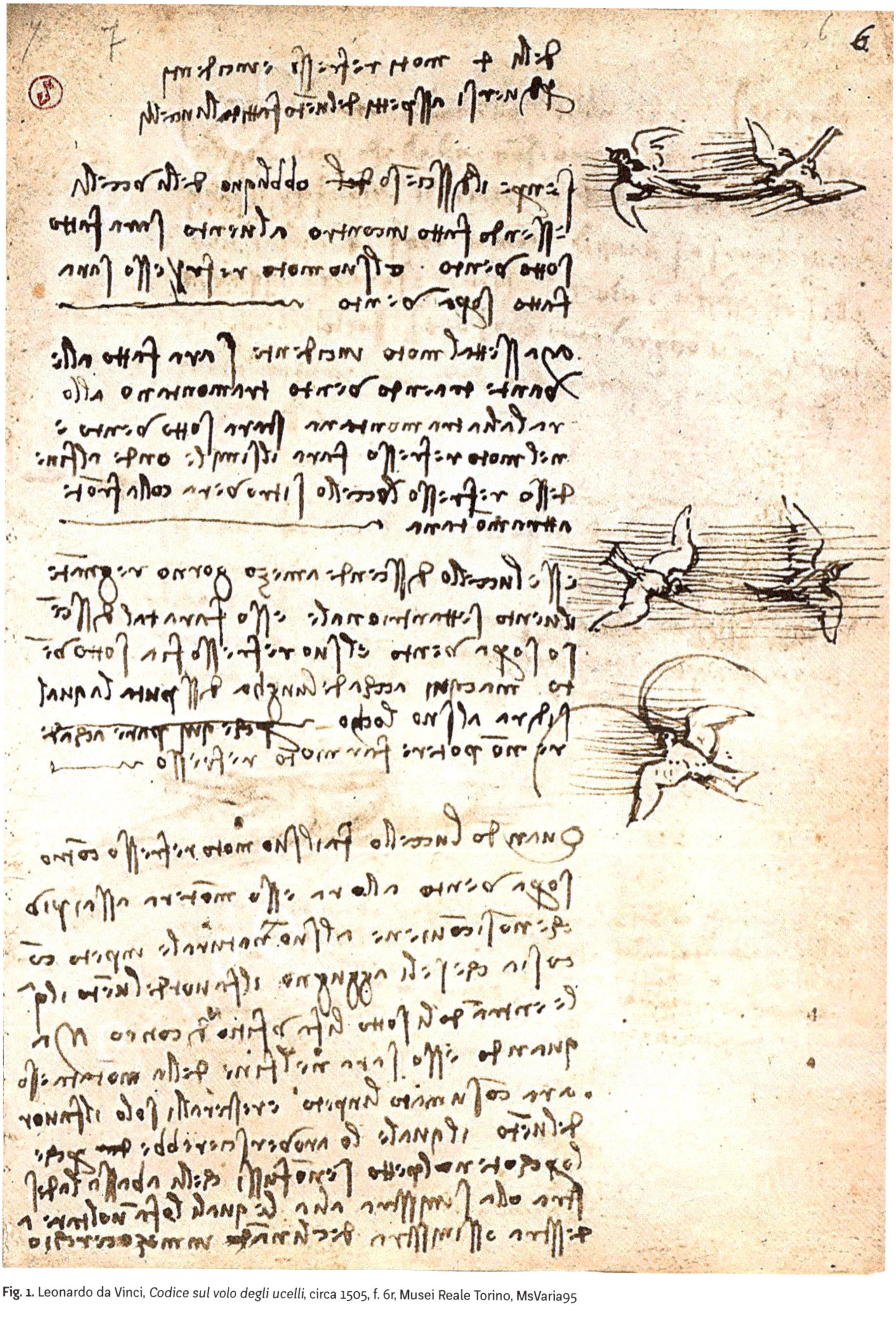

Fig. 1. Leonardo da Vinci, *Codice sul volo degli ucelli*, circa 1505, f. 6r, Musei Reale Torino, MsVaria95

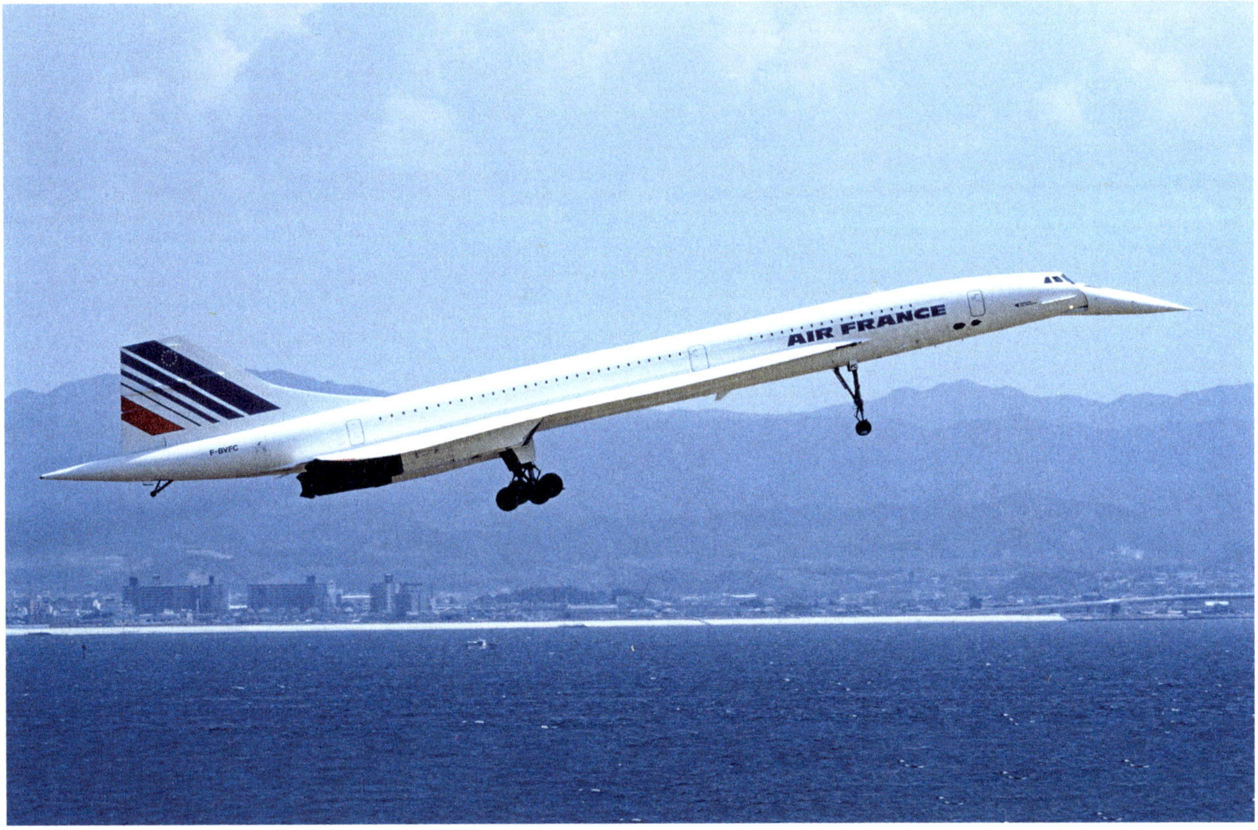

Concorde landing at Kansai International Airport in 1994

popularised this emerging science worldwide. For her, nature as mentor, model and measure are the three founding principles of biomimicry.

Biomimicry thus sits at the crossroads of multiple interdisciplinary fields: ecology and evolutionary sciences, biology and engineering, natural sciences and industry.

Biomimicry identifies natural solutions that have emerged over our planet's 3.8 billion years of evolution, drawing inspiration from living organisms to adapt them for new applications through research, development and industrialisation. Its applications span all sectors of human activity: agriculture, energy, transport, aeronautics, robotics, information technology, architecture, construction, life sciences, cosmetics and more. Biomimicry is therefore playing an increasingly vital role in business, research laboratories and think tanks, opening up new possibilities for reimagining innovation while serving as a pivotal force in the ecological transition.

Numerous examples demonstrate how much this biomimetic revolution has already transformed our view of nature and our environment, along with our technologies and systems, often yielding considerable economic and environmental benefits. Among these innovations are the Shinkansen bullet train's nose cone inspired by the kingfisher's streamlined beak [fig. 2], enabling it to reach speeds of 300 km/h while minimising noise [fig. 3]; Festo's bio-inspired drone, with wings pivoting like those of dragonflies for enhanced performance; wind turbine blades mimicking humpback whale flippers that improve energy efficiency by 20% and reduce noise; and micro-grooved wetsuits replicating the texture of sharkskin to reduce hydrodynamic drag, from

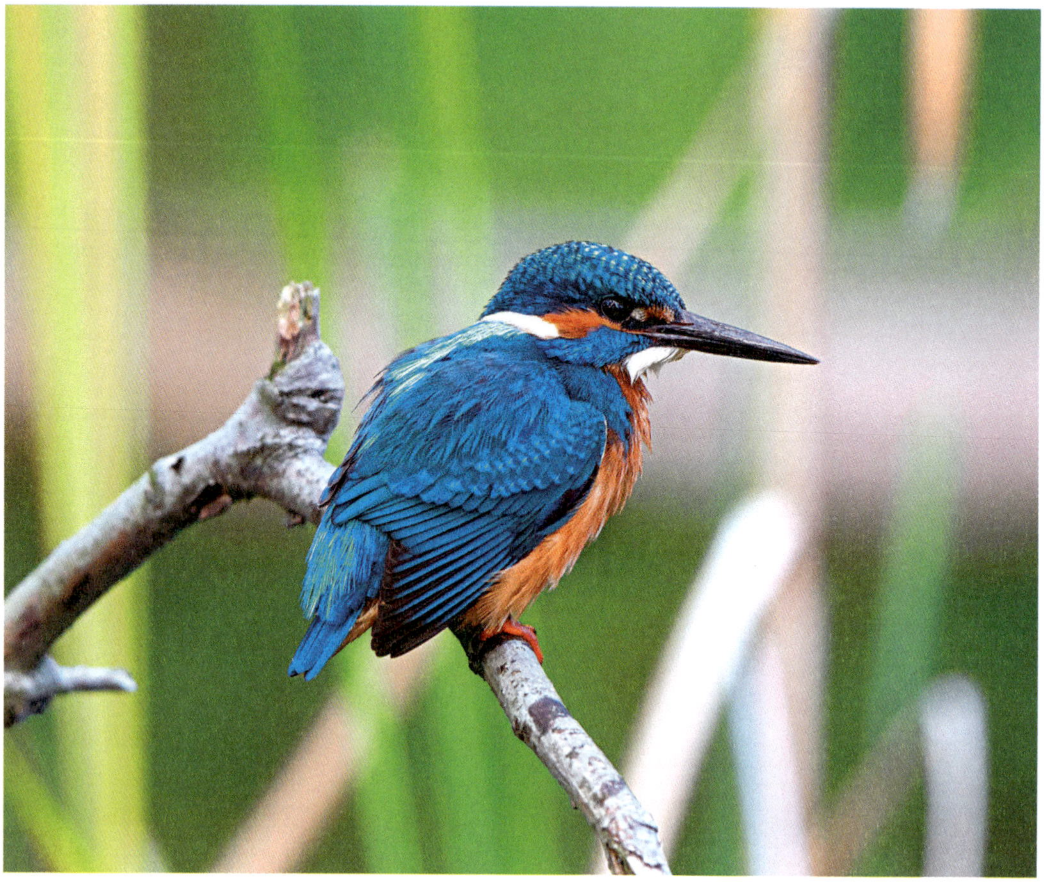

Fig. 2. Eurasian kingfisher (*Alcedo atthis*), in autumn, 2020, Germany

which Airbus drew inspiration to coat its A340-300 fuselages, thereby reducing air resistance and fuel consumption. Other examples include self-cleaning surfaces similar to lotus leaves that are used for shower screens, windows and certain aeronautical coatings; robots with feet inspired by the gecko, a small lizard capable of climbing walls and walking on ceilings, enabling adhesion to smooth surfaces; natural air conditioners ventilated vertically by means of chimneys and galleries that imitate the structure of termite mounds; and the industrial manufacture of Velcro, inspired by burdock flowers.

The unprecedented exhibition *Biomimicry: Taking Inspiration from Nature, from Leonardo da Vinci to the Present Day* reveals the intellectual process of imitating nature from Leonardo da Vinci's time to the present day through an immersive and educational visitor experience. With audiovisual productions and interactive displays presented in the form of games, it offers a unique experience throughout the length of the tour. Visitors can explore an original drawing by Leonardo da Vinci (*Codex Atlanticus*) and an engraving by Albrecht Dürer, rare 16th-century *objets d'art*, precious Renaissance manuscripts, loans from the Natural History Museum and the Army Museum in Paris, models of machines based on Leonardo's drawings, including an ornithopter with a six-metre wingspan, a mechanical dragonfly, a flying sphere, a bat wing, an operculated wing, and an aerial screw, alongside robots and numerous biomimetic machines lent

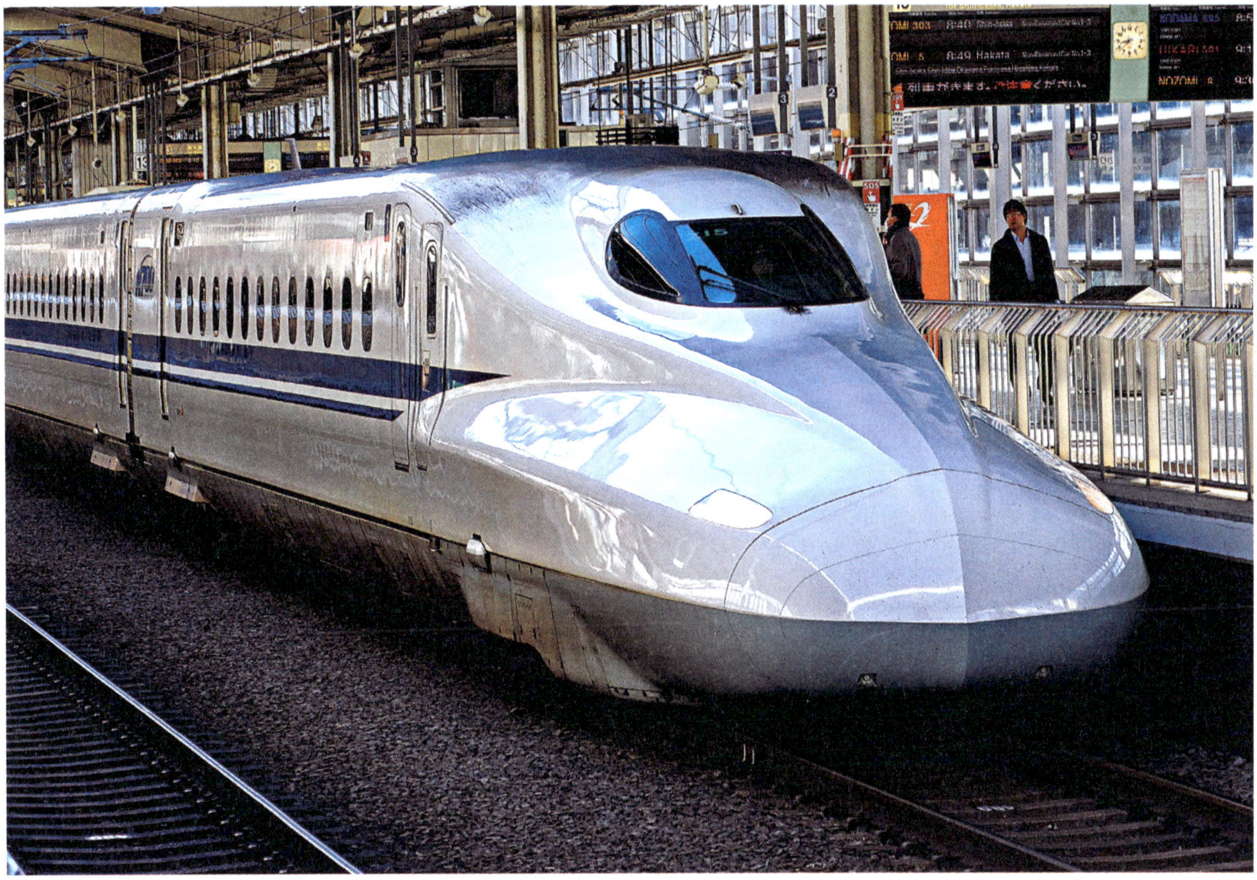

Fig. 3. Shinkansen train leaving the station, 2013, Kyoto, Japan

by various scientific laboratories, such as the Laboratory of Analysis and Architecture of Systems at the French National Centre for Scientific Research (LAAS-CNRS), the University of Lausanne, the Étienne-Jules Marey Institute of Movement Sciences at Aix-Marseille University, and the Institute of Insect Biology Research (IRBI) at the University of Tours.

The exhibition also showcases imaginative scale models by Jacques Rougerie, the world-renowned French oceanographer and architect of coastal and underwater habitats, such as the *SeaOrbiter* ocean exploration station, a solar-powered underwater vessel in the shape of a seahorse, and the fabulous herons created by François Delaroziere, Production and Artistic Director at Machines de l'Île in Nantes, and extraordinary biomimetic dresses by Dutch fashion designer Iris Van Herpen.

The exhibition is conceived, produced and presented under the direction of the Château du Clos Lucé, in collaboration with curators Andrea Bernardoni and Pascal Brioist. The exhibition catalogue, co-published by the Château du Clos Lucé and Éditions Skira, features original contributions from the following academics, researchers, and leading experts on Leonardo's work:

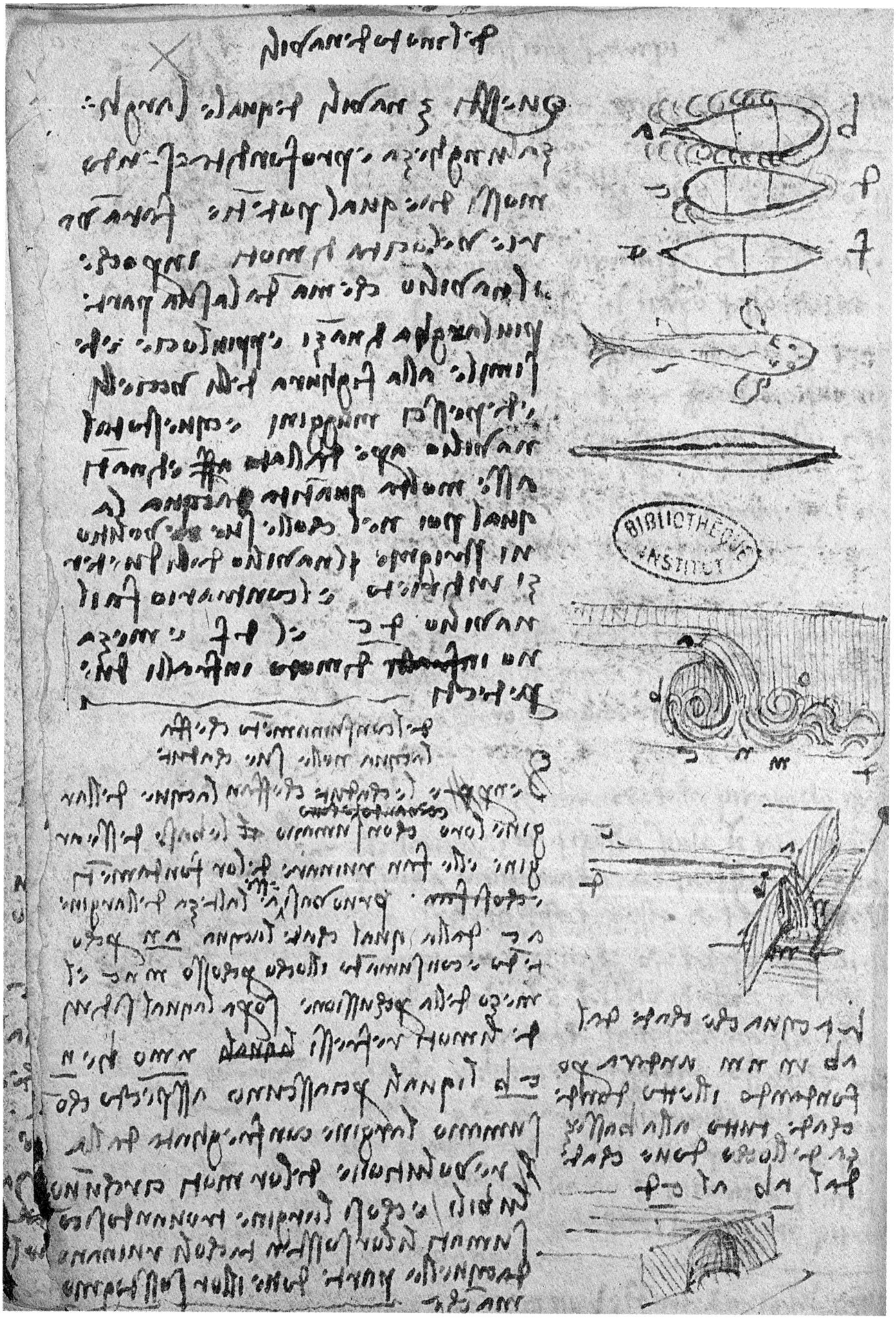

Leonardo da Vinci, *Manuscript G*, c. 1510-1511, 1515, 14.1 × 10.5 cm, Bibliothèque de l'Institut de France, Ms 2178, f. 50v

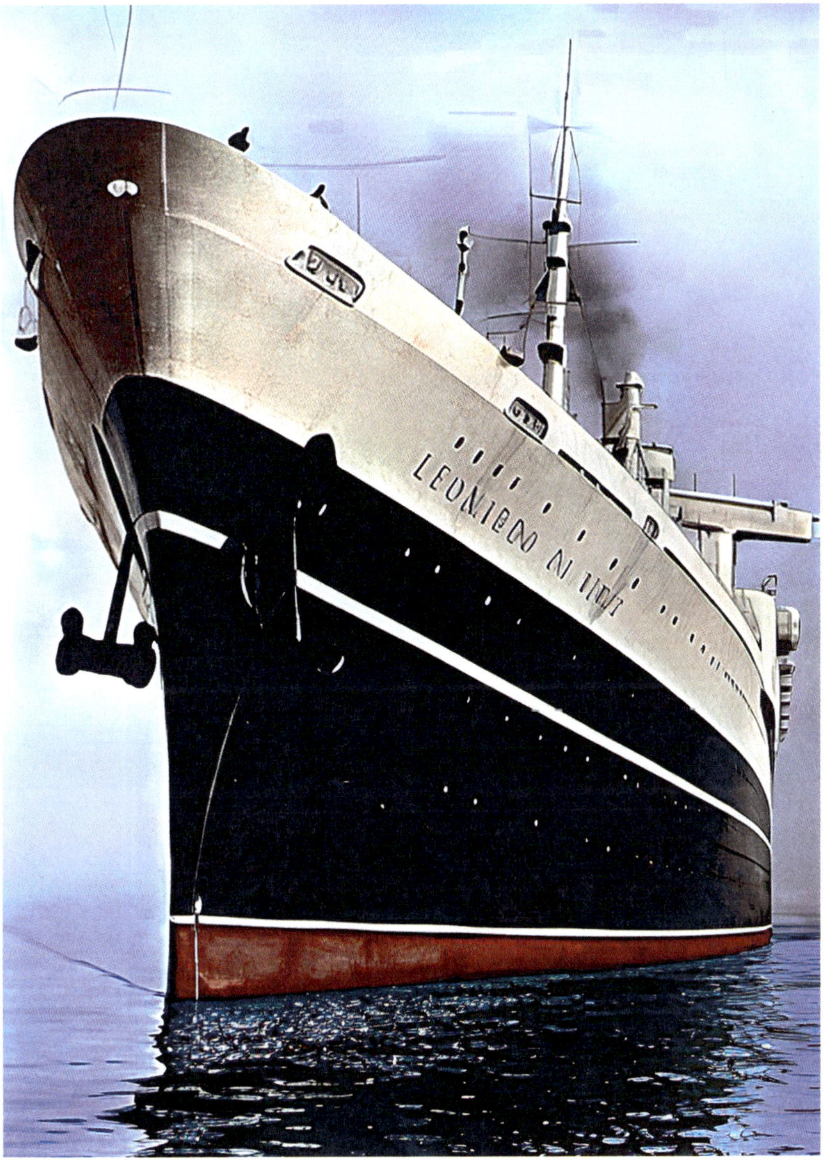

SS Leonardo da Vinci, Italian transatlantic liner built in 1960, with its innovative bulbous bow inspired by Leonardo's studies of fish hydrodynamics

- Andrea Bernardoni, Professor of History of Science and Technology at the University of L'Aquila, and Consultant at the Galileo Museum in Florence;
- Pascal Brioist, Professor of Modern History at the University of Tours and member of the Centre d'études supérieures de la Renaissance;
- François Delaroziere, Production and Artistic Director of Compagnie La Machine, founder of Les Machines de l'Ile de Nantes;
- Dominique Le Nen, university lecturer and Surgeon at the Regional University Hospital in Brest;
- Domenico Laurenza, Professor of the History of Science at the University of Padua;
- Alexander Neuwahl, architect and engineer, collaborator at the Leonardo da Vinci Museum in Vinci, expert in 3D reconstructions;
- Enrica Pagella, teacher and former Director of the Royal Museums of Turin;
- Emmanuelle Pouydebat, CNRS Research Director at the Natural History Museum in Paris;
- Jacques Rougerie, French architect and oceanographer, Academician and member of the Académie des Beaux-Arts;
- Julien Serres, researcher at the Institut des sciences du mouvement, CNRS-Aix-Marseille University;
- Vinod Kumar Saranathan, researcher at the Institute for Institut de recherche sur la biologie de l'insecte (IRBI), University of Tours;
- Philippe Souères, Director of Research at LAAS-CNRS, University of Toulouse;
- Thomas Steinmann, researcher at the Institut de recherche sur la biologie de l'insecte (IRBI), University of Tours.

Château du Clos Lucé would also like to thank the museums, foundations, and university research laboratories that have loaned works:

- Amsterdam, Iris Van Herpen
- Aix-Marseille Université, Institut des sciences du mouvement Étienne-Jules Marey
- Bry-sur-Marne, Festo
- Lausanne, École polytechnique fédérale, Biorobotics Laboratory (BioRob)
- Milan, Veneranda Biblioteca Ambrosiana – Pinacoteca
- Milan, École polytechnique
- Montevarchi, Artes Mechanicae
- Nantes, François Delaroziere
- Paris, galerie Martinez D.
- Paris, Jacques Rougerie
- Paris, musée de l'Armée
- Paris, musée de la Marine
- Paris, Muséum national d'Histoire naturelle
- Toulouse, LAAS-CNRS, département robotique
- Tours, bibliothèque municipale
- Tours, Centre d'études supérieures de la Renaissance
- Université de Tours, Institut de recherche sur la biologie de l'insecte

This exhibition has been made possible thanks to the financial support of the Centre-Val de Loire region, to whom the Château du Clos Lucé is grateful for its generosity and continued trust. Lastly, the Château du Clos Lucé would like to thank the members of its team who have worked with enthusiasm, professionalism and dedication to bring this wonderful cultural project to fruition, in particular Jacques de Tarragon, General Director; Michaël Petitjean, General Secretary; Diane Junqua, Director of Communications and Sponsorship; Sandra Chupin, Exhibition Officer; Nina Germain, Communications Officer; Jordane Mourgues, Executive Assistant; Stéphane Darras, Head of the Technical Department, and his entire team; and the NC design studio represented by Nathalie Crinière.

This exhibition attests the depth and vitality of Franco-Italian relations and illustrates the aspiration of the Chateau du Clos Lucé to share and spread a common culture inherited from the humanism of the Renaissance.

REIMAGINING OUR CONNECTION WITH THE WORLD

François Bonneau
President of the Centre-Val de Loire Region

If there is one figure who profoundly marked his era and our region, it is Leonardo da Vinci. His enduring influence has inspired artists, thinkers and scientists across the globe, and in Centre-Val de Loire in particular. We are committed to preserving this legacy and the values it embodies in terms of creativity and the relations that exist between nature, culture and the art of living.

From 7 June to 10 September 2025, the Château du Clos Lucé invites you to explore the scientific studies into biomimicry made by Leonardo da Vinci and contemporary researchers. Leonardo's transdisciplinary approach, and that of the Renaissance more broadly, resonates with a new way of inhabiting and engaging with the world. At a time when scientific inquiry and thought may be called into question, this exhibition offers a marvellous opportunity to reflect on our relationship with the living world and our place within it.

By hosting this exhibition, the Clos Lucé wholeheartedly embraces the vision the Region has been advancing since 2019 with its "Nouvelles Renaissances" (New Renaissances) initiative. Artists, philosophers and scientists are best placed to help us reimagine the world, and Leonardo da Vinci remains the timeless figure who best embodies this aspiration. This is what we are championing during the coming summer season, which will offer an exceptional encounter with the creativity, heritage, landscapes and way of life of Centre-Val de Loire.

My heartfelt thanks go to the Clos Lucé team for bringing this exhibition to fruition, and to the curators Pascal Brioist, Professor of Modern History at the University of Tours and member of the Centre for Advanced Renaissance Studies in Tours, and Andrea Bernardoni, researcher in the History of Science and Technology at the University of L'Aquila, and a collaborator with the Galileo Museum in Florence. Their efforts have enabled us to call attention to the extraordinary possibilities for cooperation between living beings.

With my best wishes for many amazing discoveries!

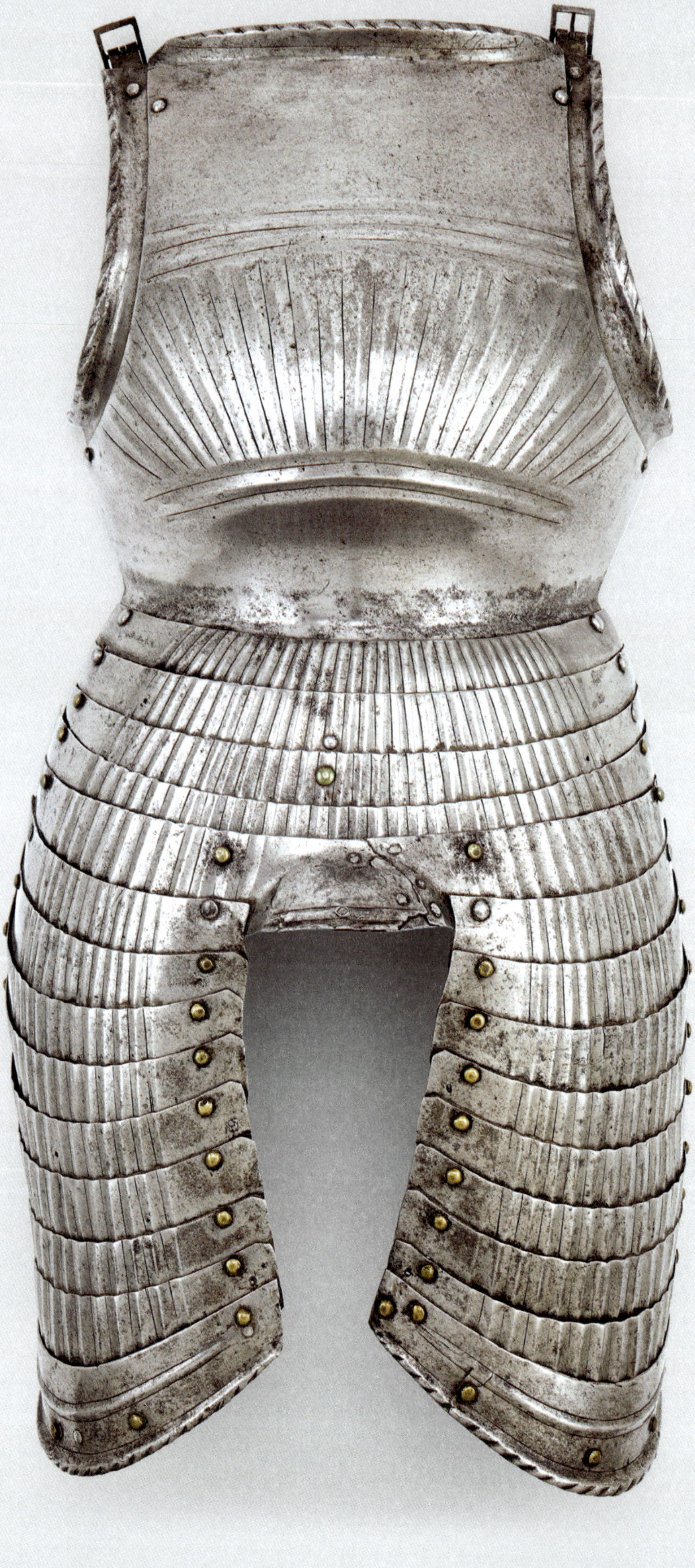

INTRODUCTION: BIO-INSPIRATION FROM LEONARDO TO THE PRESENT DAY

PASCAL BRIOIST AND ANDREA BERNARDONI

Man's natural inclination towards analogical thinking has found an inexhaustible source of inspiration for mechanical engineering in living organisms. This approach, far from being recent, has its roots in prehistory. During the Renaissance, engineers examined forms in nature and became convinced that imitating nature, or thinking analogically about nature's creatures, enabled them to find ingenious technical solutions to the problems they faced.

By 1520, the ribs of breastplates imitated the corrugated structure of scallop shells, and leg and shoulder protections (tassets) in armour borrowed heavily from the physiology of lobster shells [fig. 1]. Around 1580, a Tudor shipwright, Matthew Baker, designed a ship's hull in the shape of a giant fish [fig. 2], reflecting the fascination with what would later be called 'biomimicry'.

There is no doubt that during the Renaissance, Leonardo da Vinci was one of the keenest observers of nature. He enriched his thinking by drawing on living creatures for answers to the questions he pondered. Some authors even consider him a precursor to bionics, the merging of biology and mechanics. The intellectual process underlying Leonardo's imitation of the living world bears careful examination. The areas to explore are vast, as his inspiration was not limited to plants and birds, but extended to insects, bats and marine creatures.

The exhibition at Clos Lucé highlights the parallels between the studies of the Tuscan scholar and the latest advances in modern robotics. Observing the solutions provided by nature to a host of problems allows us to conceive of technology in a paradigm less focused on domination and more on collaboration and harmony.

To comprehend the subject, we should define the main areas where this approach can be put into practice, rather than seeking all potential applications, as bio-inspiration offers such an abundance of possibilities. Three categories stand out: the imitation of materials, the imitation of movement and locomotion, and the imitation of extra-human senses.

LEFT
Fig. 1. Demi-harnois, c. 1510-1515, iron, leather, brass, Musée de l'Armée, inv. 611PO

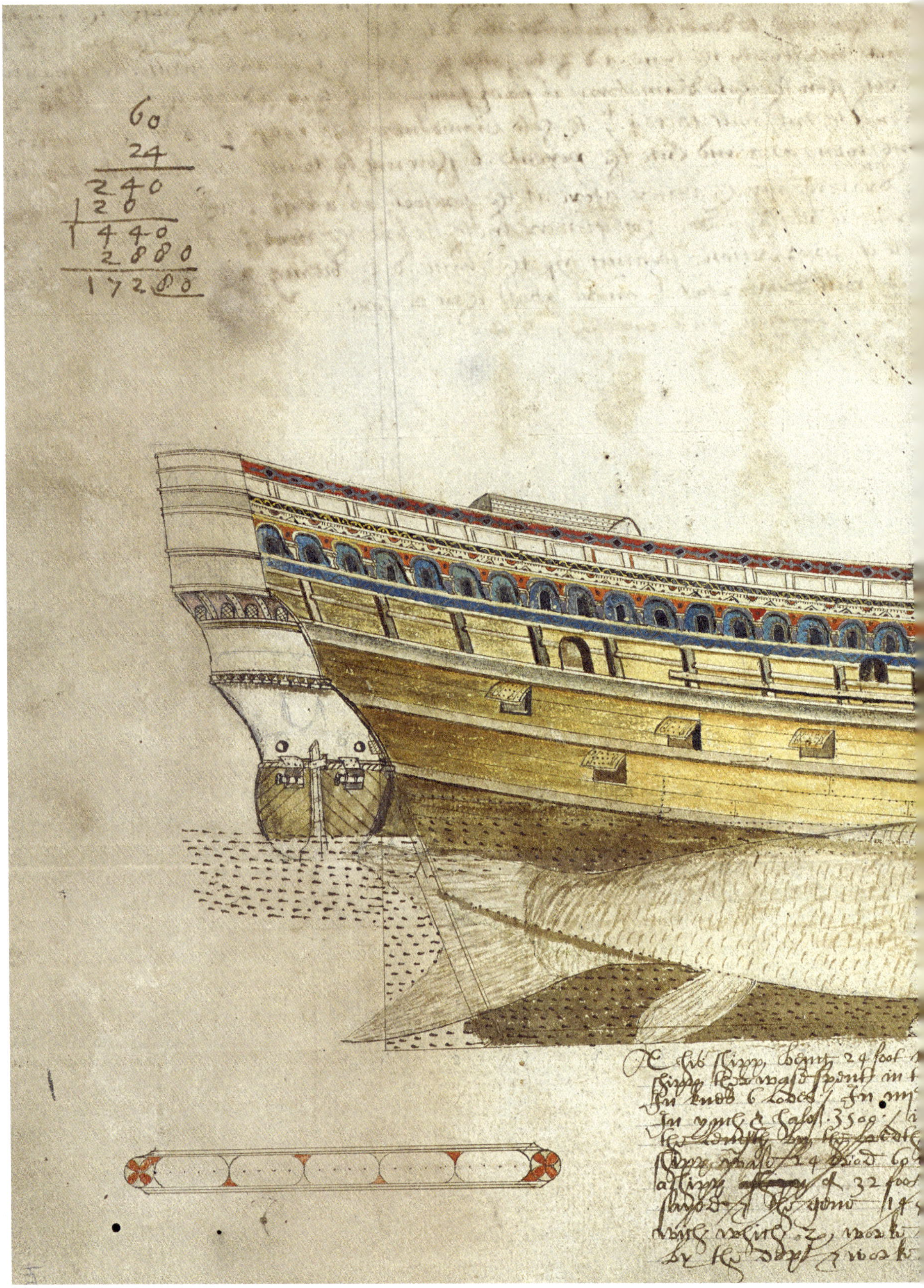

Fig. 2. Matthew Baker, *Fragments*, c. 1585, Pepys Library, Magdalene College

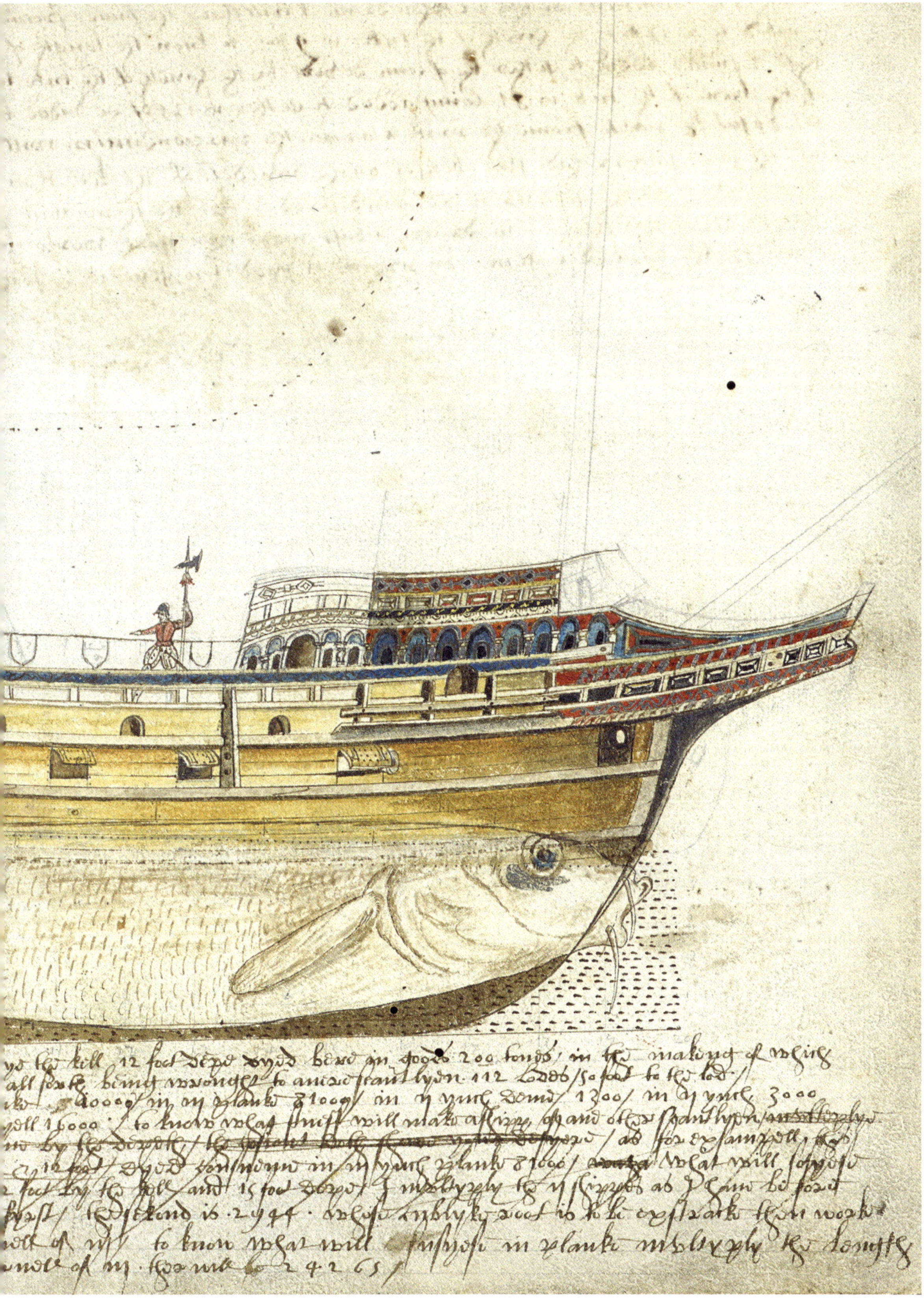

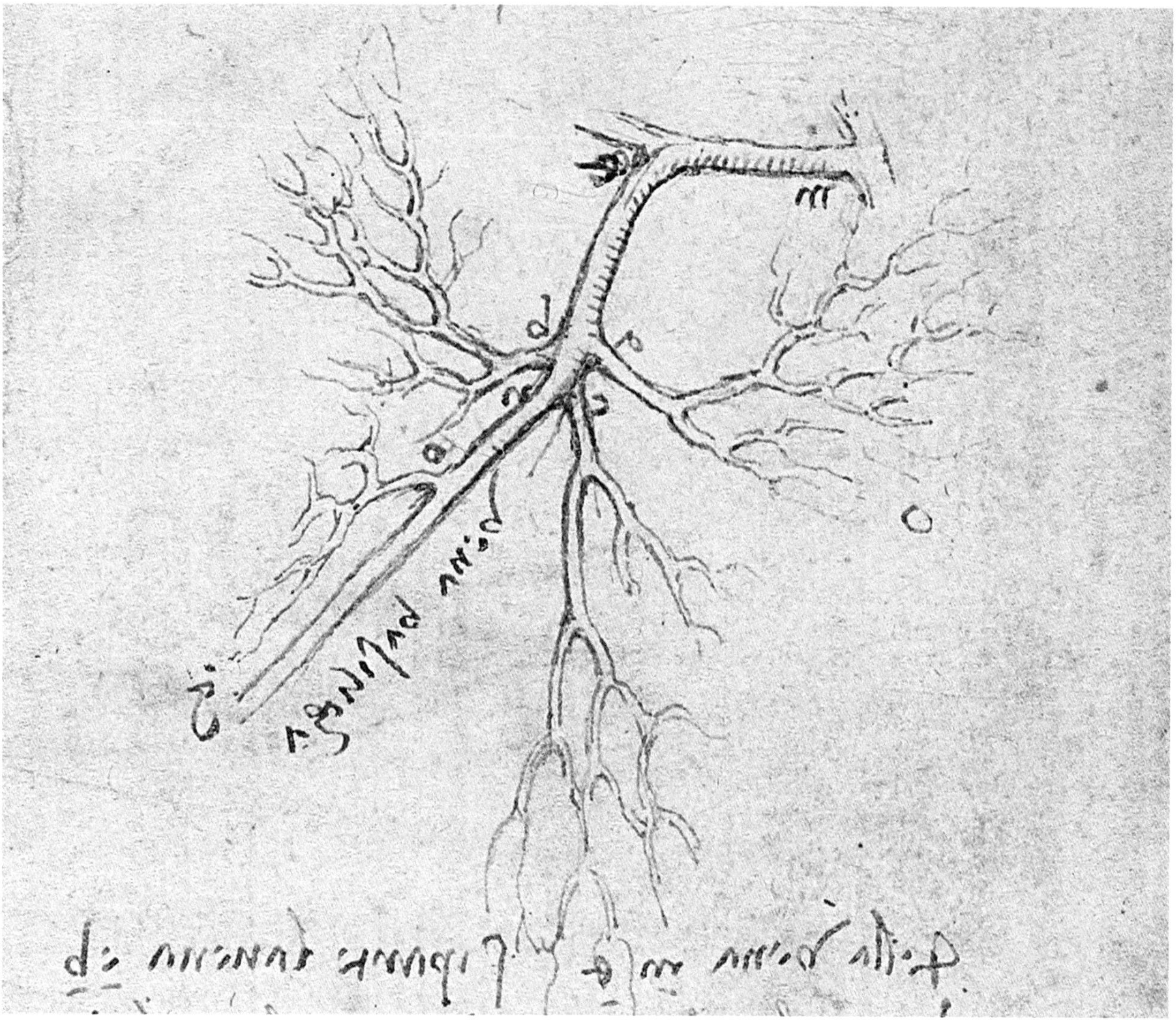

Fig. 3. Leonardo da Vinci, *The muscles of the arm, and the veins of the arm and trunk* (detail), c. 1510-1511, black chalk, pen and ink, wash, 29.9 × 19.9 cm, Windsor, Royal Collection Trust, RL 19005r

Geometric shapes found in nature form the basis for countless objects and materials. Leonardo da Vinci, a keen observer of nature, was particularly fascinated by these shapes and their constant transformations: tubes (like the hollow bones of birds, which he planned to replace with canes for his ornithopters), spiral shapes (springs), vortices, plaits in women's hairstyles, lunules or crescent shapes, branched and combined forms [fig. 3]. Living organisms use these specific geometric shapes for defence and reproduction.

Spheres can be found in dandelion flowers, fruit (such as the cherry drawn on a folio of *Manuscript B*) and sea urchins. Leonardo used this geometric form in his design of a flying sphere that protects a pilot positioned on a gyroscope.

Angular or pointed shapes traditionally offer a means of defence, such as rose thorns and animal fangs and horns, and they are common in the weapons conceived by the Tuscan master.

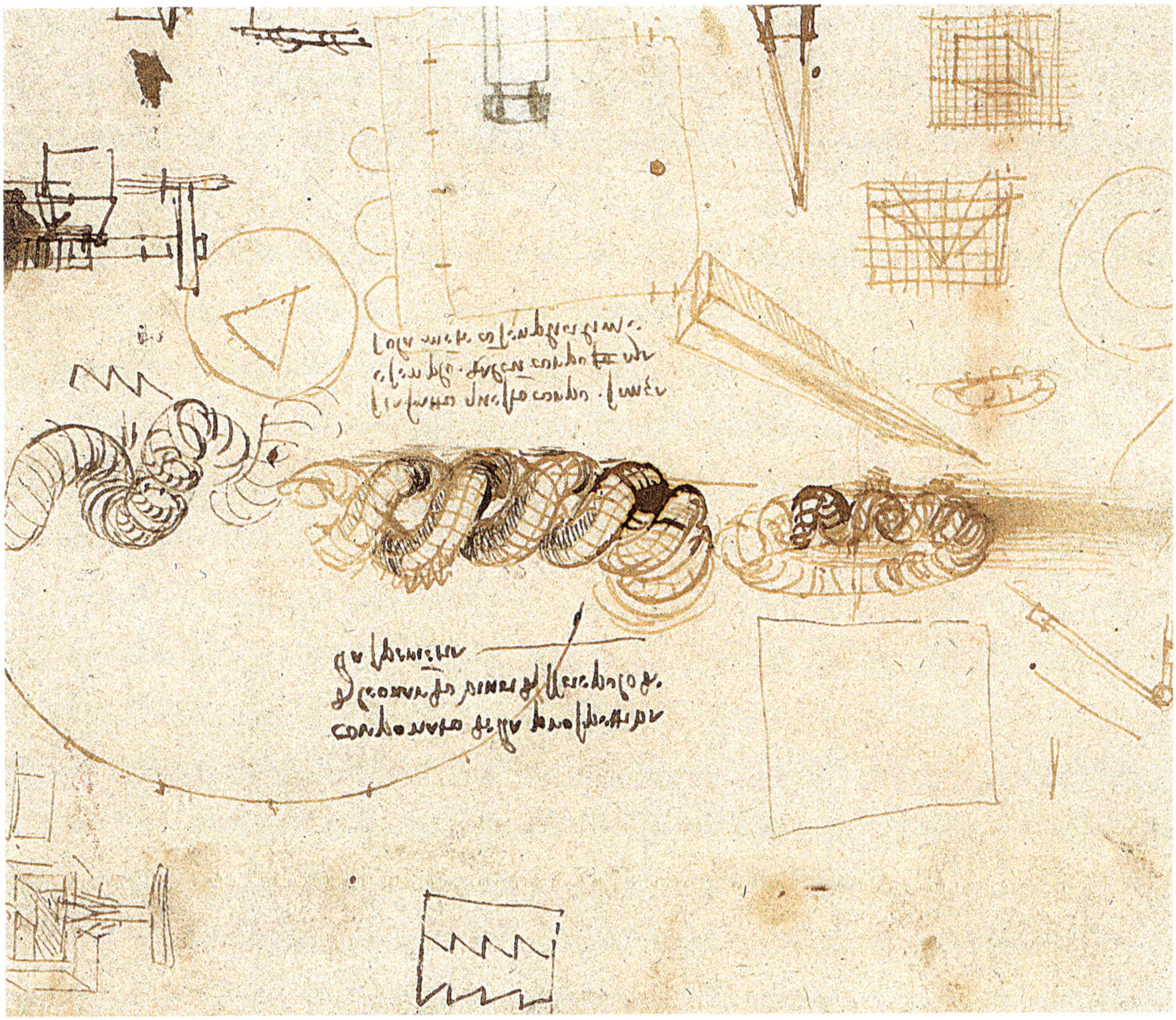

Fig. 4. Leonardo da Vinci, *Codex Atlanticus*, 1490, pen and ink, f. 520r (detail), Veneranda Biblioteca Ambrosiana

Spiral shapes allow linear forms to be contained in a confined space. In nature, they can be found in nautiluses, ammonites and chameleon tails, amongst others. In the *Codex Atlanticus*, Leonardo drew a shape inspired by a snake coiling around a stick [fig. 4].

Helical shapes allow objects to be grasped by increasing friction, similar to climbing plants. This is also the principle of the hook-like structures found in the burdock plant, the inspiration for Velcro. Leonardo discovered an analogue in what he called the cotyledons of the placenta in the foetal womb, which, he said, had "a male and a female form".

Branching structures and fractal shapes, seen in trees, veins and bronchi, enable the colonisation of space. Their matrix-like power fascinated Leonardo almost as much as interlacing patterns, which became a hallmark of his work.

The hexagon is the shape that circles take when they are packed together in a confined space. The circumference of a circle can indeed contain six tangent circles of identical radius. The

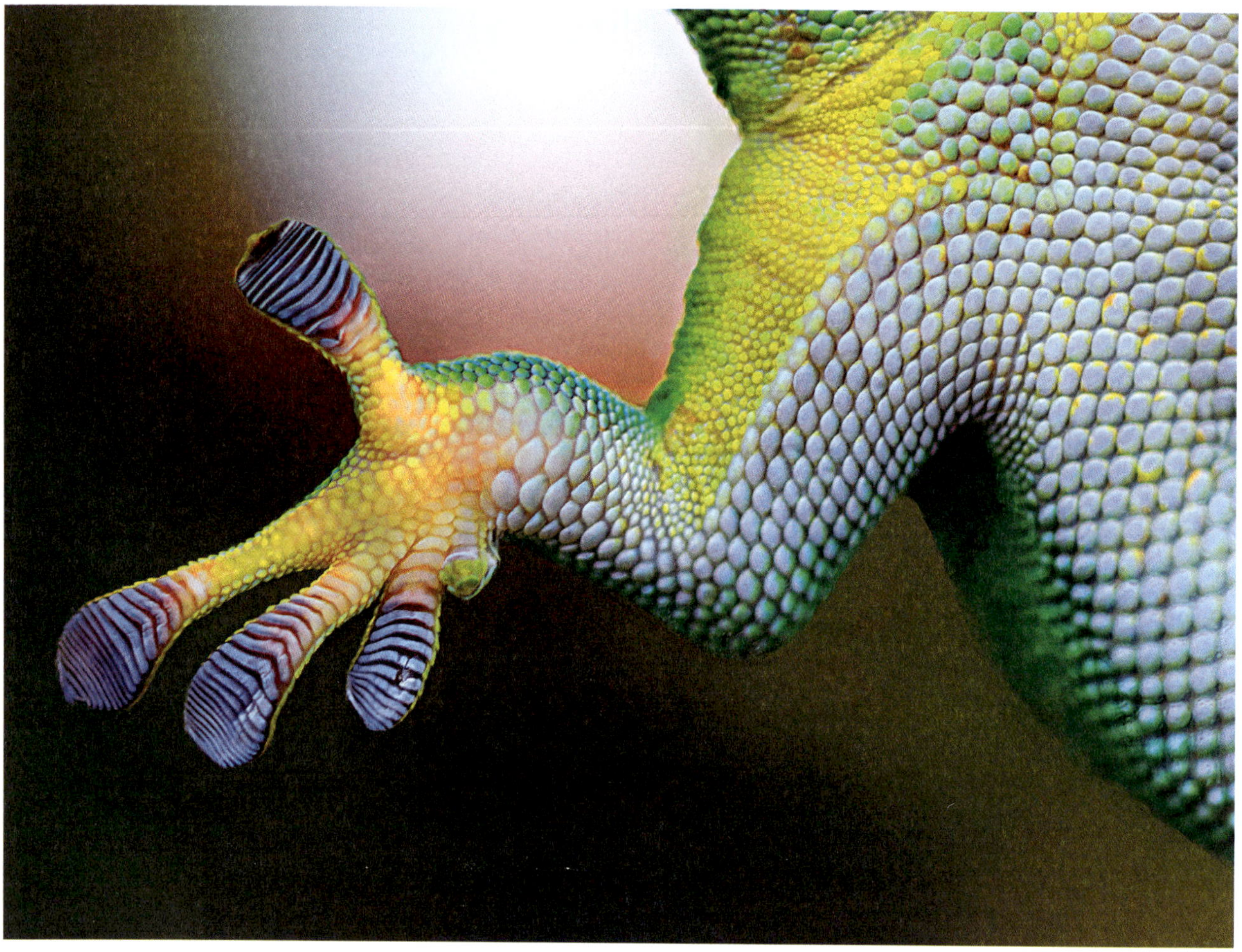

Fig. 5. Gecko paw, 2017

hexagonal structures seen in the combs of beehives, in which bees store their eggs and honey, are economical in terms of materials used, while also providing a light embossed surface that resists compression. Its use in industry is widespread, particularly in the manufacture of protective cardboard packaging and the internal structures of helicopter blades.

Similarly, the dry adhesive capacity of geckos' feet, with their microscopic hairs and reversible adhesion, which can change angle when the animal wants to detach and move forward on smooth surfaces [fig. 5], is of interest to carpet manufacturers. The manner in which ivy adheres to surfaces using tiny branched plant fibres offers a solution for composite adhesives. In the 1970s, microscopic examination of sharkskin revealed the presence of grooved denticles that significantly reduce water resistance. This property has been used to improve Airbus fuselage skins and the foils of hydrofoil racing yachts, which are themselves inspired by the fins of orcas or dolphins. The study of the hydrophobic and self-cleaning properties of lotus leaves [fig. 6] has spurred research into hydrophobic coatings for solar panels and anti-fog glass.

The intense, luminous blue used in the cosmetics industry is not derived from chemical dyes but rather by the microscopic structures of the scales on the wings of the Morpho butterfly, native to the Amazon region, which reflect only specific wavelengths of light. Other butterflies

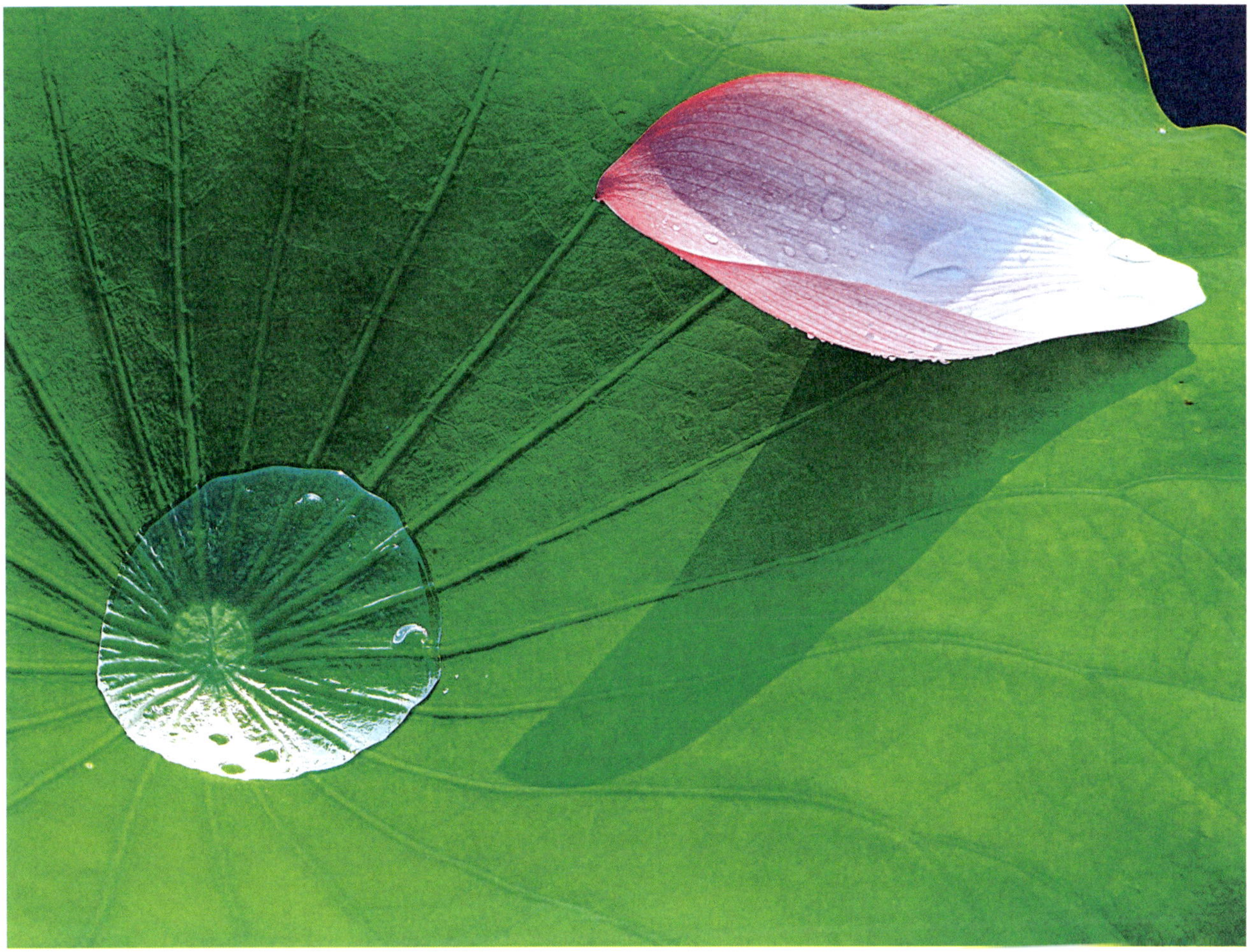

Fig. 6. Lotus leaf, 2017

boast structures that make their wings transparent. Current research in biomimetics is exploring the futuristic possibilities of nanostructures, phenomena about which Leonardo could not have known. He was particularly interested in types of locomotion, especially aerial, and wrote an entire treatise on flight (*Sul Volo*, Turin). He also designed a series of flying machines for winged flight, inspired by birds, bats, dragonflies and butterflies.

After the invention of Clément Ader's bat plane, modern aeronautics abandoned the flapping wing concept, except for certain small drones. It has, however, drawn lessons from animal forms for landing gear and for winglets, the upward-pointing fins on the wingtips of some aircraft, inspired by what Leonardo called the 'alula', or small wing, which he considered important for birds' steering.

Modern winglets are not steerable, but they reduce air drag induced by flight and, consequently, save fuel [fig. 7].

In the field of aquatic locomotion, Leonardo not only designed fins inspired by the wings of flying fish, he also developed a theory of swimming and hydrodynamics, explaining the principle of bulbous bows based on his observations of fish. Bulbous bows replaced straight bows in the 1950s, becoming standard on large cargo ships by the 1990s [fig. 8].

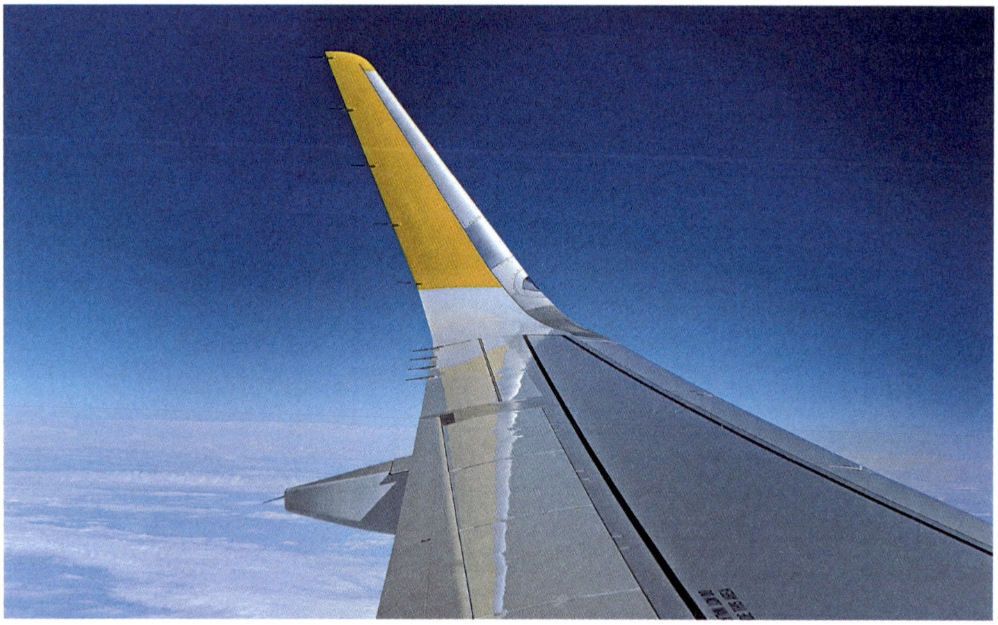

Fig. 7. Winglet of an A320 aircraft flying from Munich to Barcelona, 2018

At a time when fish and birds were far more abundant than they are today, Leonardo was captivated by the mysterious phenomenon of their collective movements, such as starling murmurations, and dedicated an entire chapter of his treatise to them. The enigma of these collective movements and the interactions between individuals remains a focus of animal biology research. The most likely hypothesis is that information is passed from one individual to the next without there being a single leader. Flying in swarms and swimming in schools provide a means of collective defence against predators.

In the field of locomotion, Leonardo designed automata of lions with articulated legs and developed a treatise on human movement that has now been lost. Today, robotics laboratories around the world produce automata with slightly bent legs capable of walking slowly on flat ground. Controlling the balance of a biped in a changing and irregular environment requires complex computer models reproducing the human nervous and muscular systems and capable of capturing information from the surroundings. Modern quadruped robots, such as Boston Dynamics' *Cheetah* and the *Sassa* from the Laboratory for Analysis and Architecture of Systems in Toulouse, are capable of imitating the movement of legs, as in Leonardo's lion, which likely moved on wheels, maintaining their balance whatever the environment and optimising load capacity and energy consumption.

Other projects focus on how salamanders crawl or lampreys move.

Finally, one promising area of biomimicry involves finding sources of inspiration in extra-human senses to be used by machines.

Leonardo had this in mind when he wrote that flying machines could not be designed unless the pilot knew how to imitate the "soul of the bird" that manages to maintain its balance in the wind. Nature offers some astonishing examples, such as the extraordinary ability of insects in flight to avoid obstacles or adjust their altitude to the irregularities of the ground, reflexively

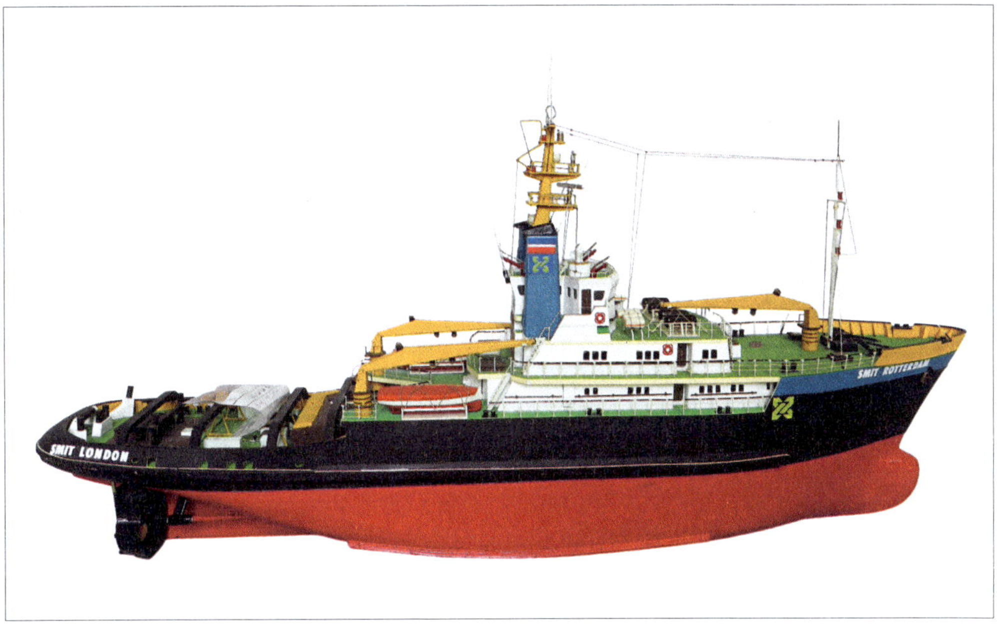

Fig. 8. Model of a cable-laying vessel with bulbous bow inspired by marine biomimicry

increasing or decreasing the frequency of their wingbeats, or abruptly changing direction. Flies are capable of observing their environment in motion, even at high speeds. Applications in terrestrial or aerial robotics are numerous. Many companies are exploring ways to build an artificial eye, like that of a fly, modelling the sensory hairs of flies, crickets and cockroaches, or imitating desert ants capable of navigating using the sun for guidance (like the AntBot robot), or bees capable of detecting, through a piezoelectric sense, whether a flower has already been visited by a fellow bee.

Bio-imitation is opening the doors of miniaturisation to drone technology, offering fascinating prospects for the future.

Bibliography

Fournier, Mathilde. *Biomimétisme, quand la nature inspire la science*. Paris: Édition Plume de carotte, 2011.

Galuzzi, Paolo (ed.). *La mente di Leonardo. Nel laboratorio del Genio Universale*. Florence: Giunti, 2006.

Giacomelli, Roberto. *Gli studi di Leonardo da Vinci sul Volo*. Rome: Assoc. Culturale Aeronautica, 1936.

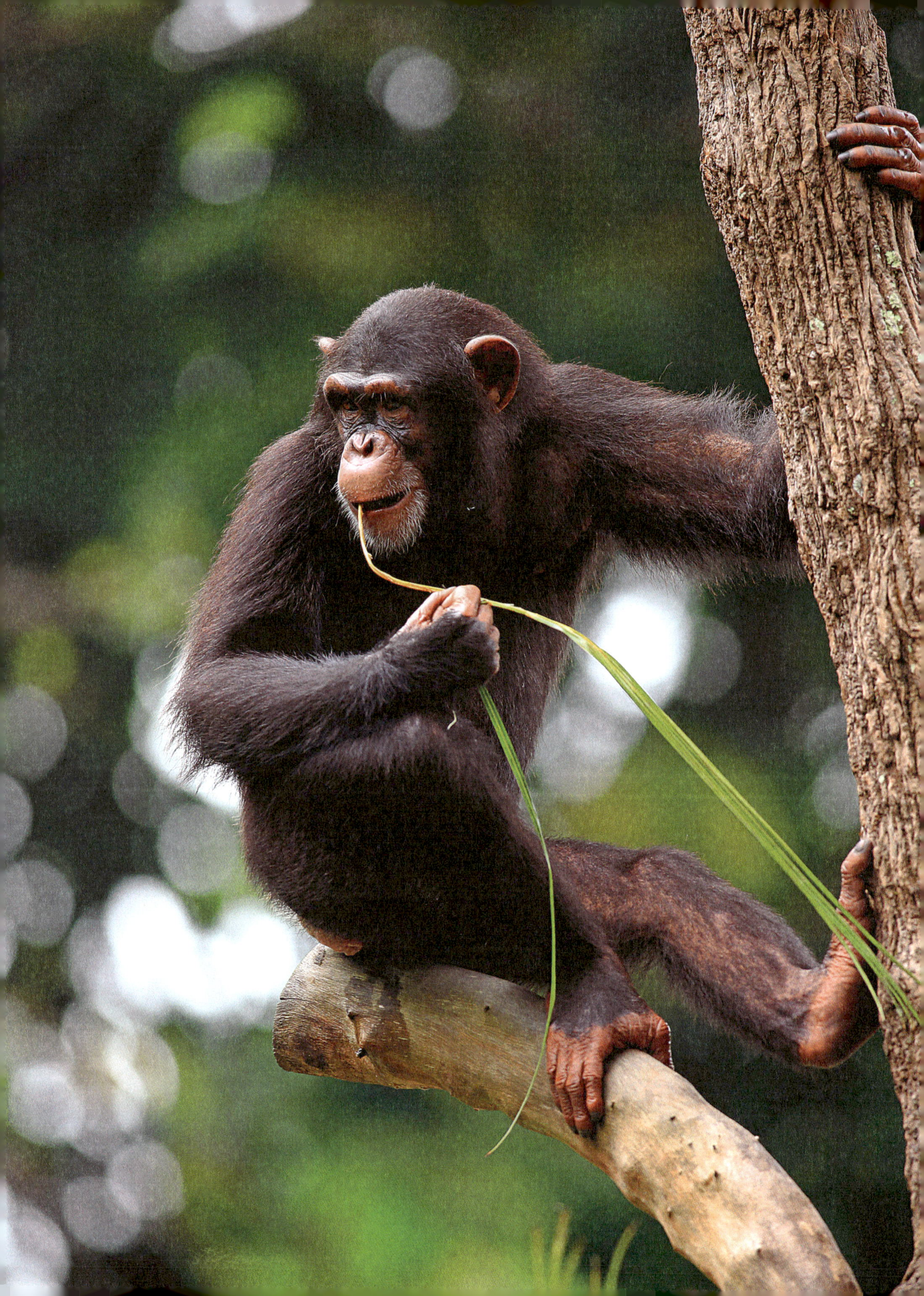

LEONARDO DA VINCI AND BIOMIMICRY: TAKING INSPIRATION FROM NATURE

EMMANUELLE POUYDEBAT

OPENING THE GREAT BOOK OF NATURE: A LABOUR OF LOVE

Living beings have been evolving for nearly 4 billion years. Through complex mechanisms, they have diversified across a wide range of environments. The result? A vast array of morphologies, performances and behaviours that encourage researchers to dream of a better world.

Their innovations, inspired by nature, have led to the development of ultra-resistant materials, adhesives that stick underwater, versatile robots, solar panels efficient at high temperatures, and solutions for purifying air, water and soil. Other projects, inspired by animals that naturally combat cancer, regenerate lost limbs, or find solutions to malaria, have contributed to new tissue regeneration technologies and other preventive and therapeutic approaches. The possibilities are endless!

Animals have developed remarkable adaptive capacities to move, conserve resources, problem-solve, protect and heal themselves, and even with regard to ageing. They are an inexhaustible source of inspiration across all fields, among which the automobile industry, chemistry, ecology, electronics, aeronautics, robotics, artificial intelligence, medicine, and more. As Antoni Gaudí suggested, shouldn't we "copy the great and always-open book of nature"? Leonardo da Vinci understood this well. Today, this vision is coming to life in biomimicry, or, more precisely, bio-inspiration. Given that the term 'biomimicry' is derived from the verb 'mimic' and means copying life, it might be more accurate and humbler to suggest that humans seek to draw inspiration from the great and open book of nature, which is too complex to be copied exactly. Hence 'bio-inspiration', the preferred term for many researchers. However we phrase it, it is incumbent on us to ensure this book does not close, that we draw ethical inspiration from living organisms and hope for a better, more harmonious life in a biodiverse world. As Montaigne wrote, "Nature can do all, and does all. If only we respect her and observe her".

LEFT
Chimpanzee feeding in a tree, Africa

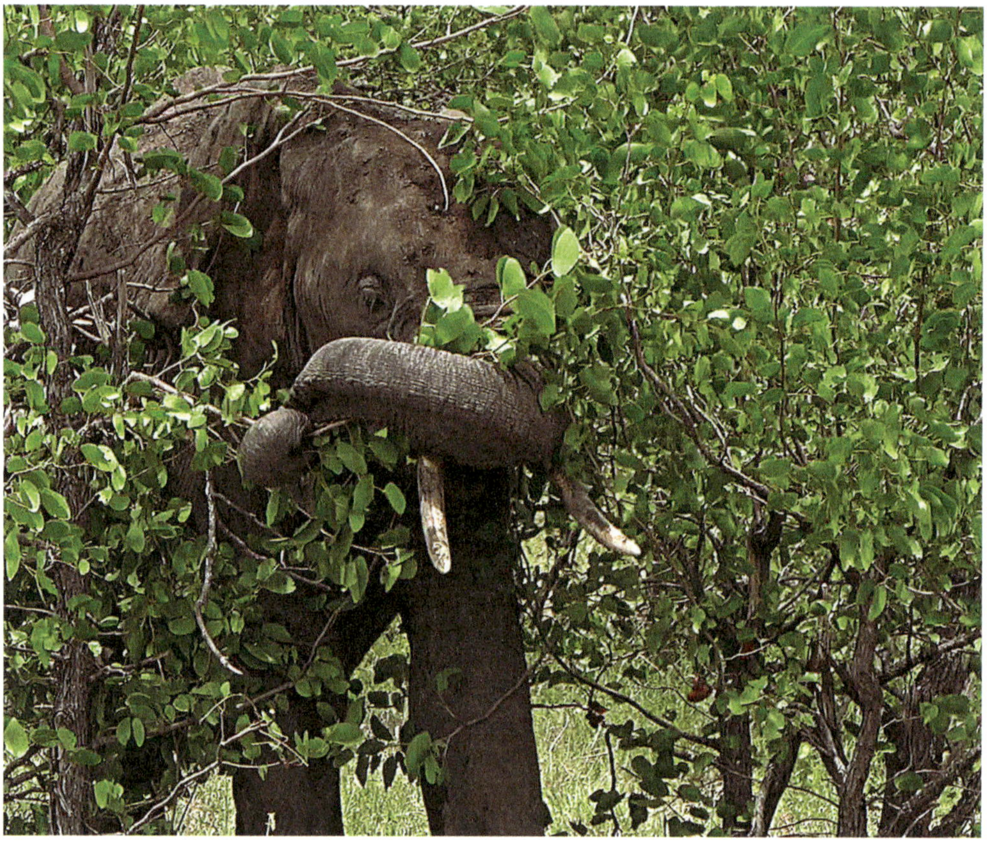

Fig.1. Elephant uprooting a tree

An Original Approach for a New Era

Bio-inspiration offers an interdisciplinary approach, marked by keen environmental awareness and a deep respect for biodiversity. In 1997, Janine Benyus transformed our relationship with nature by describing biomimicry as an innovative approach that transfers principles from living organisms and ecosystems to make human societies compatible with the biosphere. This approach to protecting nature requires scientists to develop interdisciplinary projects in collaboration with specialists from diverse fields.

Two scientific studies involving chimpanzees and elephants illustrate this symbiosis between observing nature and technological innovation. They show how these extraordinary animals can serve as inspiration for robotics and malaria prevention. A bold initiative for our future!

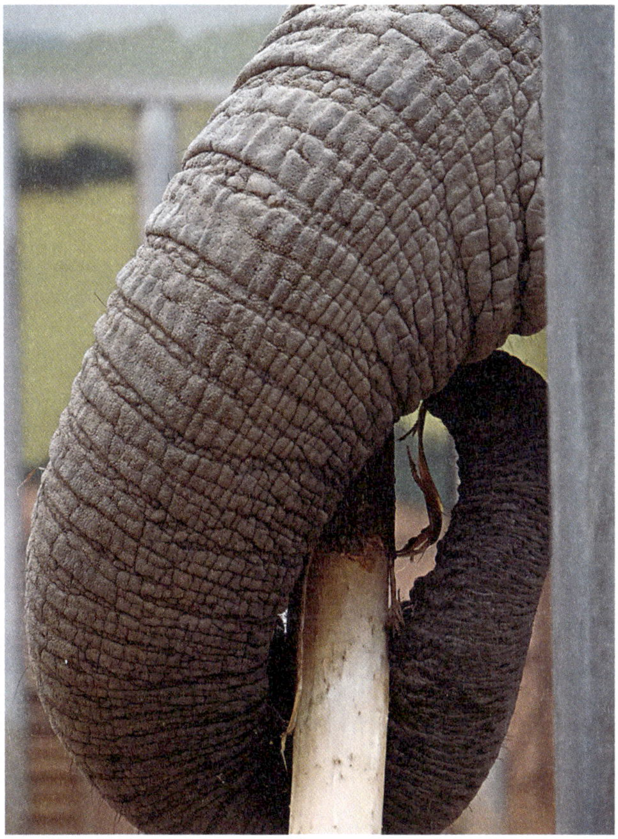

Elephant trunk

When a Trunk Inspires a Robot

The evolution of elephants and their trunks remains a mystery. The trunk is a remarkably versatile and vital organ, used for drinking, eating, communicating, moving, playing, and more. Composed of over 150,000 muscle bundles and equipped with two 'fingers' at its tip, the trunk of the African savannah elephant can uproot a tree by coiling around it [fig. 1], grasp a fruit by suction, or even manipulate a popcorn. This organ, which is precise, powerful and efficient, is a tremendous source of inspiration for modern technology. I am studying it to drive innovation in the field of industrial robotic arms. These arms, often specialised for objects of specific sizes and shapes, need to become more versatile and reliable in grasping objects of various sizes, shapes and masses to ensure human safety.

So, how can we innovate with elephants? By conducting an interdisciplinary study. The first step involves cataloguing the variety of functions of the trunk in its natural environment (South Africa and Namibia) and establishing links between these functions, trunk morphology, and tusk shape, depending on the environment. The second step involves experimentally collecting biomechanical data, at ZooParc de Beauval (France), using a novel device to quantify forces and 3D kinematics (trajectories, speeds, accelerations) without markers placed on the trunk. This is now possible thanks to neural networks. With all this data acquired, the design of a revolutionary

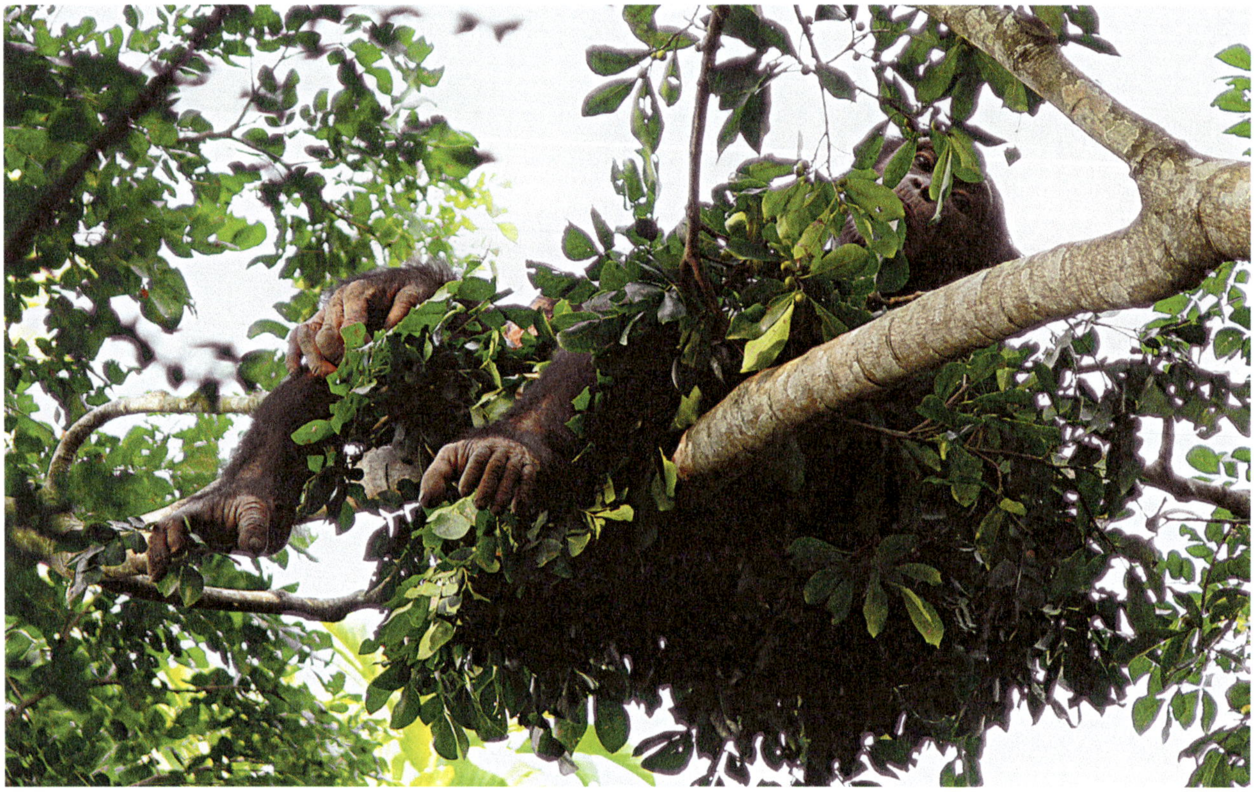

Fig. 2. A chimpanzee lounging in his nest

robotic trunk prototype is now being considered, based on real biological data rather than mere visual imitation, as in the past.

But the project has gone even further, combining science and elephant conservation. Indeed, we have shown that certain vital functions of the trunk are linked to the tusks (their size, shape, and asymmetry). However, the size of African savannah elephants' tusks is shrinking due to poaching. What will become of them? How will they survive under these conditions? How can we help them? Much work remains to be done to convince and protect.

From Chimpanzees to Mosquito Repellents

Every evening, chimpanzees build nests in trees to sleep [fig. 2]. My colleague, primatologist Sabrina Krief, observed that chimpanzees in the Sebitoli area of Uganda's Kibale National Park sometimes nest at heights of over 40 metres. This means the nest must be comfortable for peaceful sleep and sturdy at the same time, as falling from 40 metres in the middle of the night is not an option. Moreover, it appears that there were fewer mosquitoes where the chimpanzees slept. This led us to question whether chimpanzees select trees with mosquito-repellent properties and/or those that offer comfort and stability? To answer this, we initiated a large-scale project comparing ten tree species most frequently used for nesting with ten species commonly found in the chimpanzees' environment. For these 20 species, graduate researcher Camille Lacroux

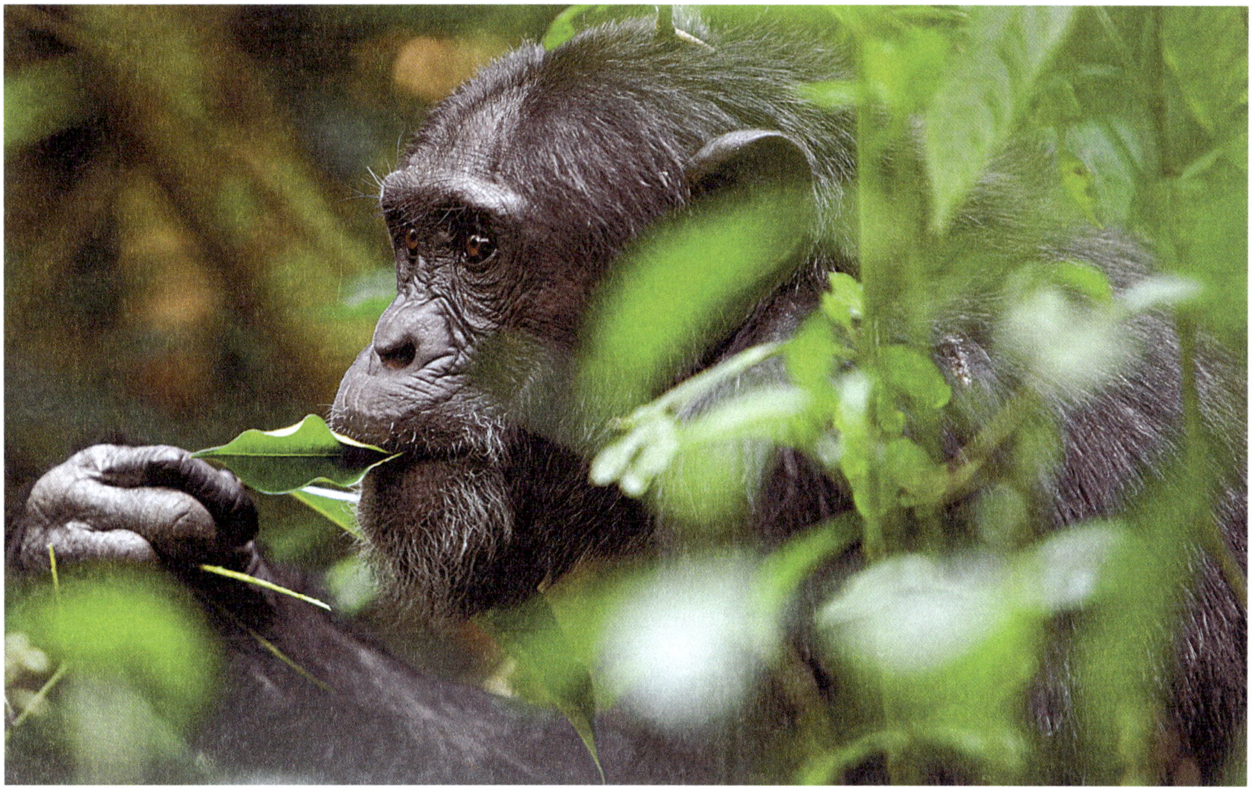

Chimpanzee feeding on leaves

determined their biomechanical and morphological characteristics, such as foliar density, leaf shape and size, and branch rigidity. Their repellent effect against the mosquito *Anopheles gambiae* was also tested. The results of five years of study are fascinating and show that chimpanzees do not choose just any tree. They prefer trees with elongated, medium-sized leaves, high foliar density, and sturdy branches, in other words, a compromise between comfort and security. But that's not all: most of these trees have leaves containing mosquito-repellent molecules. The Sebitoli chimpanzees thus sleep in nests made from trees that provide a secure, comfortable environment, free from mosquito bites. In short, a nest conducive to sleep! This discovery opens the door to new strategies for protecting human populations against the devastating effects of malaria and highlights the urgent need to protect chimpanzees, our closest relatives.

Leaving the Last Word to Leonardo da Vinci

Nothing is ever set in stone or entirely complete. When, in the 15th century, Leonardo da Vinci envisioned the future by observing and attempting to understand nature, it is unlikely that he imagined how visionary he was. His interdisciplinary outlook, both branching and convergent, moved from theory to practice, from performance to beauty. Drawing inspiration from nature, innovating, exploring, and passing on knowledge, certainly, but with an ethical reflection on our relationship with living organisms, demonstrating collective intelligence, empathy, altruism, recycling, reducing pollution, preserving water and oceans, and respecting the environment and life. It is crucial to reconcile innovation with respect for biodiversity and animal welfare, and to consider the economic and ecological impact of exploiting living organisms.

It is time for biological challenges and economic and sustainability priorities to be questioned and addressed together. Nature holds potential solutions and even more mysteries. Let us strive to unravel them with an immediate focus on maintaining biodiversity. As Albert Camus wrote, "Real generosity towards the future lies in giving all to the present".

Bibliography

Benyus, Janine M. *Biomimicry: Innovation Inspired by Nature*. New York: William Morrow Paperbacks, 1997.

Cornette, Raphaël. "The Relationship Between Distal Trunk Morphology and Object Grasping in the African Savannah Elephant (*Loxodonta africana*)". *PeerJ* 10:e13108 (2022).

Cornette, Raphaël, Delapré, Arnaud, Houssin, Céline, Mulot, Baptiste, Pouydebat, Emmanuelle. "Measuring the Force of the Distal Part of the Elephant's Trunk". *MethodsX*. https:doi.org/10.1016/j.mex.2022.101896 (2022).

Cornette, Raphaël. 'Maximum Trunk Tip Force Assessment Related to Trunk Position and Prehensile 'Fingers' Implication in African Savannah Elephants". *PLoS ONE*, 19(5) (2024), e0301529.

Costes, Pauline, Delapré, Arnaud, Houssin, Céline, Mulot, Baptiste, Pouydebat, Emmanuelle, *Quand les animaux et les végétaux nous inspirent*. Paris: Odile Jacob, 2019.

Costes, Pauline, Soppelsa, Julie, Houssin, Céline, Boulinguez-Amboise, Grégoire, Pacou, Camille, Cornette, Raphaël, Pouydebat, Emmanuelle, "Effect of the Habitat and Tusks on Trunk Grasping Techniques in African Savannah Elephants". *Ecology and Evolution*, 14(4) (2024).

Lacroux, Camille, Pouydebat, Emmanuelle, Krief, Sabrina. "Repellent Activity Against Anopheles Gambiae of Leaves of Nesting Trees in the Sebitoli Chimpanzee Community of Kibale National Park, Uganda". *Malaria Journal* 21, art. no. 271 (2022).

Soppelsa, Julie, Pouydebat, Emmanuelle, Lefeuvre, Maëlle, Mulot, Baptiste, Houssin, Céline, Lacroux, Camille, Krief, Sabrina, Douady, Stéphane, Cornette, Raphaël, Durand, Sophie, Aleeje, Alfred, Asalu, Edward, Pouydebat, Emmanuelle. "Chimpanzees Select Comfortable Nesting Tree Species". *Scientific Reports* 2023 Oct 7;13(1), 16943.

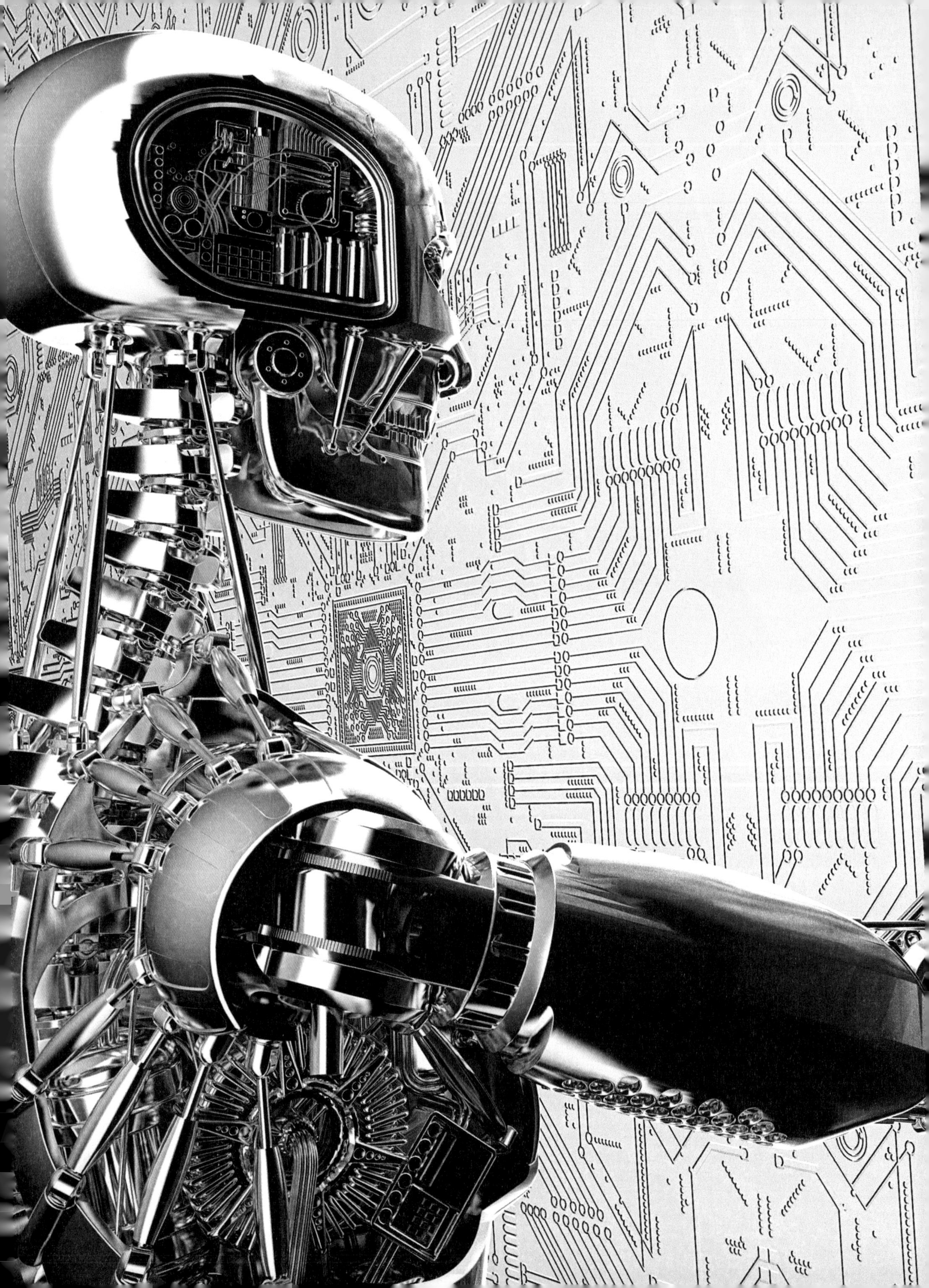

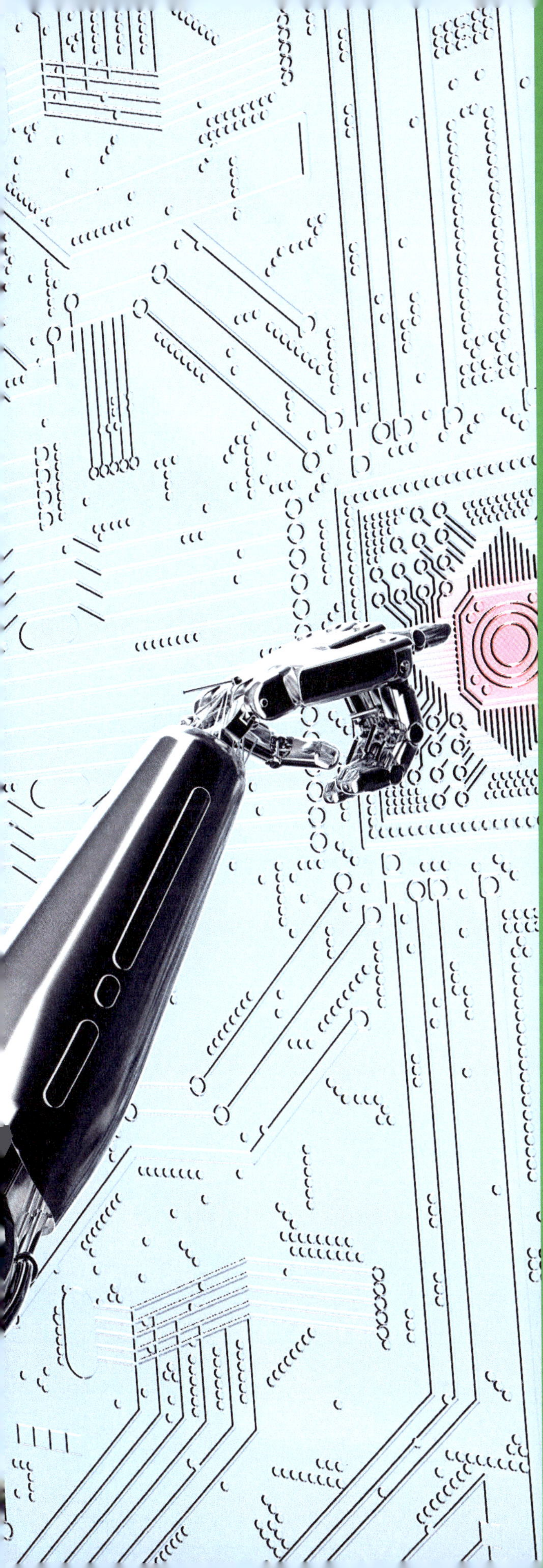

Biomimicry, Robots and Human Anatomy

CHAPTER I

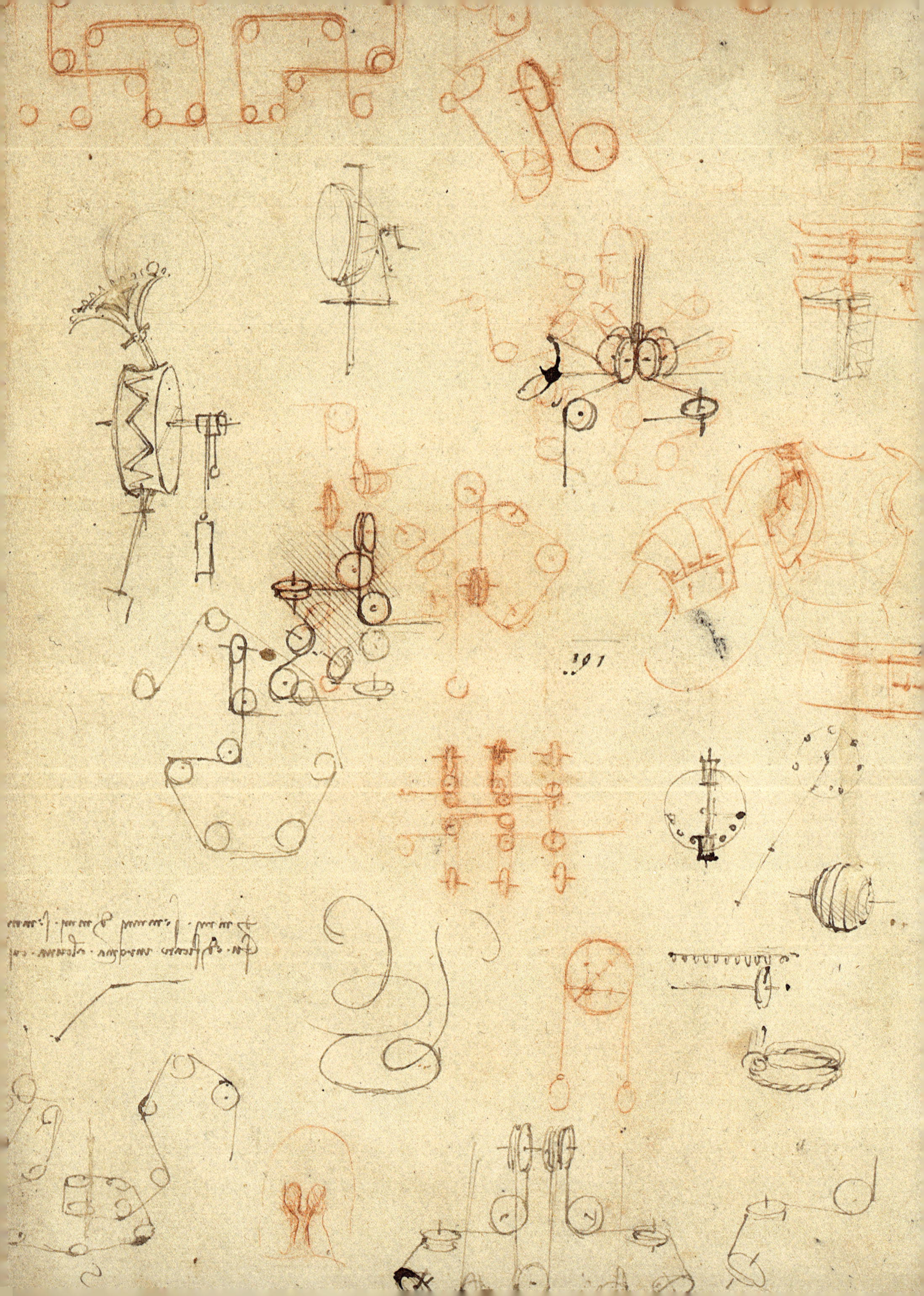
391

CONTINUOUS QUANTITY. LEONARDO AND THE MECHANICS OF THE HUMAN BODY: NUANCE IN ART AND MECHANICAL ROTATIONS

DOMENICO LAURENZA

Renaissance art, through its realistic imitation of nature, was in some ways biomimetic, even though the term did not yet exist. The fact that many Renaissance artists, like Leonardo, were also engineers helps us better understand the creative spirit of the period. At that time, imitating nature was not limited to painting, but extended to the design of machines and engineering projects. For example, Leonardo's hydraulic engineering replicated natural dams composed of stones and wood in order to harness the natural motion of water as a source of energy. Similarly, machine designs often drew inspiration from, and enhanced, the forms and movements of human or animal bodies.

In this way, artistic mimesis (the imitation of nature) and mechanical invention were often guided by fundamental principles like that of "continuous quantity", essential for understanding Leonardo and his vision of a fluid, dynamic, natural world. To understand this concept, it is essential to begin with the connection between the anatomical study of the human body and the study of machines.

PREVIOUS PAGE
Humanoid robot on a computer network, 2016

LEFT
Fig. 1. Leonardo da Vinci, *Codex Atlanticus*, "Studies on the humanoid automaton", 1497, pen and ink, f. 579r, Veneranda Biblioteca Ambrosiana

The *Codex Madrid I* (c. 1495) marks a key stage in Leonardo's treatises on machine elements. In it, he dissects machines into their fundamental components (screws, joints, wheels, springs, etc.), going beyond the purely empirical understanding of individual parts. From a theoretical standpoint, this systematic approach represents the most innovative aspect of his research. In this, the anatomical model influences the mechanical model: the machine undergoes a true 'dissection', revealing its distinct components [fig. 1]. But then mechanics in turn inspires anatomy: "Provide that the book on the elements of machines, with its practice, comes before the demonstration of the movement and force of man; and by these means you will be able to prove all your propositions", he notes in a folio dated 1509–10 (Windsor, RL 19009r).

In his research, Leonardo gradually transitioned from a quantitative (mathematical) approach, dominant in 15th-century Tuscan art, to a qualitative (physical) one.

This exploration culminated in the most innovative element of Leonardo's painting: *sfumato*. A technique employing layered glazes to endow subjects with softly blurred contours, it transcends what Giorgio Vasari called the "dry manner", that is, the practice of defining forms with crisp, unmodulated contours.

The *sfumato* in Leonardo's paintings creates seamless transitions between forms and shadows. Although the term rarely appears in his theoretical writings, a passage from the *Libro di Pittura*, based on a study in *Manuscript G* (folio 26r), reveals his thinking. He criticises contemporary painters for exaggerating muscular definition.

In other extracts from the now-lost *Book A*, compiled by Melzi, he describes the motions of the shoulder and hand as "continuous quantities", that is, near-infinite motions that trace circular arcs [fig. 2]. He studies the dynamics of the hand and how it is perceived from different angles.

This vision of nature as a continuous, curvilinear reality can also be found in his mechanical inventions. In the *Codex Madrid I*, he analyses mechanical joints through this lens: some are capable of limited, distinct movements (up/down; left/right), while others are capable of infinite, circular motions ("universal joints"), like those in the human body. The shoulder joint, for instance, behaves exactly like a universal joint.

Few drawings of Leonardo's humanoid robot survive, but from those that do, we can see that he sought to build a machine capable of effortless, fluid, and continuous movements [fig. 1]. At times, fine lines depict what appears to be the robot's articulated frame, composed of numerous overlapping and mobile plates to enable these smooth motions.

Curved, continuous movement is central to Leonardo's design for a crane intended to lift earth excavated from a canal bed [fig. 3]. The ramp for raising the debris forms a spiral, and the transmission mechanism uses human or animal power to turn a large wheel.

For this project, Leonardo studied the dynamics and anatomy of a human body hauling a weight up a hill using a wheel and a rope. His drawing reveals that the knee joint appears more limited in its range of motion than the shoulder joint.

In this crane design, human movements become fluid thanks to mechanical elements, such as wheels and ropes.

Finally, Leonardo praises the cart, pulled by animals via a system of gears, which he considers the greatest human invention: "For my part, I have yet to find anything in the inventions of others that is more practical than carts turned by animals [...] It is certain that the cart is unique compared to all other human inventions [...]". For Leonardo, a fundamental principle of mechanics – the transformation of reciprocating motion into continuous motion – becomes a broader reflection: it is a way of overcoming the limitations of human and animal movements to achieve smooth and continuous motion.

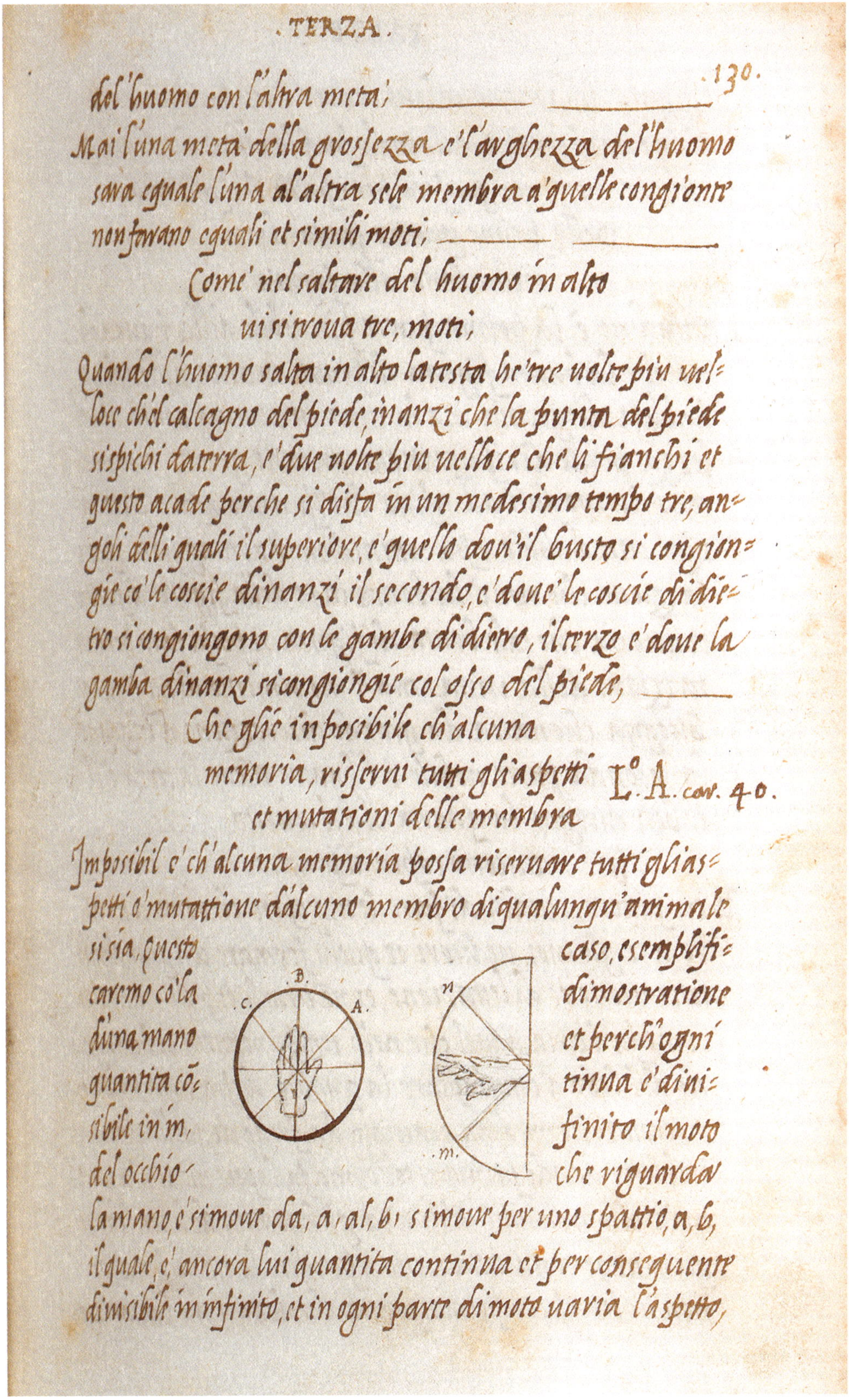

.TERZA.

.130.

del'huomo con l'altra metà; ———— ————

Mai l'una metà della grossezza e l'arghezza del'huomo sara eguale l'una al'altra sele membra a quelle congionte non faranno eguali et simili moti; ———— ————

Come nel saltare del huomo in alto ui si troua tre, moti;

Quando l'huomo salta in alto la testa he tre uolte più ueloce ch'el calcagno del piede, inanzi che la punta del piede si spichi da terra, e due uolte più uelloce che li fianchi et questo acade perche si disfa in un medesimo tempo tre, angoli delli quali il superiore, e quello dou'il busto si congiongie co'le coscie dinanzi il secondo, e doue le coscie di dietro si congiongono con le gambe di dietro, il terzo e doue la gamba dinanzi si congiongie col osso del piede, ————

Che gli è inposibile ch'alcuna memoria risserui tutti gli aspetti et mutationi delle membra

L.° A. car. 40.

Imposibil e ch'alcuna memoria possa riseruare tutti gli aspetti e mutattione d'alcuno membro di qualunqu'animale si sia, questo caso, esemplificaremo co'la dimostratione d'una mano et perch'ogni quantita continua e diuisibile in infinito il moto del occhio che riguarda la mano, e si moue da, a, al, b, si moue per uno spattio, a, b, il quale, e ancora lui quantita continua et per consequente diuisibile in infinito, et in ogni parte di moto uaria l'aspetto,

Fig. 2. Leonardo da Vinci, *Diagram on representation from multiple viewpoints and hand dynamics*, f. 130r, Biblioteca Apostolica Vaticana, Cod. Urb. Lat. 1270

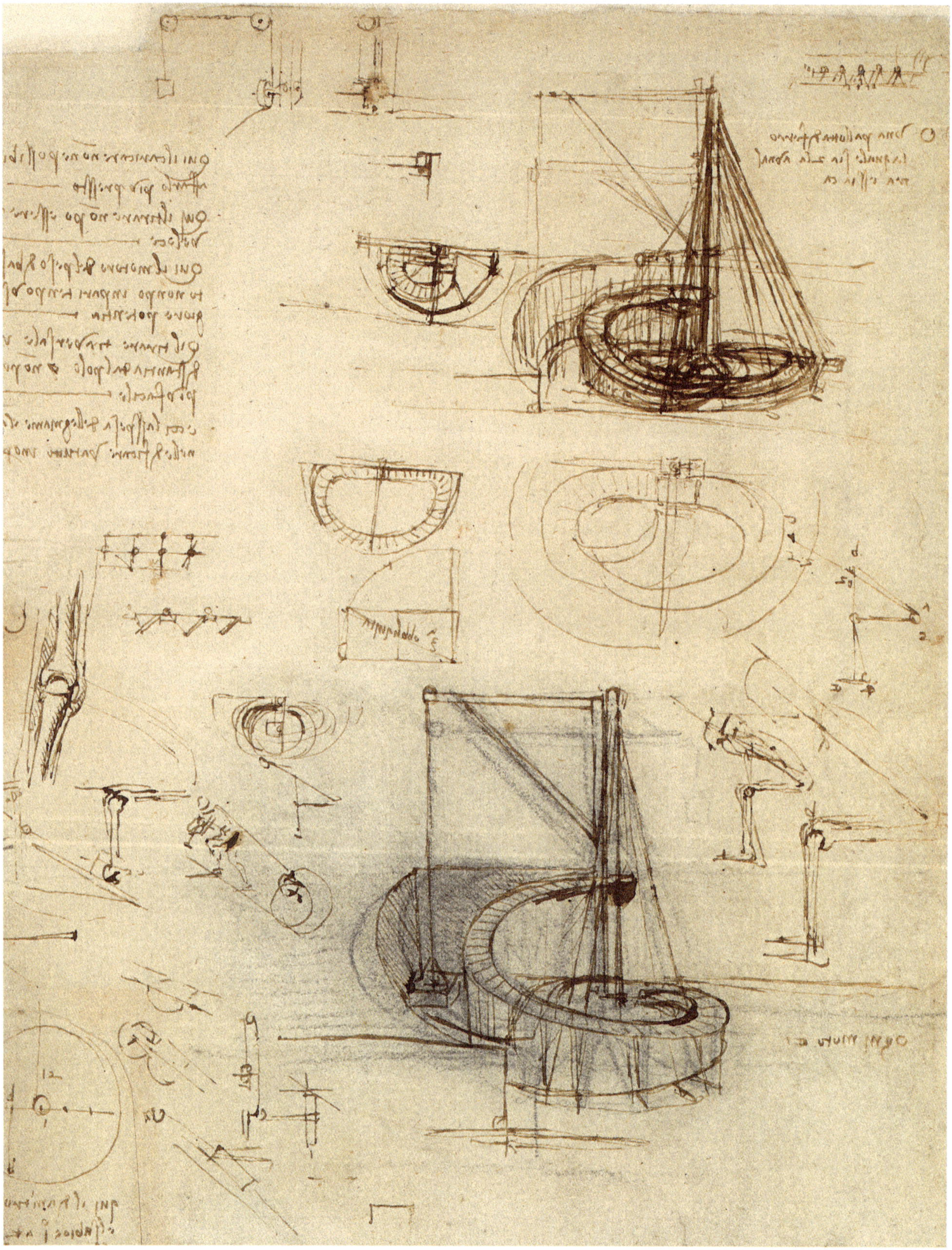

Fig. 3. Leonardo da Vinci, *Codex Atlanticus*, "Studies on the excavator and anatomy and dynamics of the human body", 1497, pen and ink, f. 444r, Veneranda Biblioteca Ambrosiana

Bibliography

Bernardoni, Andrea, Neuwahl, Alexander. "Lavoro manuale e soluzioni tecnologiche nello scavo dei canali", in Galluzzi, Paolo (ed.). *L'acqua microscopio della natura. Il Codice Leicester di Leonardo da Vinci*. Florence: Giunti, 2018, pp. 134-53.

Laurenza, Domenico. *Leonardo. L'anatomia*. Florence: Olschki, 2005, pp. 143-45.

Laurenza, Domenico. *Una sfida al limite: il robot di Leonardo tra anatomia ed elementi macchinali*, in Garai Luca (ed.). *I dilettevoli teatrali spettacoli di Leonardo da Vinci*. Bologna: Feltrinelli, 2019, pp. 55-70.

Rosheim, Mark E. *L'automa programmabile di Leonardo*. Florence: Giunti, 2000.

Taglialagamba, Sara. *Automation and Robotics by Leonardo da Vinci*. Milan: CB Edizioni, 2010.

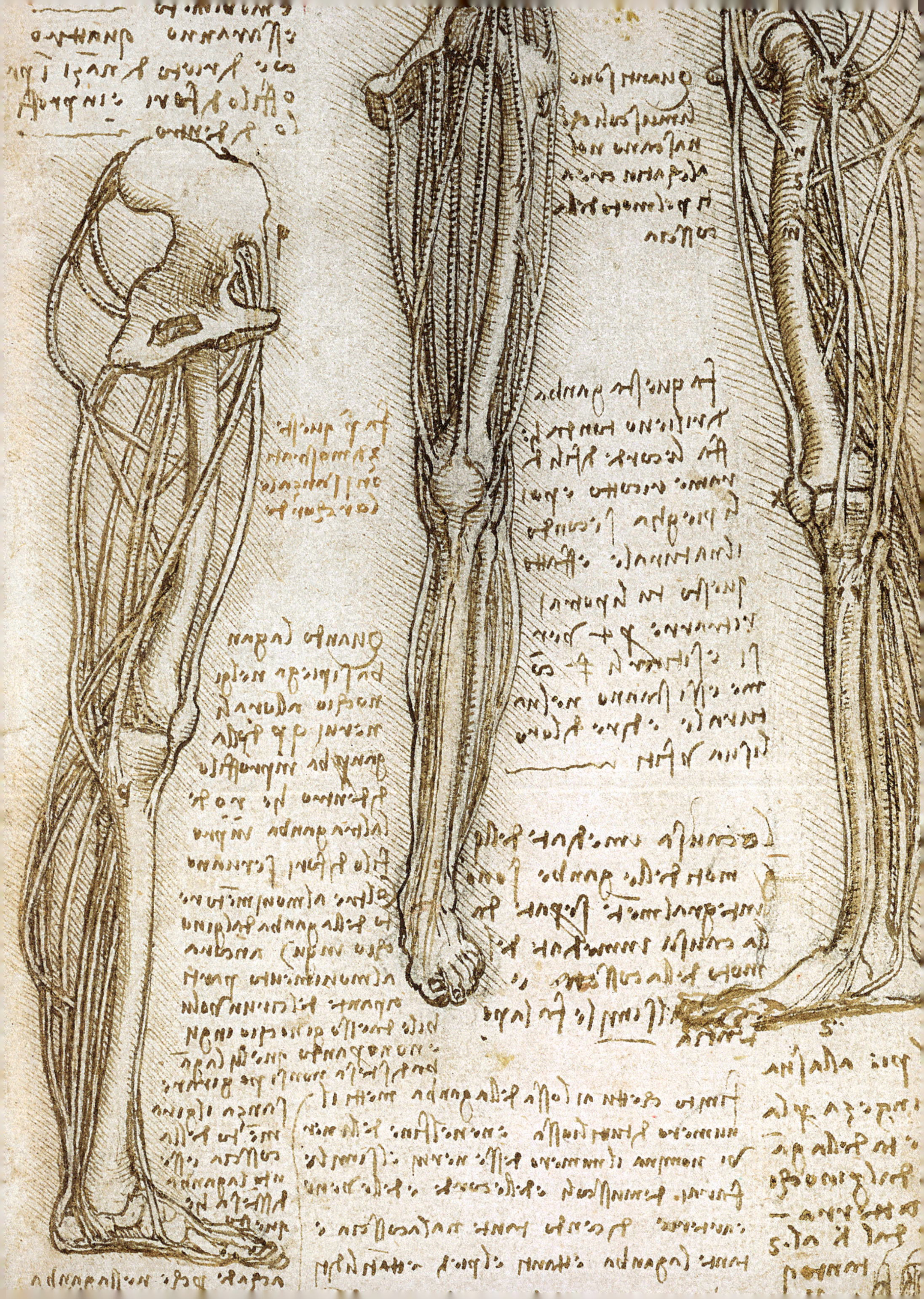

LEONARDO AND THE MODELLING OF THE HUMAN BODY

Dominique Le Nen, Domenico Laurenza

In addition to his artistic genius, Leonardo da Vinci was a scientist and engineer with a passion for research and experimentation. His exceptional observational skills and insatiable curiosity naturally led him to explore and replicate the biological phenomena around him. As a result, he designed casts, models and mechanical devices, and modelled functions with striking clarity, always with the aim of fostering understanding, sharing his knowledge, and teaching.

Copper or Brass Wires to Model Muscles

Leonardo da Vinci was genuinely fascinated by the study of muscles and their functions, far more so than other painters of his time, who focused merely on the contours they create beneath the skin. In his sketchbooks, he combined art with science to explore in detail the muscles, nerves and their functions. Confronted with the morphological and functional complexity of various muscles, he described their actions and positions by modelling them with the use of copper or brass wires. He created skeletons which he covered with these wires, *modelli* that enabled him to identify the muscles, their attachments to bones, how they intersect with one another, and how they move different parts of the body [fig. 1].

Leonardo was probably inspired by the ideas of Galen, the ancient Greek physician, who aptly compared the action of tendons at the joints to the strings that control puppets. The anatomical research of both Leonardo and Galen is rich with such analogies, although only Leonardo translated them into drawings or sculptures.

His models were not mere automata designed to amaze, but powerful cognitive tools that placed art at the service of science.

LEFT
Fig. 1. Leonardo da Vinci, *The bones and schematised muscles of the leg*, c. 1510, pen and ink over traces of black chalk, 21.5 × 11 cm, Windsor, Royal Collecction Trust, RL 12619r

A Glass Aorta to Observe Blood Flow

Leonardo studied the heart extensively, producing over twenty highly detailed plates. He dedicated himself to this organ very late in life, beginning by dissecting the hearts of oxen, drawing the atria, ventricles, papillary muscles, coronary vessels and valves with remarkable accuracy. While he did not discover the principle of 'blood circulation' as described by William Harvey in the 18th century, he came very close.

Thanks to a practice common in Tuscany, which involved killing a pig by driving a spike into its chest, Leonardo visualised and drew the movements of the heart chambers as they filled (diastole) and emptied (systole) (Windsor, RL 19065r). Observation of the passage of blood from the left ventricle through the aortic valve, which prevents backflow, inspired Leonardo to build a model. He began by pouring wax into an ox's aorta just where it emerges from the heart, revealing a widening, known as a 'sinus', above the aortic valve. These sinuses would later be described by the Italian anatomist Valsalva in the late 17th century, who gave them their name. Leonardo then created a delicate glass mould with an aortic orifice incorporating this bulge to replicate the sinuses. By injecting water and millet seeds into it, he could observe their flow through the aorta and deduce from his experiments that the vortices in the sinuses were partly responsible for closing the valve as the heart filled [fig. 2]. In the *Codex Leicester* (f. 9v), Leonardo planned to have a ceramicist construct a similar device to study the movement of sea waves: by blowing into a terracotta vessel with transparent glass walls and using millet seeds, the motion of an object submerged in agitated water can be observed.

Model of Bellows to Explain and Imitate Respiration

In his quest to understand the mechanism of respiration and replicate it using technology, Leonardo da Vinci envisioned creating a model of furnace bellows [fig. 3]: "... the air which is breathed in by lungs enters continually dry and cold and issues forth moist and warm" (Windsor, RL 19081r). This clever device reproduced the movement of warm and cold air, thus imitating the workings of the lungs.

In the diagram of this device, the warm exhaled air exits through a window (*m*), which is closed by a valve or flap (*b*, *d* in the diagram, following the mirrored writing used by Leonardo), and is then expelled through the chimney. The fresh inhaled air is drawn into the other chimney and passes through the other window (*n*) to enter the box, which represents the lung. The valve or flap (*a*) then closes, and once this air has been heated, it exits through the first window, and so on.

Leonardo explains in the text accompanying the folio that if breathing is short and rapid, it suffocates the breather, because the heated air is not completely expelled.

Leonardo's work on respiration and the heart – in other words, on the links between the movements of air and blood – evolved and adapted over the course of his studies and discoveries, though he never completely broke free from the works of Galen. Thus, in 1508, to describe the mechanism of the heart's action, Leonardo followed Galenic theory, according to which the heart sends a mixture of air from the lungs and blood towards the aorta. He called this mixture 'vital spirit', 'vital heat', or 'innate heat', generated by the friction of blood moving within the chambers

RIGHT
Fig. 2. Leonardo da Vinci, *The aortic valve*, c. 1512-1513, pen and ink on blue paper, 28.3 × 20.4 cm, Windsor, Royal Collection Trust, RL 19082r

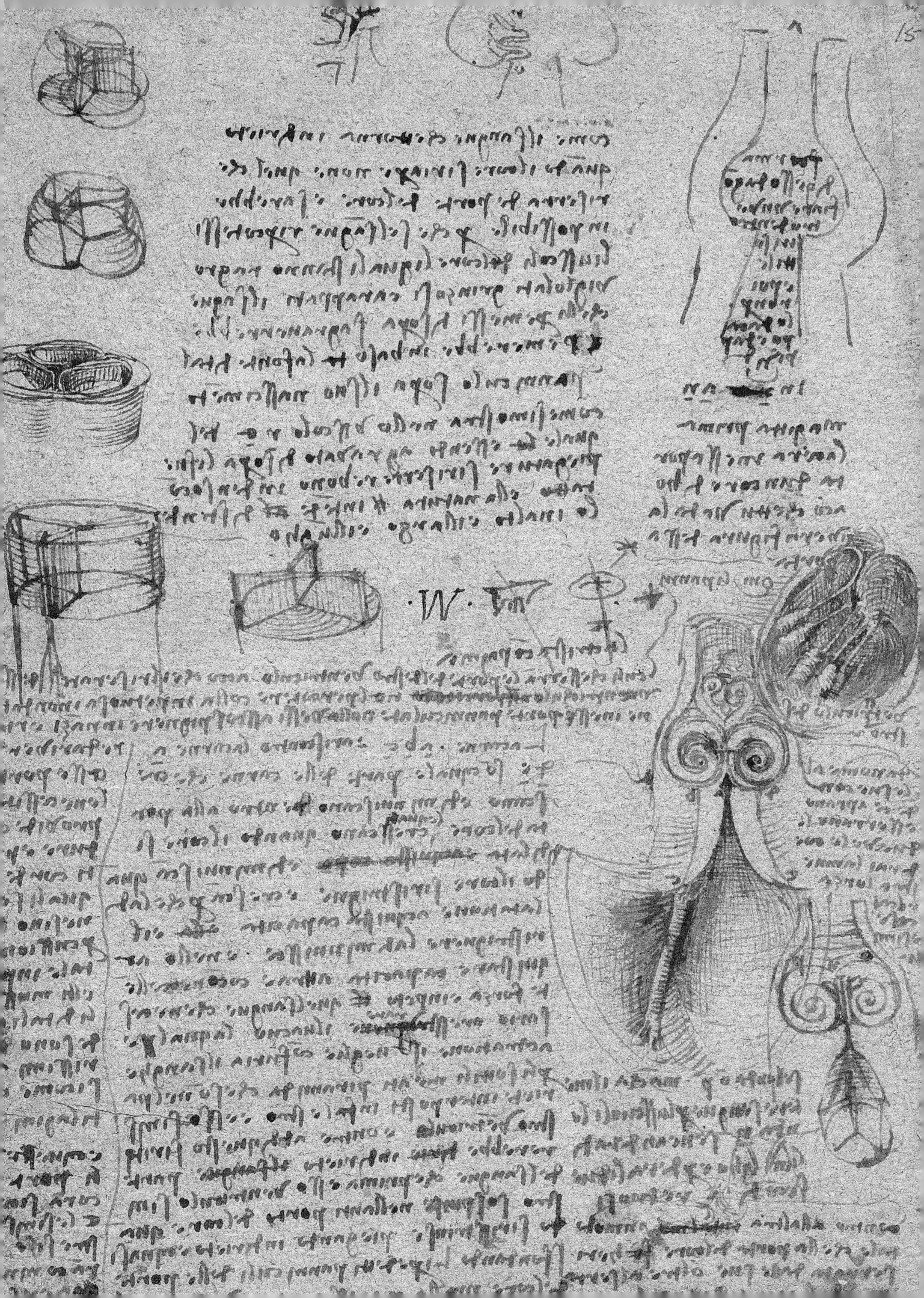

of the heart. The air in the lungs thus serves to cool the heat produced by the heart's movements, because, for Leonardo, the faster it beats, the more the heat increases, "as proven by the pulse of feverish individuals, which is driven by the beating of the heart" (Windsor, RL 19029r). This bellows model served as inspiration for another invention, namely, a more efficient furnace.

This same approach can be seen on the verso of the folio (*Codex Arundel*, f. 24v), where the design of an underwater breathing apparatus represents a biomimetic amplification of respiration [fig. 4]. The drawing appears to depict two tubes through which air flows in both directions between the diving mask at the bottom and the floating dome at the top. As with the furnace, the machine mimics the dual anatomical structure of the respiratory organs, the heart and the lungs, with the former being an integral part of the respiratory system.

These two inventions are thus forms of biomimicry, one related to fire, the other to water.

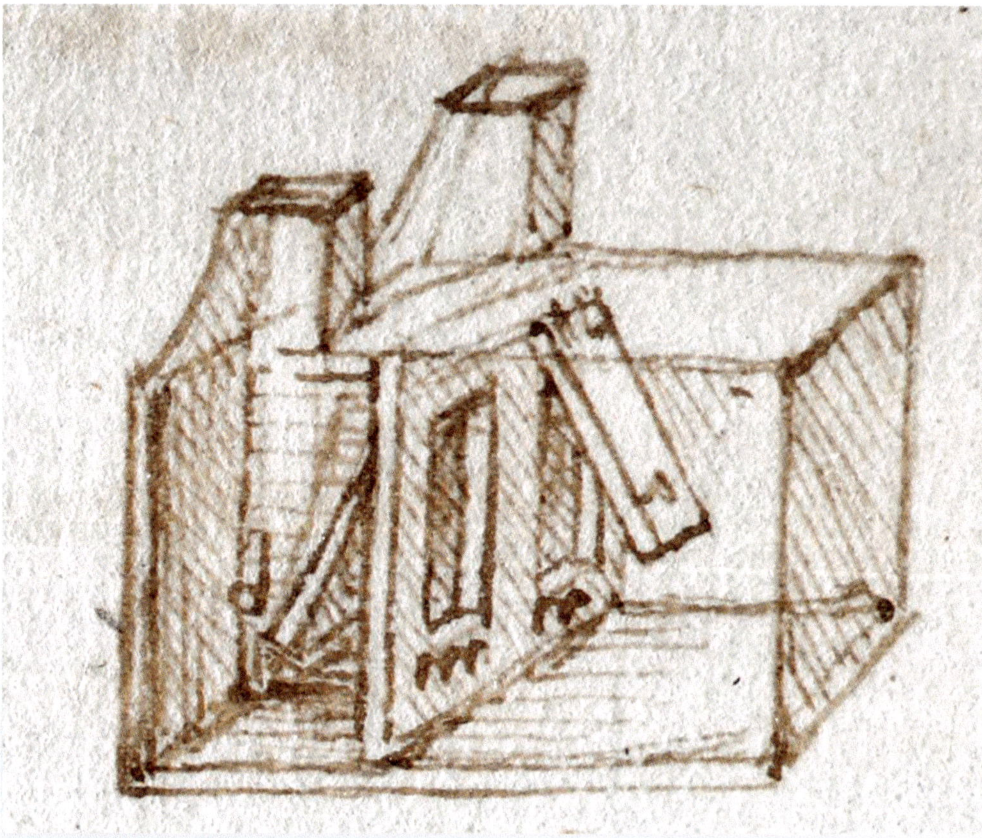

Fig. 3. Leonardo da Vinci, *Codex Arundel*, c. 1480-1518, f. 24r (detail), British Library, Arundel 263

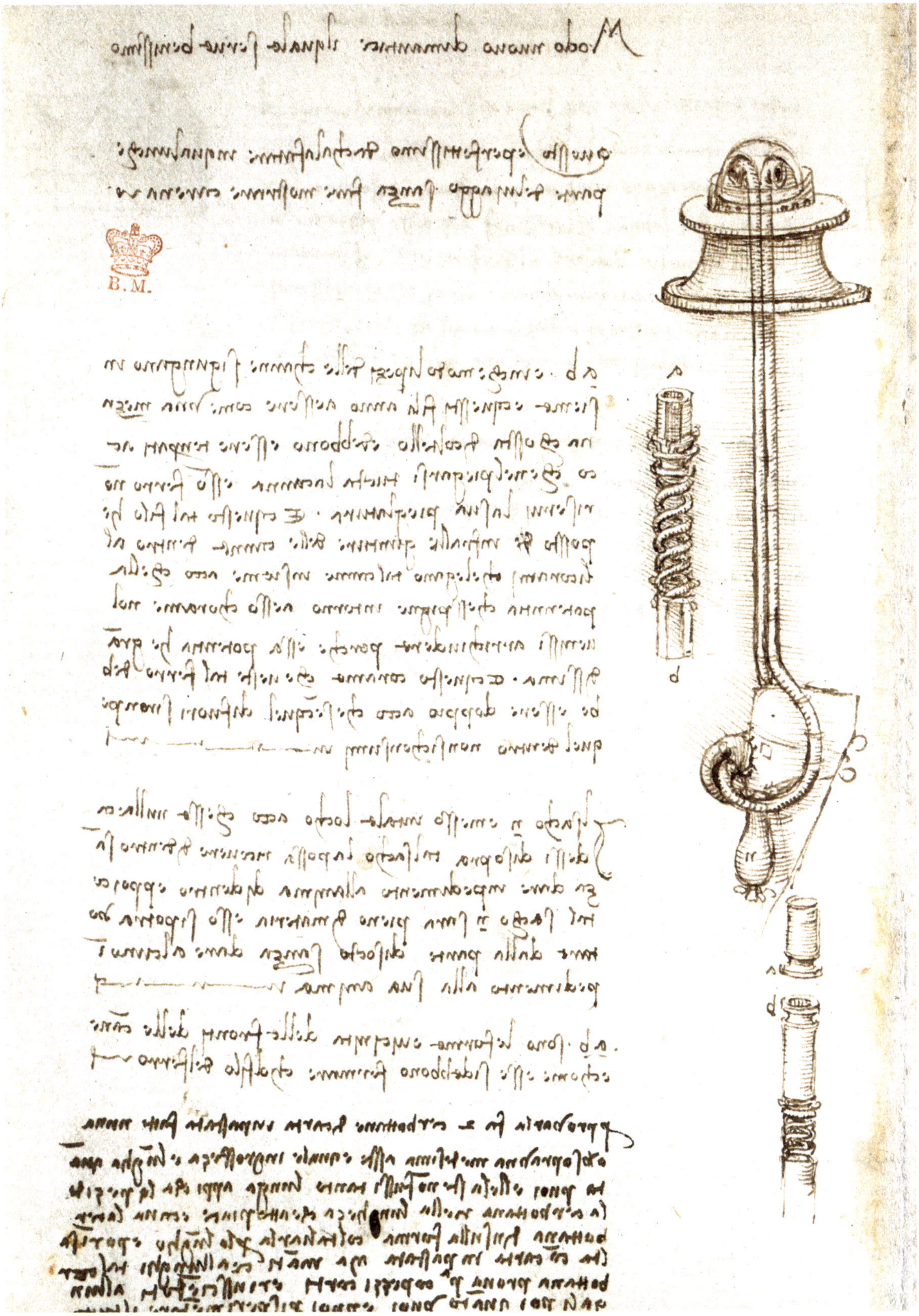

Fig. 4. Leonardo da Vinci, *Codex Arundel*, 1508, pen and ink, f. 24v, British Library, Arundel 263

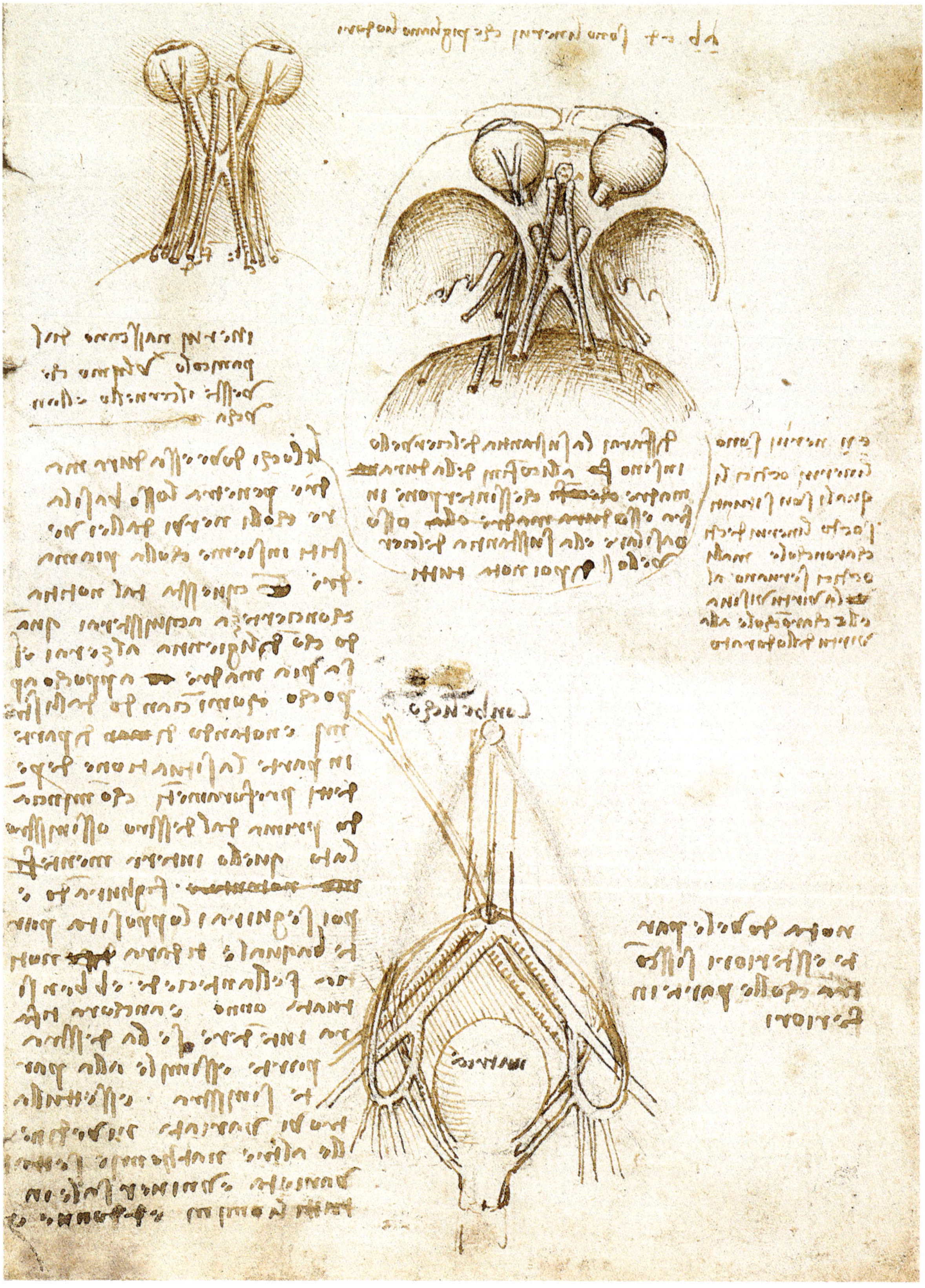

Leonardo da Vinci, *The cranial nerves*, c. 1508, pen and ink over traces of black chalk, with scratching out, 19 × 13.6 cm, Windsor, Royal Collection Trust, RL 19052r

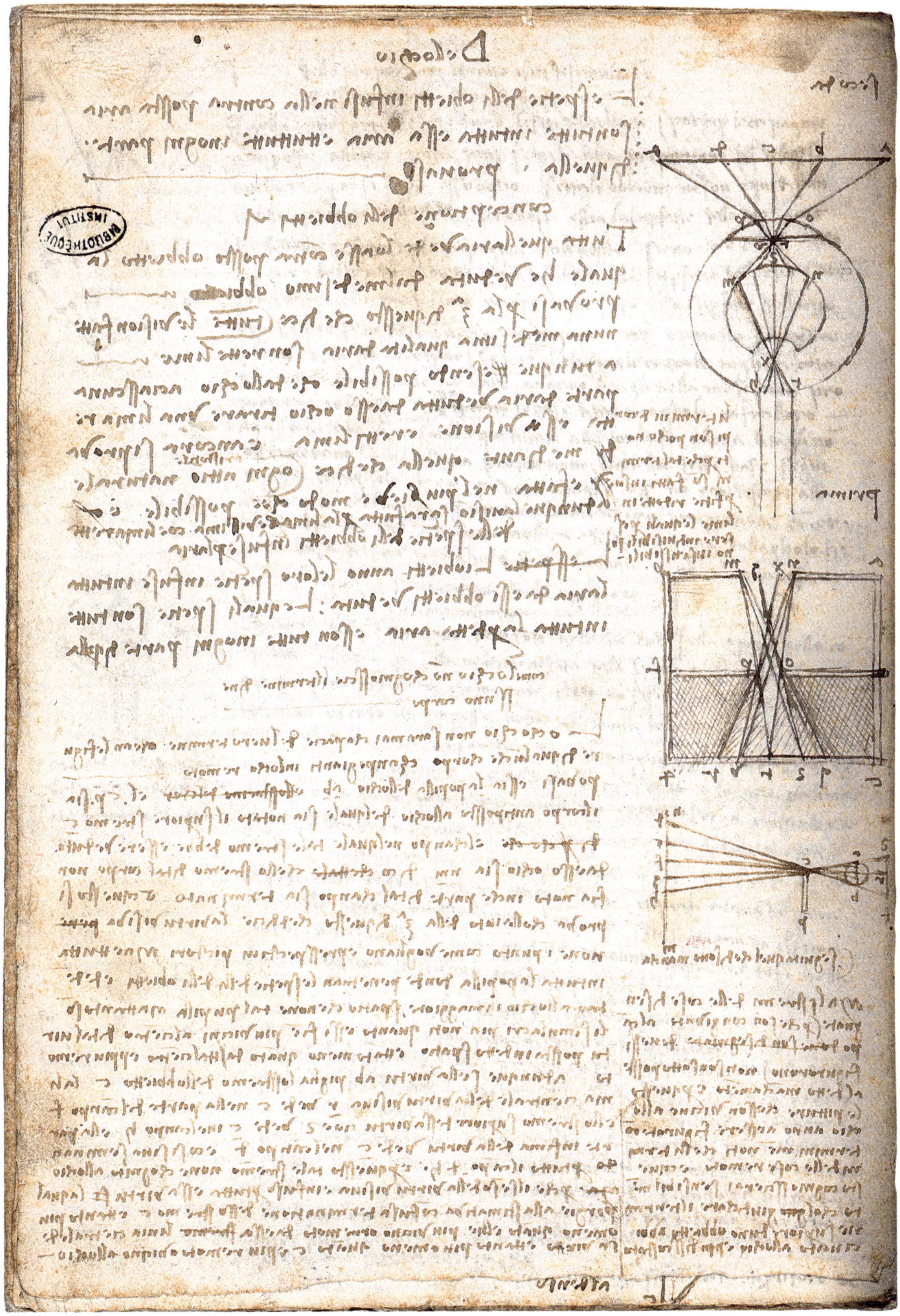

Fig. 5. Leonardo da Vinci, *Manuscript D.*, c. 1508-1509, 23.1× 16.5 cm, f. 10v, Bibliothèque de l'Institut de France, Ms 2175

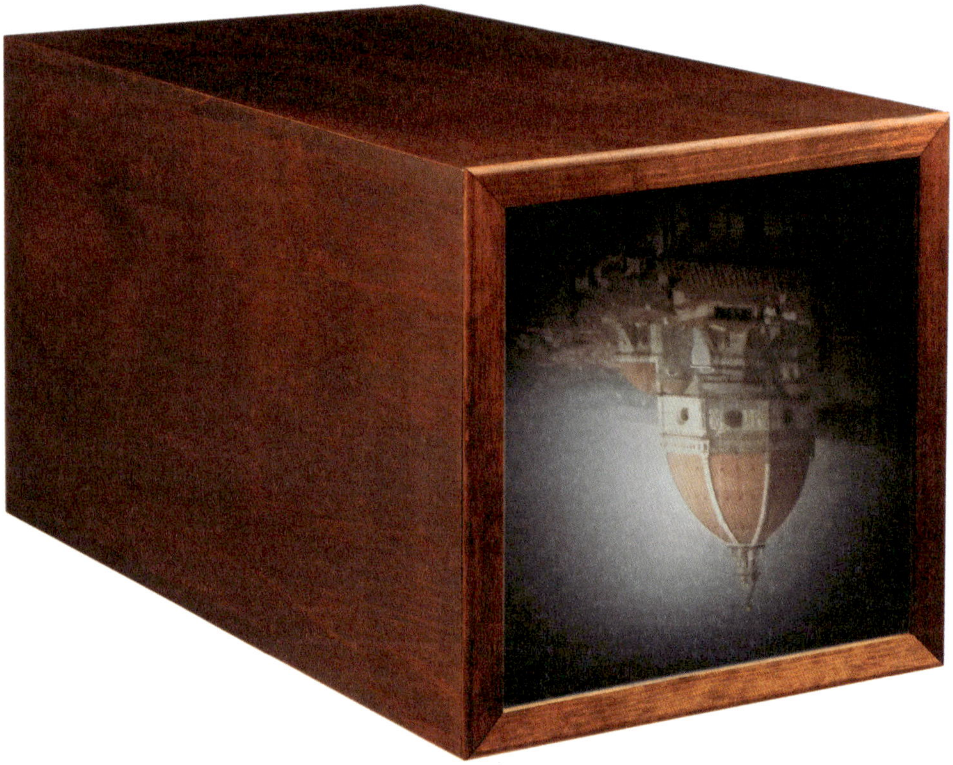

Fig. 6. Jean-Louis Pironio, model of the *camera obscura*, after Leonardo's drawing in *Manuscript D*, Bibliothèque de l'Institut de France (f. 10v)

The Camera Obscura: Revealing the Mystery of Vision

Leonardo da Vinci was obsessed with the mystery of vision, to which he devoted a great many studies spread across various codices, as evidenced by the ten folios of *Manuscript D* in Paris, including folio 10v devoted to the construction of a *camera obscura*. For Leonardo, the eye represented a "window onto the soul" (*Codex Ashburnham*, folio 19r). He dissected the eye, identifying its components by function: the pupil and lens, optic nerves and brain [fig. 5]. On the role of the pupil, a true lens, he wrote: "... The black or near black border that surrounds the pupil serves no other purpose than to increase or reduce its size; to increase it when the eye looks toward a dark place, and to reduce it when it gazes upon brightness or some luminous object. And you shall conduct the experiment of bringing a light close to the eye; do this when you are looking into darkness and then turn your eye toward this light, and the experiment will convince you" (*Codex Atlanticus*, f. 345r).

The *camera obscura* is a black box into which light enters through a small hole on one side and is closed on the opposite side by a thin sheet of white paper or frosted glass. If the opening is sufficiently small, the observer's eye placed in front of it will see an inverted image of the external scene on the opposite wall [fig. 6].

This principle, known since antiquity thanks to Aristotle, fascinated Leonardo. He reflected on how the inverted image projected by the *camera obscura* could be perceived as upright by the eye, hypothesising that the pupil inverted the image and that the lens then "inverted it back". Although this theory is incorrect, it reflects Leonardo's scientific approach, always seeking to understand the mechanisms of the human body, whether it be blood circulation, respiration, or vision.

Bibliography

Brioist, Pascal, Le Nen, Dominique. *Léonard de Vinci et l'anatomie, la mécanique de la vie*. Paris: Skira Paris, 2023.

Clayton, Martin, Philo, Ron. *Leonardo da Vinci: Anatomist*. London: Royal Collection Trust, 2017.

Laurenza, Domenico. *Leonardo, l'anatomia*. Florence: Giunti, 2009.

Le Nen, Dominique. *Léonard de Vinci, l'aventure anatomique*. Vanves: Éditions E/P/A, 2019.

O'Malley, Charles Donald, de Cusance Morant Saunders Bertrand, John. *Leonardo da Vinci on the Human Body*. New York: Gramercy Books, 1982.

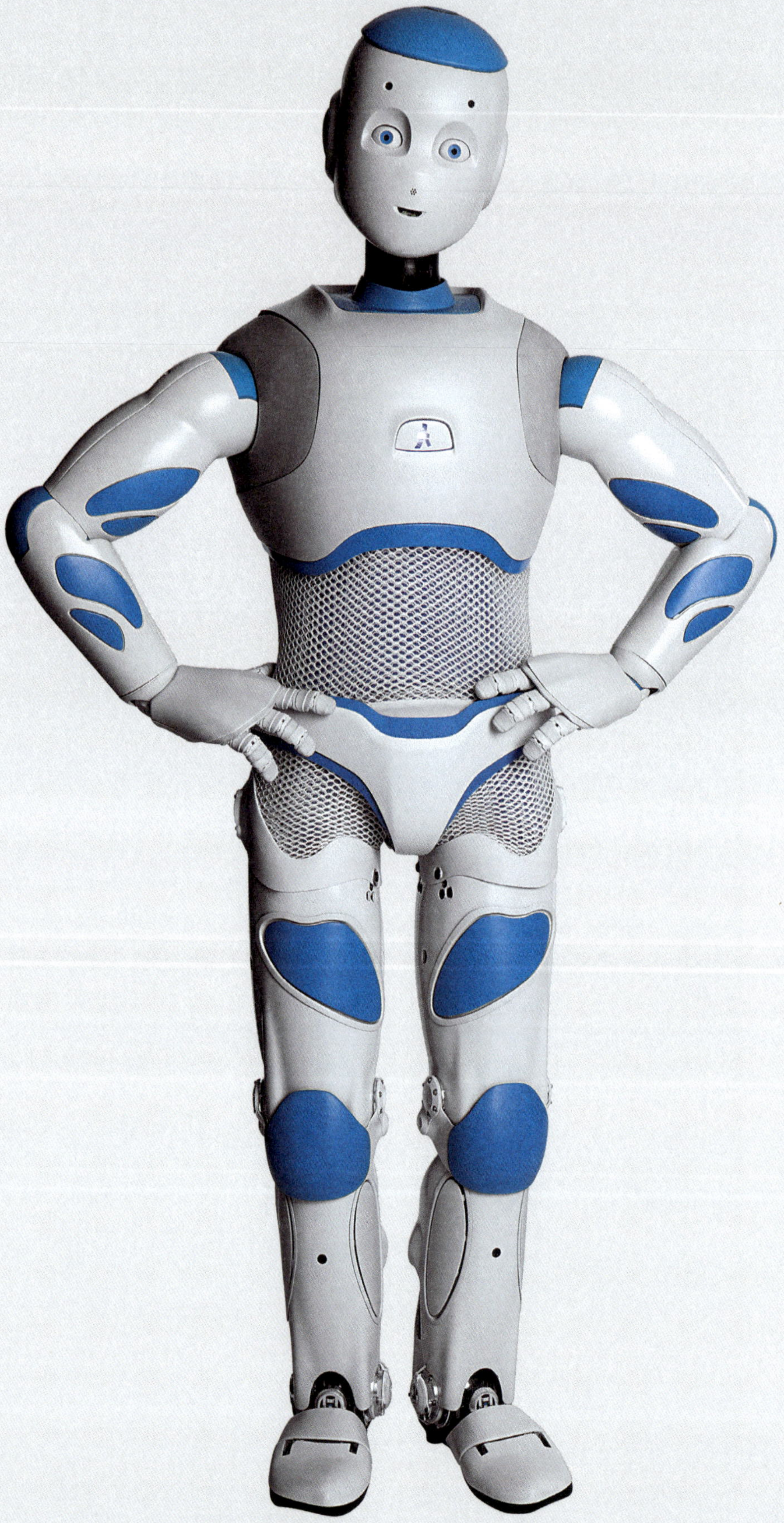

BUILDING AND OPERATING ROBOTS TO UNDERSTAND LIVING ORGANISMS

PHILIPPE SOUÈRES
WITH THOMAS FLAYOLS, MICHEL TAÏX,
OLIVIER STASSE

The design of robots is primarily motivated by the desire to free humans from having to perform arduous, repetitive tasks, or tasks that require speed and precision.

Robots are used in countless fields, from manufacturing to disaster response, surgery and daily assistance. For many robotics researchers, however, the challenge goes much further. Through robotics, these scientists are studying humans and animals, continuing the work of the pioneers of cybernetics in the late 1940s. Their goal is to create machines that resemble living beings and possess similar capabilities, in order to understand how these creatures manage to function in their environments. Combining engineering and interdisciplinary knowledge, they build in order to understand.

Taking inspiration from animals and humans to build robots means not only imitating their appearance, but also replicating their systems of perception, information processing and movement control, on which their ability to act is based. Unlike mere automata or software, robots are machines that can adapt their behaviour. They are equipped with sensors that provide information about their environment and internal state, processors that enable them to execute programs based on perceived and stored data, and actuators to interact with the real world.

The combination of perception, decision-making, and action gives the robot a level of autonomy that enables it to perform a variety of tasks. Although these robotic systems are just rudimentary imitations of living beings, they offer researchers a remarkable opportunity to address issues traditionally confined to the life sciences.

The Gepetto team at LAAS-CNRS has been conducting research since 2006 on the movement of anthropomorphic systems and, more generally, legged robots. Their work raises important questions:

LEFT
Fig. 1. The humanoid robot Romeo, 2016

- How can these machines be equipped with the ability to analyse their environments and adapt to them in order to plan their movements?
- How can the movements of each of the body's joints be coordinated to produce effective overall coordination?
- How can optimal contact points be selected to navigate complex environments such as stairs, narrow passages, and sloped or uneven terrain while maintaining balance?
- How can objects, whether solid or fragile, be manipulated with the dexterity of a living being?

To determine the forces to be applied to each joint of the robot in order to accomplish a task, an effective technique involves solving an optimisation problem. This technique echoes discoveries in neuroscience related to human motor control, which demonstrate that the central nervous system optimises our movements in accordance with certain criteria, the exact nature of which remains a subject of debate.

These optimisation techniques are at the heart of the achievements of Boston Dynamics' Atlas robot, capable of performing jumps and movements worthy of a human athlete. In this vein, the Gepetto team has carried out a series of demonstrations with the humanoid robots HRP-2 and Talos, as well as with quadruped robots.

In recent years, advances in artificial intelligence, driven by the increasing power of computers and access to huge databases, have revolutionised robot programming. It is now possible to equip robots with motor skills through experience accumulated by virtual robots in advanced simulations, using machine learning algorithms. These action policies are the result of reinforcement learning algorithms that optimise reward functions by adjusting the parameters of artificial neural networks, systems whose operation is loosely inspired by biological neurons.

Alongside this software revolution, the hardware design of robots has made significant progress in recent years. On the one hand, mechatronics is opening new horizons with increasingly powerful actuators and sensors for processing information. On the other hand, innovative materials and 3D-printing techniques are offering new possibilities for optimising the structure of robots.

Despite these advances, a major challenge remains in the quest to imitate animal movement: the lack of artificial actuation processes capable of matching the performance of biological muscles. The majority of current legged robots use electric motors coupled with reduction systems, a solution that struggles to replicate the flexibility and sensitivity of muscles and tendons. More than ever, robotics is advancing by drawing on interdisciplinary expertise, and it is highly likely that it will become an indispensable pillar of medicine and life sciences in the future.

To illustrate our research work, we have chosen to present two very different robots, which correspond to two phases of the team's scientific journey. The first, Romeo [fig. 1], is a humanoid robot designed in 2014 by the company Aldebaran Robotics as part of a national programme involving a large number of industrial and academic partners, including LAAS-CNRS.

The design of this first French prototype of a life-sized humanoid robot was highly ambitious. The goal was to incorporate a large number of innovations into the machine, such as an original spinal column mechanism, an articulated foot, legs actuated by a system of screws and cables, and a stabilised gaze inspired by the human vestibulo-ocular system. The project did not, unfortunately, achieve its objectives owing to the significant gap between the ambitions and mastery

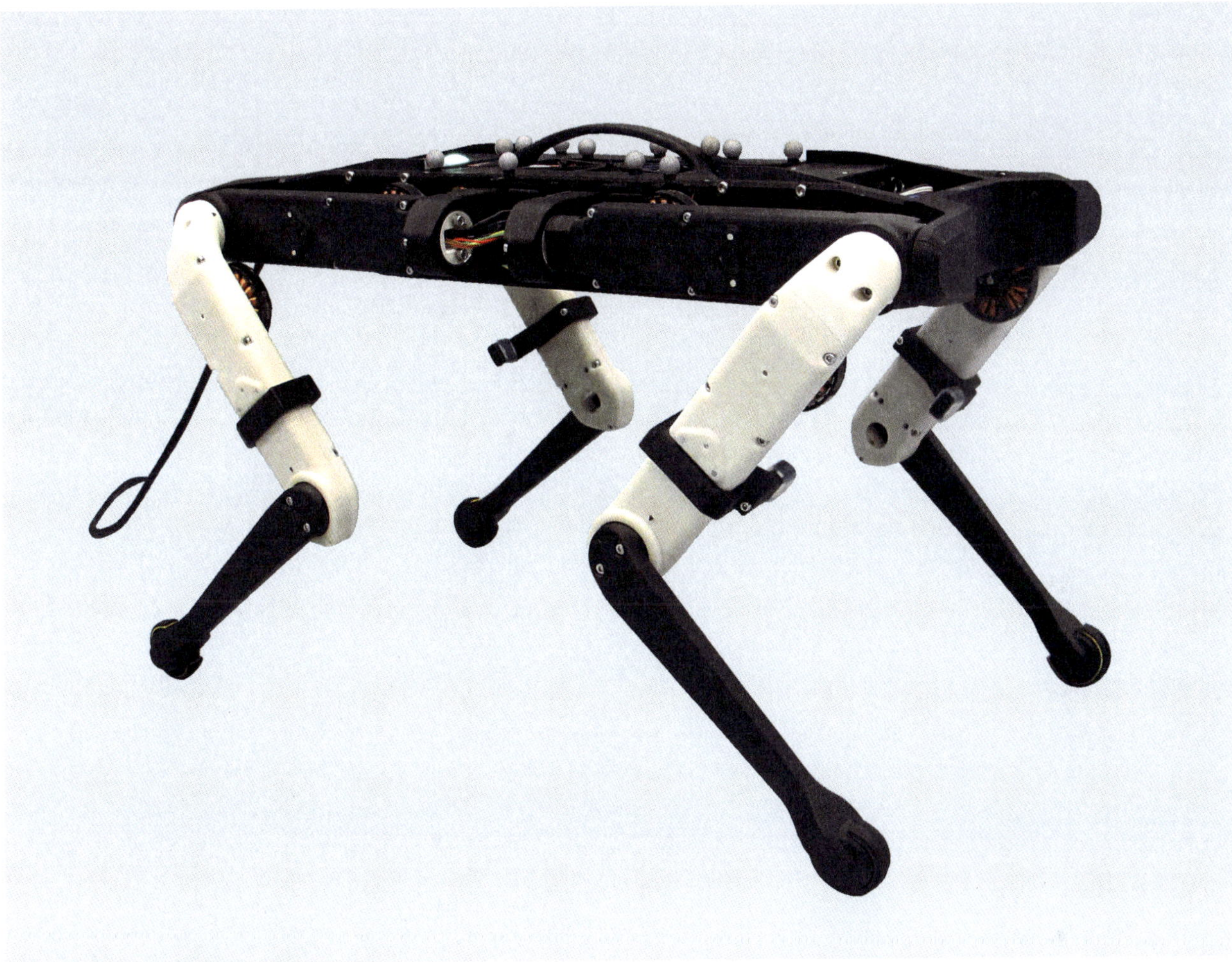

Fig. 2. The Solo12 quadruped robot, 2020

of the technologies employed. This robot, which was intended to be capable of both communicating with humans, particularly through its gestures and ability to interpret the environment, and physically interacting with them to assist in their daily lives, was never fully functional.

This setback highlights the challenges of humanoid robotics, which requires the consideration, from the design stage, of countless hardware and software constraints essential for the proper functioning of perception, decision-making, and control systems. This compels researchers to proceed modestly, step by step, in their attempts to replicate the incredible performance of biological systems.

The second robot is the small quadruped Solo12 [fig. 2], developed through a partnership between the Max Planck Institute in Tübingen, Germany, and the Gepetto team at LAAS-CNRS in Toulouse, as part of the Open Dynamic Robot Initiative (ODRI).

This robot features 12 degrees of freedom, three per leg, each powered by the same reversible and innovative actuation module. Thanks to this actuator, this lightweight robot is capable of performing highly dynamic movements, including large-amplitude jumps, and actively cushioning impacts upon landing.

Solo12's dynamic capabilities have enabled the research team to develop innovative new approaches, such as collaborative design, predictive trajectory optimisation, and machine learning for locomotion. Building on this success, a new, slightly larger quadruped prototype, Sassa, is currently under development at LAAS, which should soon be equipped with a head, supported by an articulated neck, featuring a 'mouth'-like gripper for grasping and manipulating objects, as well as vision and inertial sensors to stabilise its perception.

Bibliography

ACKERMAN, Evan, "Aldebaran Robotics Introduces Romeo, Finally". *IEEE Spectrum*, 2012. https://spectrum.ieee.org/aldebaran-robotics-introduces-romeo-finally

ARACTINGI, Michel, FLAYOLS, Thomas, LÉZIART, Pierre-Alexandre, PEREZ, Julien, SILANDER, Tomi, SOUÈRES, Philippe. "Controlling the Solo12 Quadruped Robot with Deep Reinforcement Learning". *Scientific Reports* (13) (2023), 11945.

CHANE-SANE, Elliot, FLAYOLS, Thomas, LÉZIART, Pierre-Alexandre, MANSARD, Nicolas, SOUÈRES, Philippe, STASSE, Olivier. "CaT: Constraints as Terminations for Legged Locomotion Reinforcement Learning". *IEEE/RSJ Int. Conf. on Intelligent Robots and Systems*, Abu Dhabi, 2024.

DANTEC, Ewen Louis et al. "Whole Body Model Predictive Control with a Memory of Motion: Experiments on a Torque-Controlled Talos". *IEEE Int. Conf. on Robotics and Automation*, Xi'an, China, 2021.

FADINI, Gabriele, FLAYOLS, Thomas, DEL PRETE, Andrea, SOUÈRES, Philippe. "Simulation Aided Co-Design for Robust Robot Optimization". *IEEE Robotics and Automation Letters* 7(4) (2022), 11306-13, 14.

FLAYOLS, Thomas, GRIMMINGER, Felix, LÉZIART, Pierre-Alexandre, MANSARD, Nicolas, SOUÈRES, Philippe. "Implementation of a Reactive Walking Controller for the New Open-Hardware Quadruped Solo-12". *IEEE Int. Conf. on Robotics and Automation*, Xi'an, China, 2021.

GRIMMINGER, Felix et al. "An Open Torque-Controlled Modular Robot Architecture for Legged Locomotion Research". *IEEE Robotics and Automation Letters*, Vol. 5(2) (2020).

GUIGON, Emmanuel, SOUÈRES, Philippe, TAÏX, Michel and TRAN, Tuan Minh. "Generating Human-like Reaching Movements with a Humanoid Robot: A Computational Approach". *Journal of Computational Science*, Vol. 4(4) (2013).

LAUMOND, Jean-Paul, SOUÈRES, Philippe, SREENIVASA, Manish. "Walking to Grasp: Modeling of Human Movements as Invariants and an Application to Humanoid Robotics". *IEEE Transactions on Cybernetics*, Part A, Vol 99 (2012), 1-14.

LÉZIART, Pierre-Alexandre, CORBÈRES, Thomas, FLAYOLS, Thomas, TONNEAU, Steve, MANSARD, Nicolas, SOUÈRES, Philippe. "Improved Control Scheme for the Solo Quadruped and Experimental Comparison of Model Predictive Controllers". *IEEE Robotics and Automation Letters* (2022).

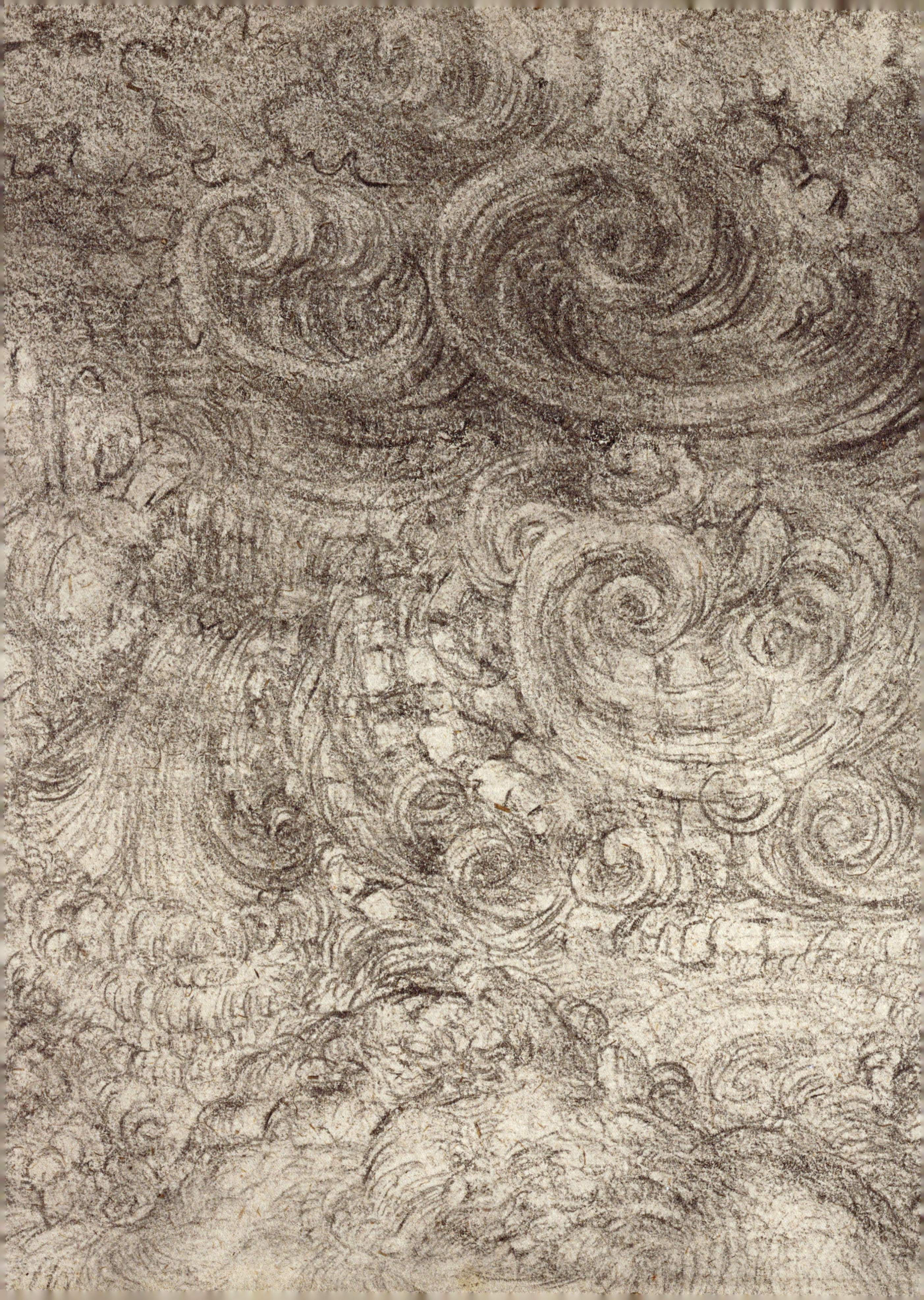

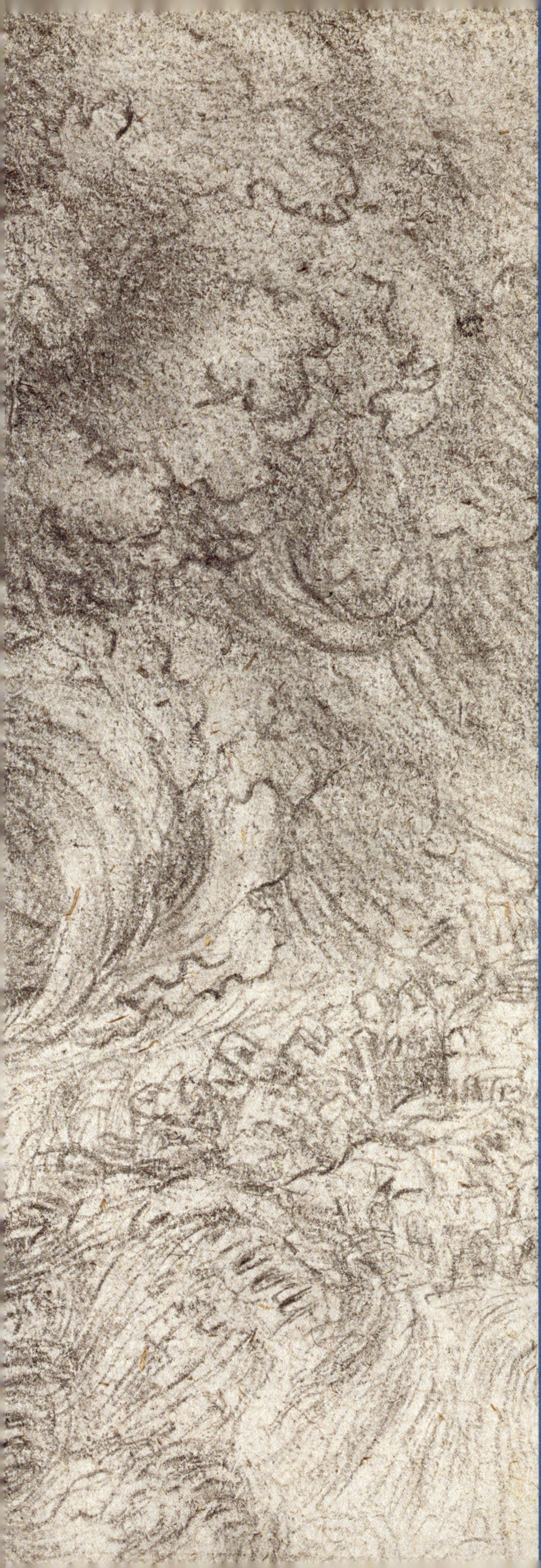

Biomimicry and Fluid Mechanics

Chapter II

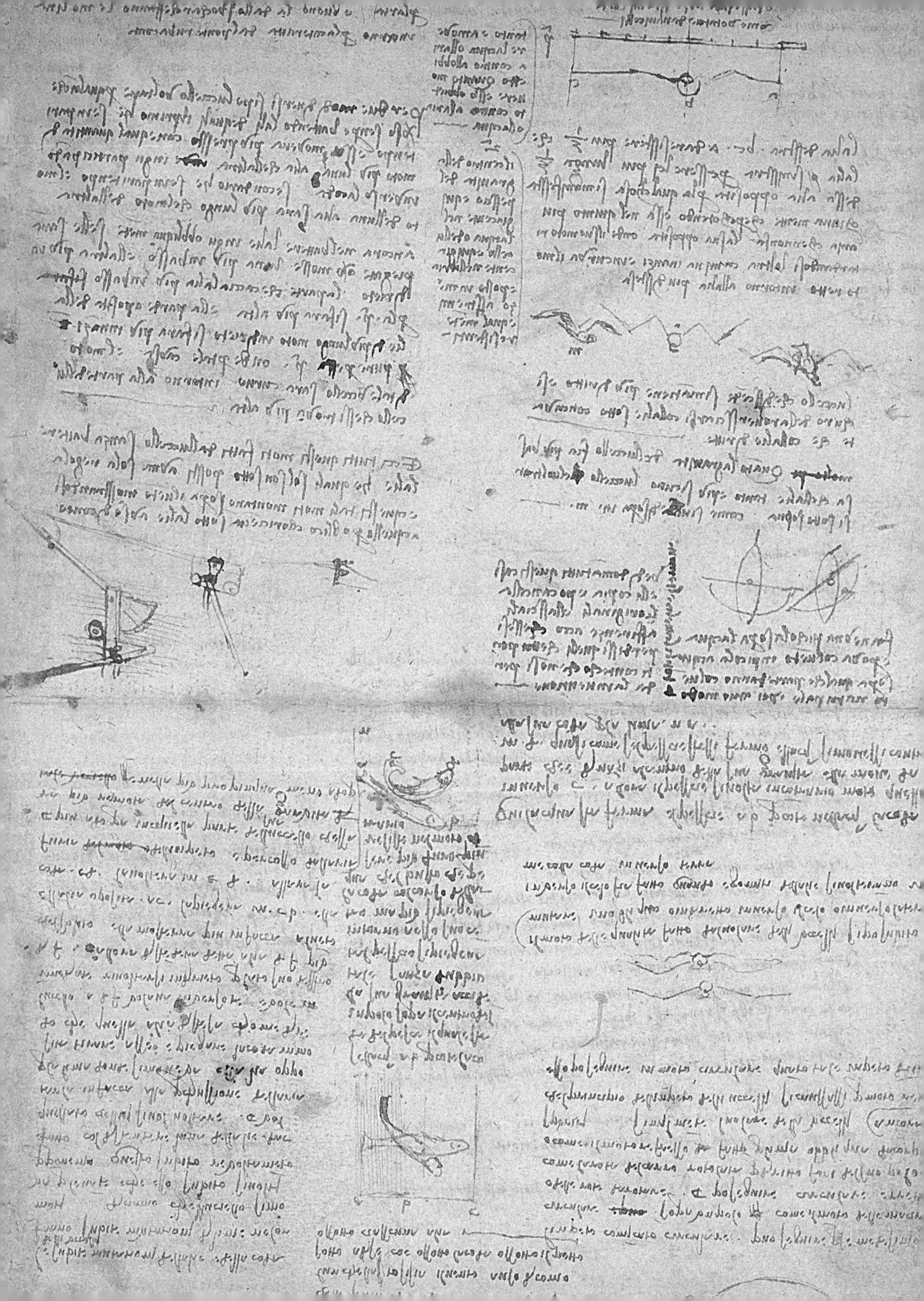

WATER AS A MODEL FOR FLUID MOTION

ALEXANDER NEUWAHL

In the mid-16th century, knowledge of hydraulics still remained restricted to the principles formulated by Archimedes.

Throughout the Middle Ages, science, confined to the monasteries, struggled to move beyond mere philosophical speculation, deprived of the liberating catalyst of experimentation. Yet this era also saw the emergence of irrigation systems of remarkable technical ingenuity, driven by the empirical brilliance of exceptional craftsmen whose work profoundly affected cities and entire regions.

In the field of hydraulics, Leonardo had strong intuitions that could not be implemented at the time owing to the lack of suitable technical and mathematical tools. For him, vortices were central to understanding fluid motion and the possibilities arising from its control.

In very simple experiments, he examined vortices simply by moving his hand in water and observing the stages of vortex formation (*Manuscript F*, f. 13r). Following a mental process typical of him, Leonardo immediately wondered about the utility of the vortex, trying to imagine ways to harness its energy, perhaps to turn a mill.

Among the experiments described in Leonardo's codices, one of the best-known is designed to study the movement of water in a vortex by immersing a rod in it (*Manuscript A*, f. 60v); another highlights the analogy between the barely distinguishable movements of air passing over an object and those of dust suspended in water stirred by an object (*Codex Leicester*, f. 29v).

Leonardo sought to uncover the common and divergent laws of vortices in water and air. Between 1510 and 1513, while observing a boat's wake, he noted in a folio (Windsor, RL 12660v) that eddies are more pronounced below the surface than on the surface itself.

The turbulence in water caused by the advancing bow of a ship appears to be more clearly defined, and thus more easily observable, beneath the surface than at the water's surface. For Leonardo, this difference stemmed from the fact that below the surface, water is at rest: it naturally 'floats'. At the surface, on the other hand, it is in contact with air, which is lighter, so it has to use energy to maintain its position. Below the surface, all the energy imparted to the water by the

PREVIOUS PAGE
Leonardo da Vinci, *A deluge*, c. 1517-1518, black chalk, 16.1 × 20.7 cm, Windsor, Royal Collection Trust, RL 12382r

LEFT
Leonardo da Vinci, *Codex Atlanticus*, "Studies on the flight of birds", 1507, pen and ink, f. 571r, Veneranda Biblioteca Ambrosiana

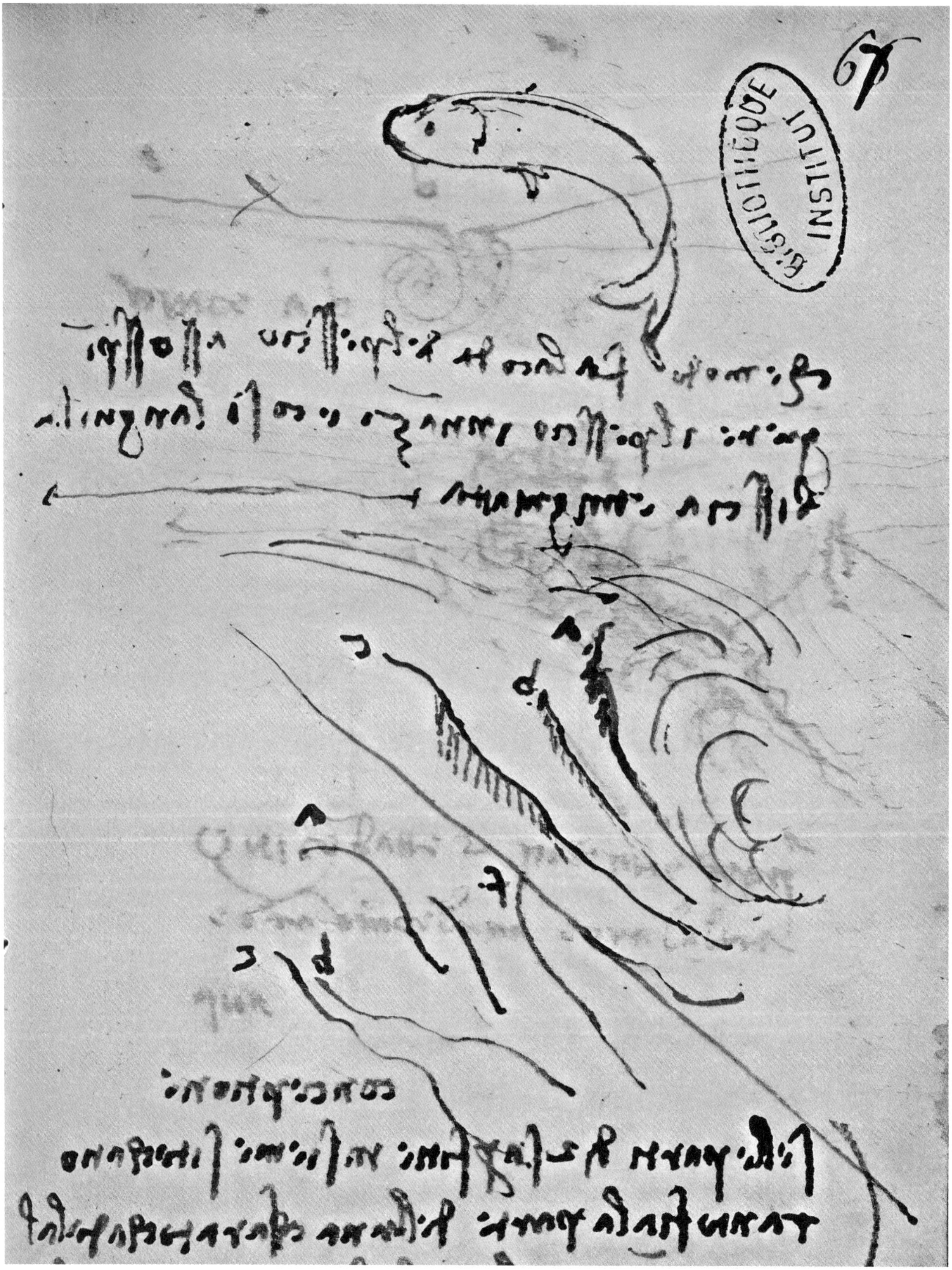

Leonardo da Vinci, *Manuscript M.*, c. 1495-1500, 10.1 × 7.2 cm, f. 67r, Bibliothèque de l'Institut de France, Ms 2183

ship's bow is used to generate turbulence. In contrast, on the surface, less energy is available to produce these vortices, as some of it is used to maintain the water there.

To identify the similarities and differences between the behaviour of water and air, the reasoning in folio 299r of the *Codex Atlanticus* is particularly illuminating. Leonardo proposes an experiment to demonstrate that water is incompressible, unlike air, which he argues can be compressed. While a container can hold no more water than its volume allows, the same is not true of air, which can, for instance, be compressed inside a vessel along with a quantity of water, causing the latter to be expelled through a hole under pressure. Similarly, Leonardo states that water does not compress as a fish moves through it but relentlessly fills the void left behind, thereby propelling the fish forward. This principle accounts for the fish's wake, with the bubbles revealing the water that fills its path.

Leonardo initially relied on theories from the Middle Ages to study the movement of an object in a fluid. According to these theories, air, by its nature, is capable of moving very rapidly; it was also for this reason that it had been defined as a 'subtle' substance. When a body passed through air, it left a void behind it; this void was immediately filled by the rapidly moving air, which 'chased' the body, propelling it from behind.

This Aristotelian theory, known as 'antiperistasis' (an action by which the force of a quality is intensified in the presence of an opposing quality), appeared repeatedly in Leonardo's studies. For example, in folio 732rb of the *Codex Atlanticus* (1508), which depicts a cube in free fall with air flowing around it, forming a small vortex and filling the void left in the cube's wake.

In one of the later folios of the *Codex Atlanticus* (460v), dated to 1516–17, Leonardo pondered why a fish moves faster in water than a bird does in air. The opposite should be true, since water is denser and heavier, and therefore harder to penetrate; a fish, too, is heavier and therefore slower; finally, its fins are smaller than a bird's wings, providing less propulsion.

The reason, he argued, lay in the fact that the liquid's greater density allows it to fill the void left by a moving body more quickly, generating greater thrust. Moreover, a bird also faces air resistance, which, unlike water, is compressible.

These observations enabled an understanding of what Leonardo wrote in folio 50v of *Manuscript G*, in which he sketched three boat hulls. Two of them, mirror images of each other, are rounded at one end and tapered at the other, while the third, tapered at both ends, resembles the outline of a fish – a mullet – seen from above and from the front. The three hulls, Leonardo wrote, of equal size and propelled by the same force, moved at different speeds owing to their shapes. The fastest was the one with a rounded bow, having a silhouette similar to that of a bird and a mullet. Thus, it generated more vortices as it cleaved through the water, which propelled the boat with greater force.

As in many other fields, Leonardo drew parallels between fish and boats. In folio 38r of *Codex Forster III*, he asserted that fish, owing to the continuous pressure water exerted on their skin, secreted a viscous substance between their scales, which adhered to their body's surface, serving the same purpose as pitch on a ship's hull. He devoted further reflections to the rudders of ships.

In folio 52v of *Manuscript E*, he focused on the '*alulae*' of birds, small appendages positioned at the leading edge of the wings, useful for stabilising flight in vortices [fig. 1]. According to Leonardo, it was simpler to manoeuvre this small surface than the whole wing, as when a ship is steered when only the rudder is turned. Why, wondered Leonardo, were the rudders of ships not

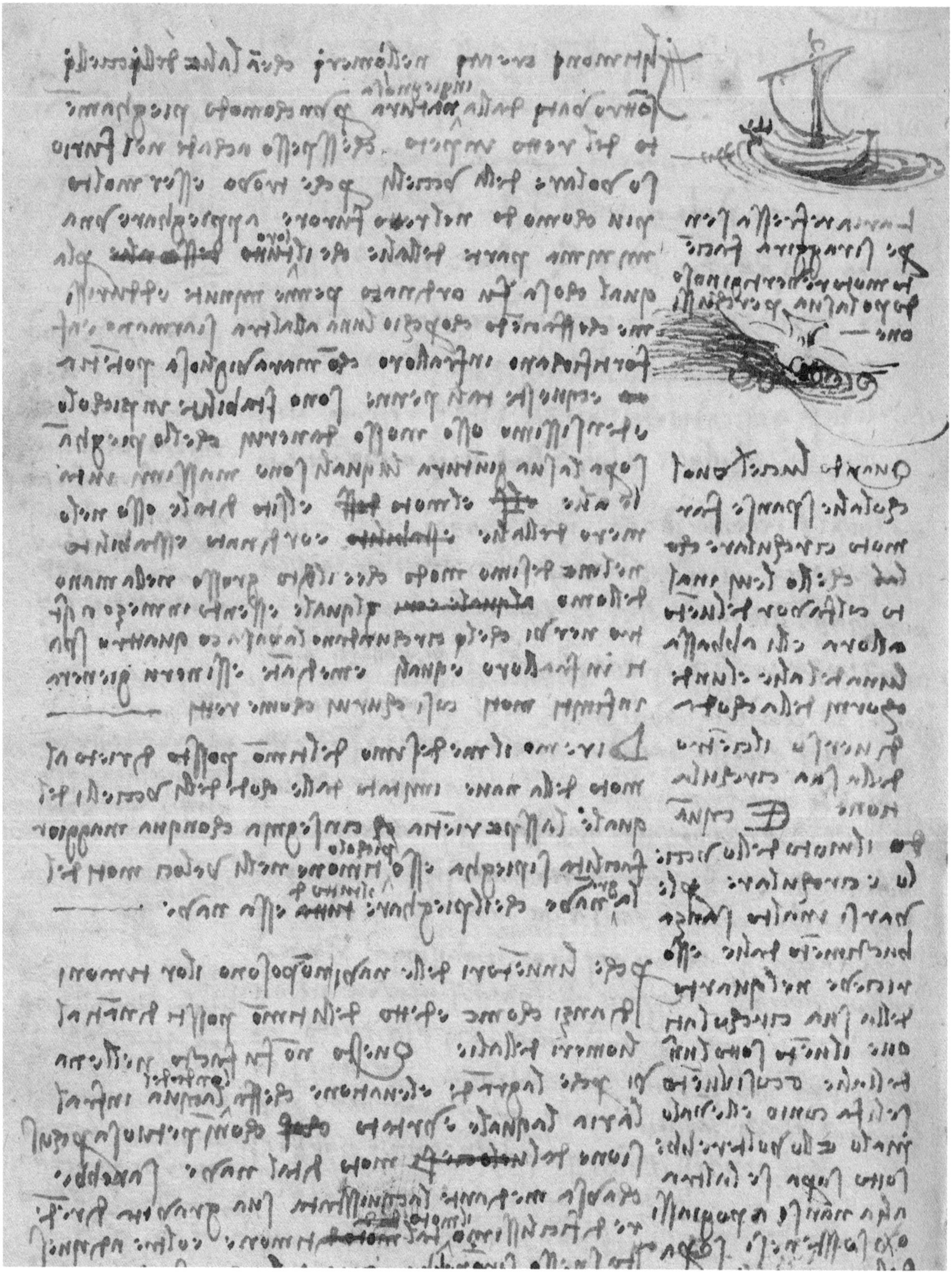

Fig. 1. Leonardo da Vinci, *Manuscript E.*, c. 1513-1514, 15.2 × 11.2 cm, f. 52v, Bibliothèque de l'Institut de France, Ms 2176

placed at the bow, to exploit their advantages? If the rudders were so placed, the waves generated by the movement of the ship, striking against them, would make manoeuvring very difficult, with the consequent risk of their breaking. This was not the case for birds: air, unlike water, compresses and offers resistance only at the wings.

While Leonardo began his studies in the wake of the Aristotelian tradition, his experiments and observations gradually distanced him from it. A passage in folio 71v of *Manuscript E* of 1513 confirmed this transition: in contradiction to what is cited above, Leonardo identified the greater density of water as a limitation on a fish's movement. While these animals are indeed endowed with much more powerful muscles than birds, they must move continuously, or their movement ceases.

It was perhaps observations of this kind that raised a doubt in Leonardo's mind about the theory of movement driven by vortices propelling an object forward. In a famous experiment that Leonardo conducted to definitively refute the classical theory of antiperistasis, it was the passage of a projectile from air into water that clearly revealed the need for a different explanation of its movement. If aerial vortices were propelling the projectile, once it entered the liquid, it should indeed have stopped, which it did not.

Leonardo observed that the air supposedly pushing a body from behind was itself displaced by the body. He concluded that the phenomenon must be explained by a different principle: "It is impossible that at the same time the mover drives its mobile and the mobile its mover" (*Codex Leicester*, f. 29v).

Ultimately, the air that, through turbulent motion, had filled the void left by a moving body was understood by Leonardo to be the air flowing beside and behind the object, air that, as it rarefied, filled the void. He offered a simple demonstration of this in folio 74v of *Manuscript F*: by throwing a stone into a sunbeam radiating into a dark space, it was possible to observe the illuminated dust swirling in the space without following the stone.

Bibliography

Bellincioni, Giovanni. *Leonardo da Vinci fondatore della scienza idraulica*. Florence: COSPIT, 1952.

Bernardoni, Andrea, Neuwahl, Alexander. *I progetti di Leonardo per Vinci*, in Barsanti, Roberta (ed.) *Leonardo a Vinci. Alle origini del genio*. Florence: Giunti, 2019, pp. 119-34.

Gombrich, Ernst Hans. *The Form of Movement in Water and Air*, in O'Malley, Charles Donald (ed.), *Leonardo's Legacy. An International Symposium*. Berkeley, CA: Univ. of California Press, 1969, pp. 171-204.

Maffioli, Cesare. *La via delle acque (1500-1700) Appropriazioni delle arti e trasformazione delle matematiche*. Florence: Olschki, 2010.

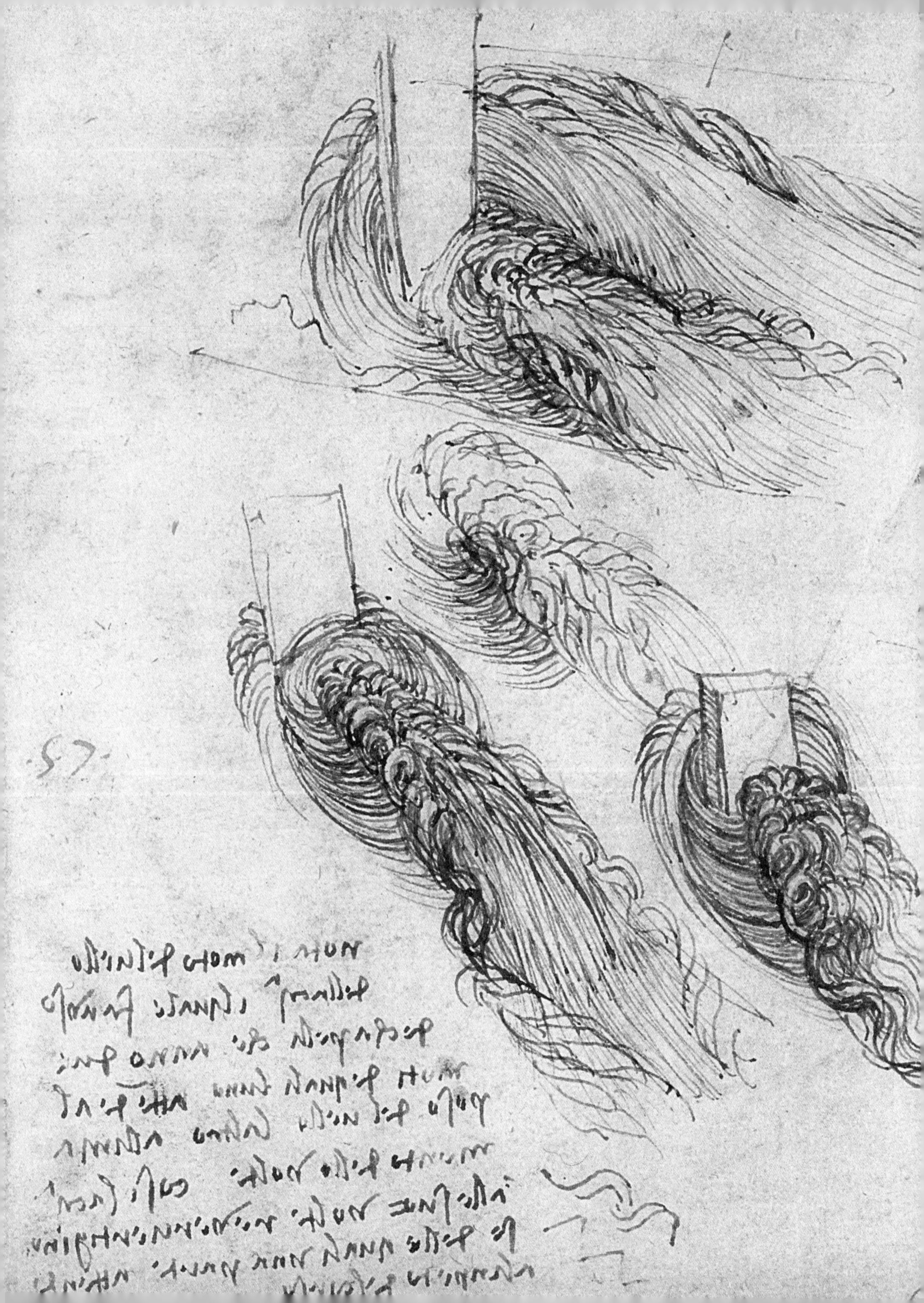

IN WATER AS IN AIR

THOMAS STEINMANN

Write of swimming underwater, and you shall have the flight of birds in the air (*Codex Atlanticus*)

Leonardo da Vinci was a forerunner in understanding fluid dynamics: whether liquid or gaseous, fluids move in similar ways. His notebooks contain sketches and detailed descriptions of experiments using tanks in which he observed fluids, employing dyes, seeds, and other light particles to trace water movements.

Today, mathematical formulae and computer programs allow us to simulate fluid movements at various scales. Engineers test models of aeroplanes, wind turbines, and other machines in wind tunnels or water channels to visualise flows around objects. Contemporary experimental fluid mechanics relies on the precise tracking and analysis of fluid motion.

These methods are just as essential in the biomimicry of locomotion, a field where biologists and engineers strive to replicate animal movements. A remarkable experiment in this domain was conducted by Michael Dickinson and his team at the California Institute of Technology. They built a large-scale robotic model of a fly moving through a viscous solution. Video footage of this experiment revealed the formation of a large vortex at the wing's edge. This vortex alters the pressure at the wingtip, increasing the forces generated by the insect. This phenomenon provides sufficient lift for the fly to remain airborne.

Modern research confirms Leonardo da Vinci's intuition about the role of air pressure on wing surfaces. As early as 1505, in his *Codex on the Flight of Birds*, he analysed the interactions between birds' wings and the air: "When the bird that is beating its wings wishes to rise, it strikes the tips of them backwards against itself, which compresses the air that lies between the ends of the wings and the breast, and this compression gives it elevation".

LEFT
Leonardo da Vinci, *Studies of water, and a seated old man* (detail), c. 1512-1513, pen and ink, 15.2 × 21.3 cm, Windsor, Royal Collection Trust, RL 12579r

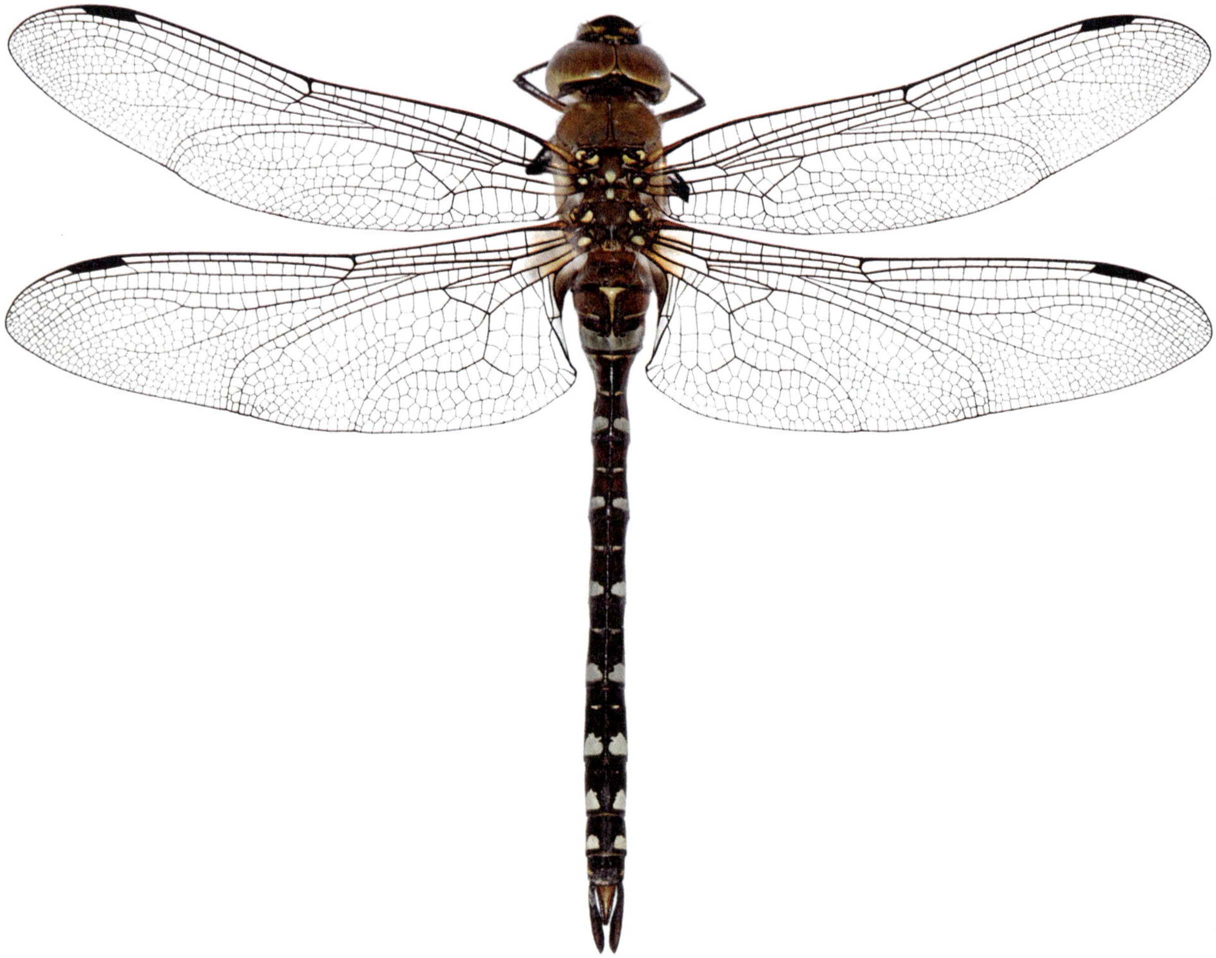

Dragonfly (*Brachytron pratense*), 2012

Complex structures, particularly vortices in watercourses, fascinated Leonardo. By analysing Leonardo's deluge drawings (c. 1517–18) [pp. 66-67], researchers have made two particularly interesting observations.

First, the vortices are depicted as a unique spiral form, replicated at different scales, illustrating, in scholarly terms, the concept of geometric self-similarity.

Second, these forms have a distinctive distribution. They do not appear randomly arranged yet exhibit a certain irregularity. These traits are mirrored in modern numerical simulations, demonstrating the accuracy of Leonardo's drawings.

Leonardo highlighted the crucial role of vortices that are often difficult to observe. Towards the end of his life, he combined his knowledge of anatomy, sculpture and fluid mechanics to create a cast of a bull's aorta to study blood vortices in the heart.

From this experiment, he concluded that these vortices aid in closing the heart valve, an intuition only validated in the 21st century thanks to advanced medical imaging techniques like magnetic resonance imaging (MRI) [fig. 1].

Leonardo's work on fluids predated modern discoveries by centuries. Today, 500 years later, researchers apply the same scientific approach, combining observation, modelling, scale adjustment and measurement to study the physical mechanisms of insect life.

The dragonfly, with its exceptional aerial ability, fascinated Leonardo and inspired magnificent sketches in *Manuscript B*.

Unbeknownst to him, lurking at the bottom of ponds, the larvae of this same dragonfly possess a remarkable technique for capturing prey. They have a labial mask that functions as an ultra-fast catapult to surprise and seize their targets [fig. 2.a], its concave shape enabling the larva to grasp and retain their prey.

Recent studies (Koehnsen et al., 2025) on the hydrodynamics of this jaw reveal the critical role of water vortices in the larvae's hunting efficiency. After scanning the larvae's labial mask using micro-radiography to obtain 3D digital models, simulations allowed researchers to analyse water flows around the mask and understand the impact of its shape and motion on its efficiency [fig. 2.b].

These simulations were then validated by experiments on large-scale models replicating the process of capturing prey [fig. 2.c]. The results suggest that the shape of the jaw is remarkably hydrodynamic, generating vortices that create a suction effect similar to that observed in certain fish [fig. 2.d]. This finding could be applied to manipulators for small autonomous underwater vehicles.

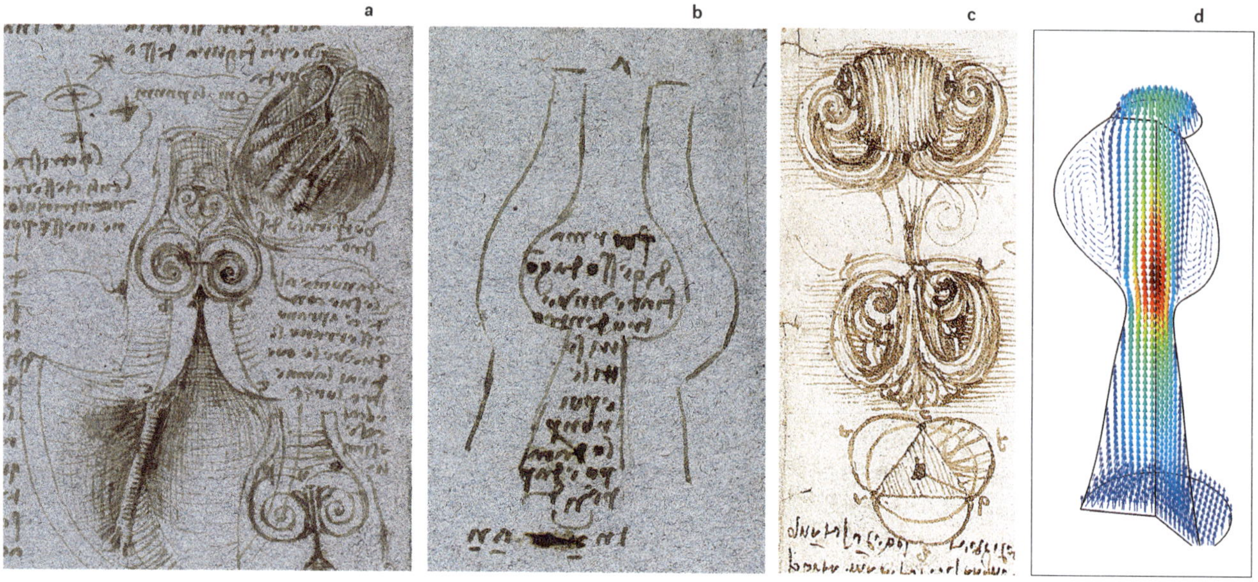

Fig. 1. a. and b. Leonardo da Vinci, *The aortic valve* (detail). c. Leonardo da Vinci, *Studies of the nerves and muscles, the heart, and optics* (detail) d. Numerical simulation of the flow in an aorta

Friction in fluids, odour transport

When a fluid flows near a solid surface, friction slows its movement. Leonardo da Vinci refers to the distribution of velocities in flow on numerous occasions, as in the *Codex Arundel*, where he writes: "The part of the liquid that moves fastest is that furthest from friction with a denser material".

He recognised this was particularly important for liquid flow in pipes, where the fastest movement occurs at the centre: "In water rising through a pipe, that which rises highest will be furthest from the pipe's walls". Known today as the no-slip condition, this concept was not formalised by scientists until the late 19th century. Leonardo's notes remain the earliest known references to this phenomenon.

Biologists studying insect antennae, which are highly sensitive olfactory organs, clearly understand the importance of this friction, which influences odour transport. One of the animal kingdom's most sensitive 'noses' is the pectinate antenna, found in several families of moths [fig. 3.a]. This type of antenna, developed and perfected over thousands of years of evolution, enables males of certain species to detect minute quantities of pheromones emitted by females [fig. 3.b]. By mimicking this extraordinary odour receptor's shape, one could envision the creation of an ultra-efficient sensor. However, the crucial role of friction between air and the solid antenna must not be overlooked.

In our example, accounting for this phenomenon means that the larger the sensor structure, the greater the friction [fig. 3.c], making it harder to capture pheromones. 3D-printed moth antenna models were tested in airflow simulations. Studies of these flows revealed the need to balance surface area and porosity to maximise odour capture. It appears that each speed corresponds to a specific antenna shape that optimises odour detection [fig. 3.d]. Thus, there is no single ideal form but several, each suited to a particular speed.

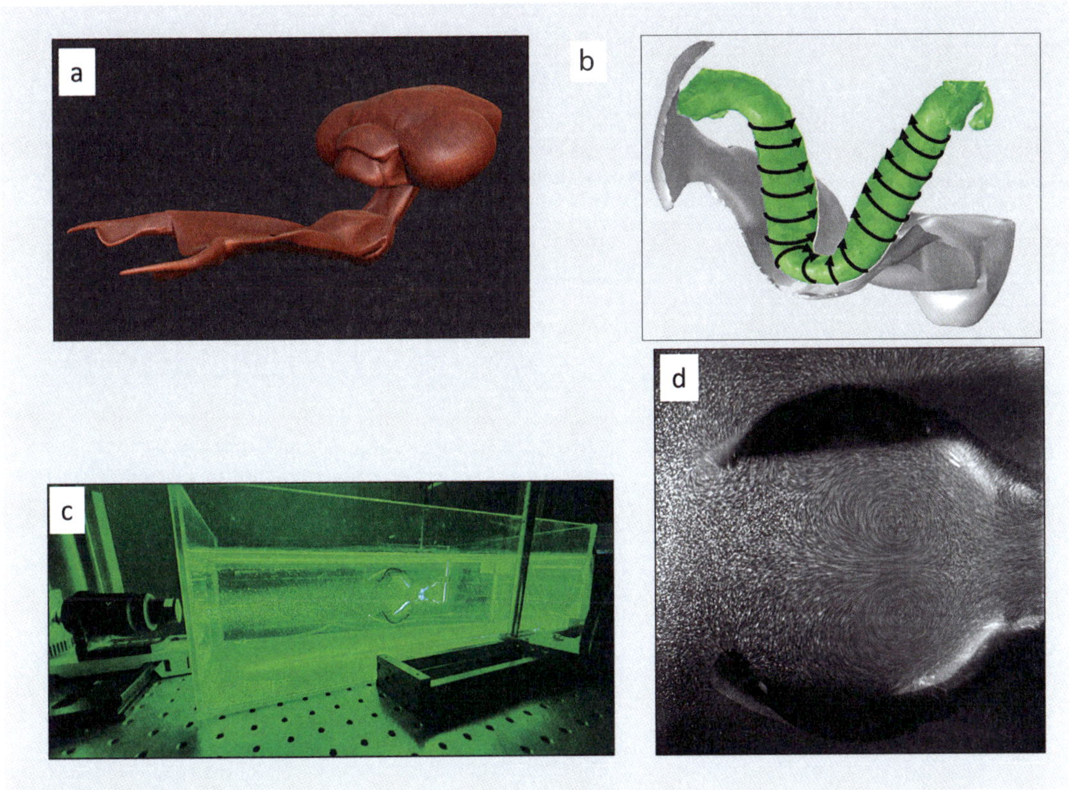

Fig. 2. a. Three-dimensional model of a dragonfly larva's labial mask
b. Vortex ring appearing as the labial mask is projected, results from simulations
c. Experimental apparatus for measuring flow on a 3D-printed model of a labial mask
d. Visualisation of the vortex ring appearing as the labial mask is projected

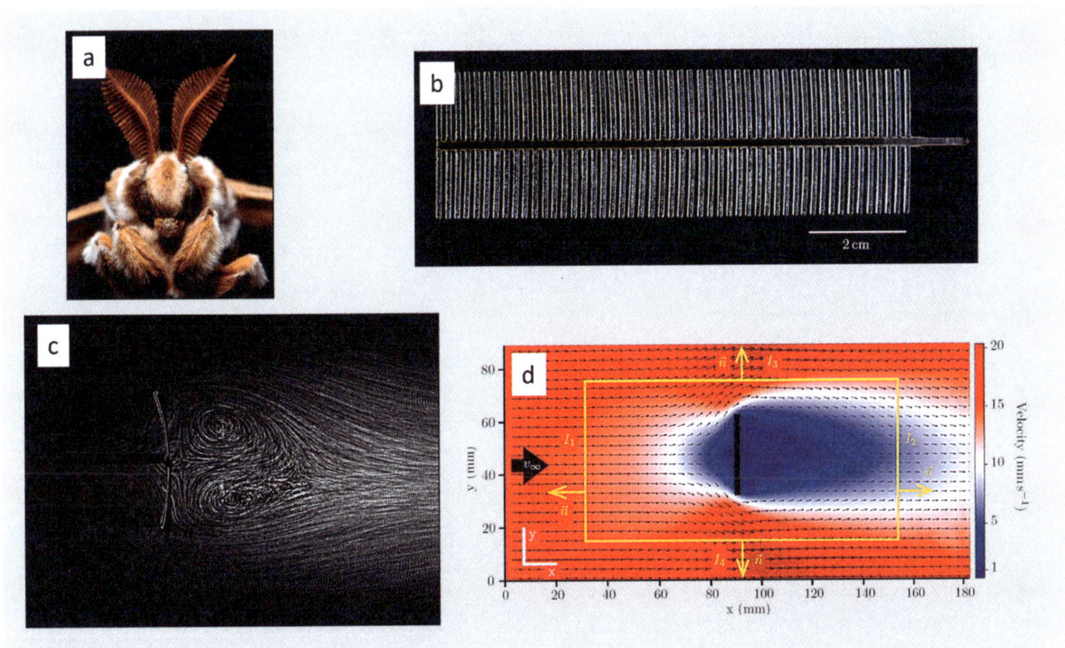

Fig. 3. a. Branched antennae of the saturniid moth, *Samia cynthia*
b. 3D-printed model of a simplified moth antenna
c. Separated vortex in the wake of a moth antenna
d. Results of flow analysis and odour capture by a biomimetic antenna

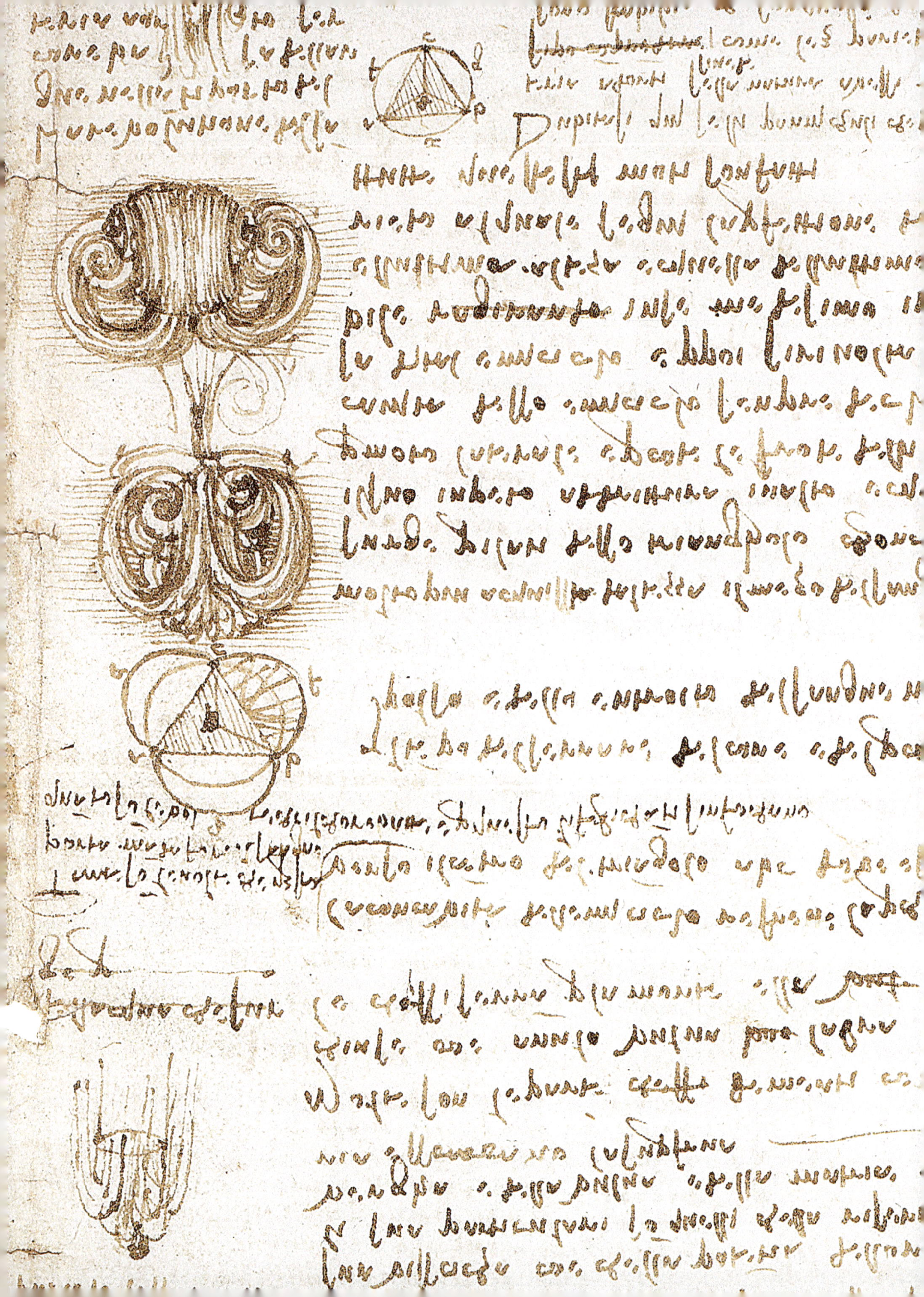

Natural moth antennae seem the most efficient.
All that remains is to draw inspiration from their shape for future applications.

Bibliography

Dickinson, Michael H., Lehmann, Fritz-Olaf, and Sane, Sanjay P. (1999). "Wing Rotation and the Aerodynamic Basis of Insect Flight". *Science* no. 284 (1954).

Gharib, Morteza, Kremers, Dymphy, Koochesfahani, Manoochehr, Kemp, Martin. "Leonardo's Vision of Flow Visualization". *Exp. Fluids* 33 (2002): 219–23.

Jaffar-Bandjee, Mourad, Steinmann, Thomas, Krijnen, Gijs, and Casas, Jérôme. "Insect Pectinate Antennae Maximize Odor Capture Efficiency at Intermediate Flight Speeds". *Proceedings of the National Academy of Sciences of the United States of America* 117 (45), 28126–28133 (2020a).

Jaffar-Bandjee, Mourad, Steinmann, Thomas, Krijnen, Gijs, and Casas, Jérôme. "Leakiness and Flow Capture Ratio of Insect Pectinate Antennae". *Journal of the Royal Society Interface* 17 (167) (2020b).

Koehnsen, Alexander, Steinmann, Thomas, Brede, Martin, Gorb, Stanislav N., Casas, Jérôme, Pincebourde, Sylvain, and Büsse, Sebastian. "Computational Fluid Dynamics Provide Evidence for a Compensatory Suction Feeding-Like Effect in the Predatory Strike of Dragonfly Larvae». Forthcoming 2025.

Marusic, Ivan, Broomhall, Susan. "Leonardo da Vinci and Fluid Mechanics". *Annual Review of Fluid Mechanics*, 2, 53:1–25 (2021).

Sharp, Nicole. "Fluid Dynamics, as Leonardo Saw Them". *Spiraling Upwards* (2024).

LEFT
Leonardo da Vinci,
Studies of the nerves and muscles, the heart, and optics, c. 1511-1513,
pen and ink, 10.7 × 43.8 cm,
Windsor, Royal Collection Trust, RL 19117r

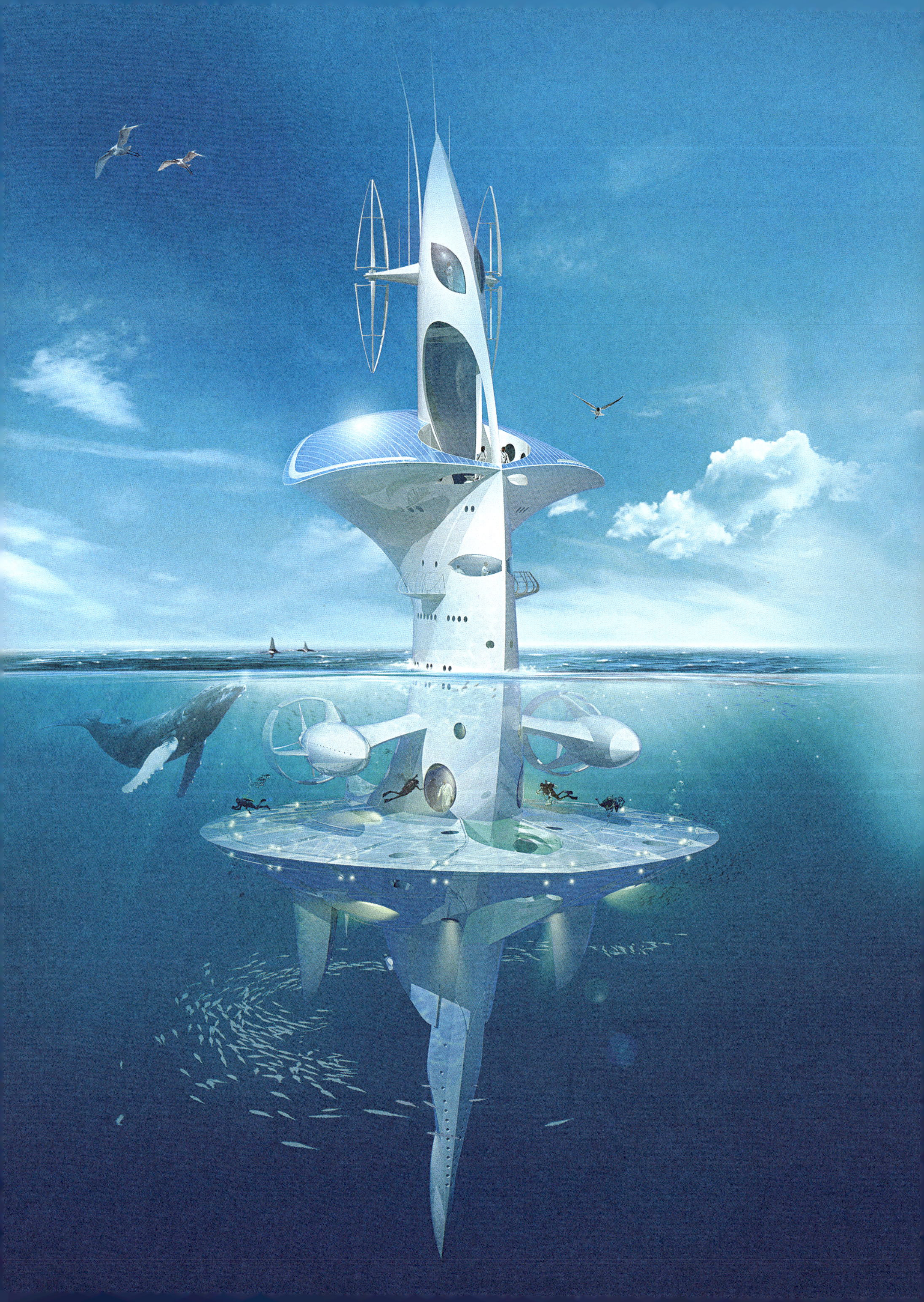

BIOMIMETIC INSPIRATION AND THE SEA

JACQUES ROUGERIE

BIOMIMICRY APPLIED TO ARCHITECTURE: A MODERN AND FORWARD-LOOKING VISION OF MARINE ECOSYSTEMS

For millennia, humans have maintained a complex relationship with the ocean, seeking to explore its mysteries while striving to navigate an environment as fascinating as it is forbidding. Coastal societies have learned to adapt. However, significant transformations are emerging, radically redefining the relationship we have with the marine environment, as well as with the living spaces, architecture, design and technologies we develop.

At the heart of the new relationship, the design of habitats and infrastructures that function in symbiosis with water takes inspiration from the existence of marine organisms. This biomimetic approach appears to offer an innovative and sustainable response to the challenges of coastal, marine and underwater worlds.

More than just a trend, it is a genuine philosophy that is developing, advocating greater harmony between the terrestrial and marine worlds, founded on the principles of sustainability, efficiency, and balance.

Biomimetic architecture marries nature and technology, offering solutions that protect the planet and safeguard future generations.

INSPIRATION FROM MARINE ECOSYSTEMS

Marine ecosystems constitute an inexhaustible reservoir of biomimetic innovations. The study of underwater nature, where organisms are endowed with unique survival strategies, opens avenues for designing structures capable of adapting to this dynamic and ever-changing environment, as highlighted by Janine Benyus in *Biomimicry: Innovation Inspired by Nature* (2002).

She demonstrates how the natural mechanisms of seashells or corals can inspire more environmentally friendly architectural designs.

The inspiring example of corals, capable of growing and adapting to changing conditions,

LEFT
SeaOrbiter

FOLLOWING PAGES:
Left, Jellyfish
Right, Pulmo

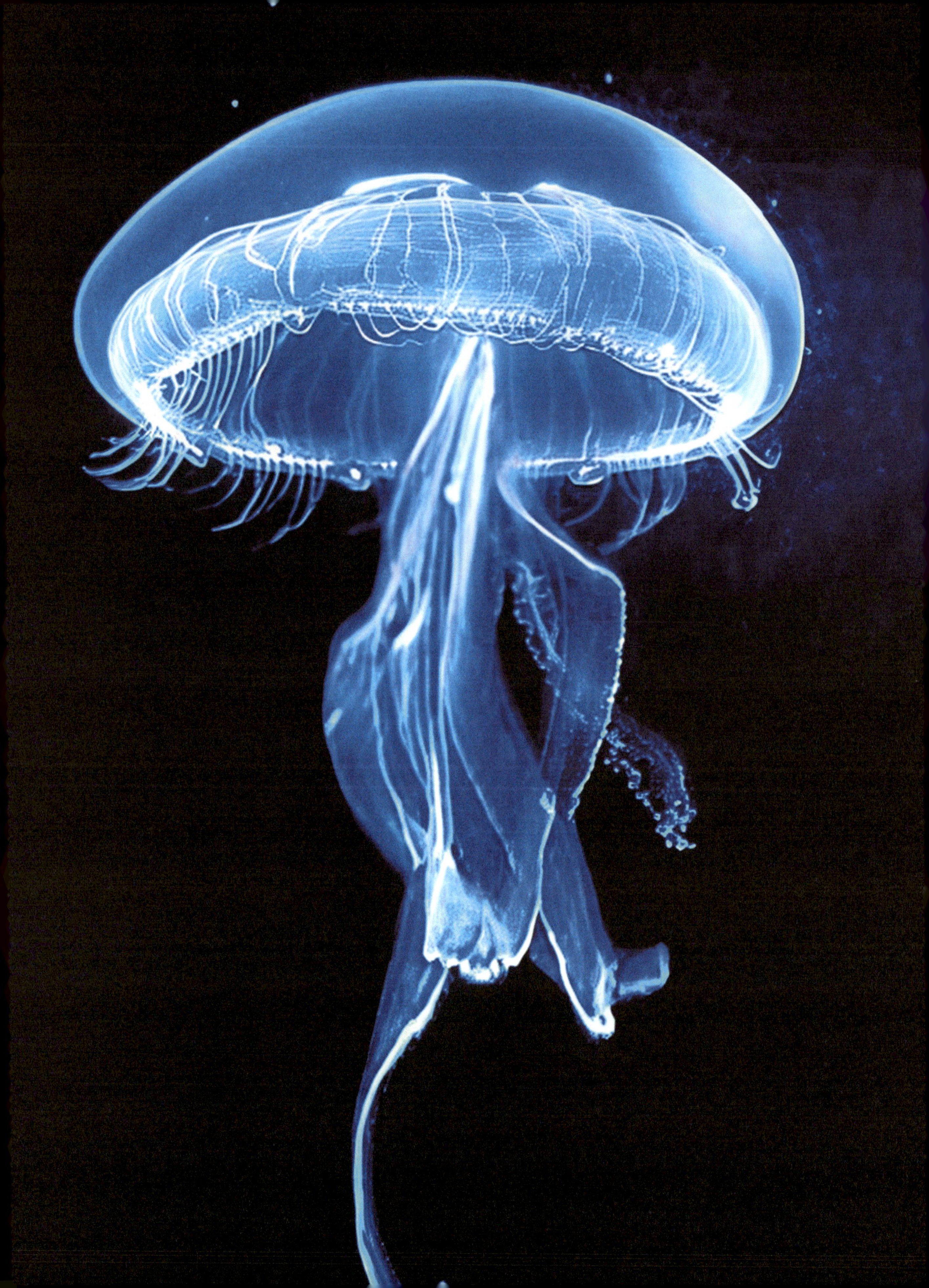

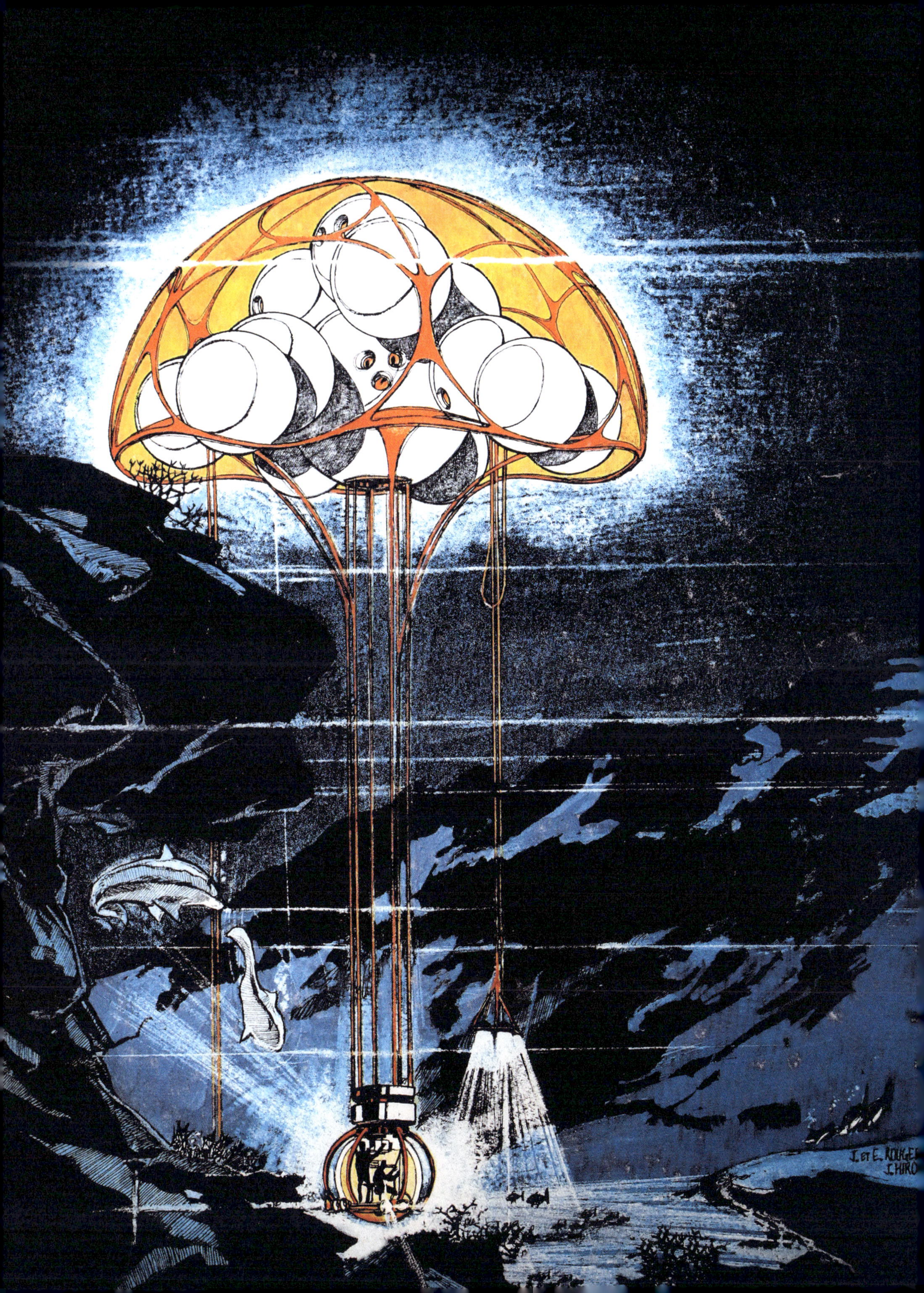
J. et E. ROUGE
J. HIRO

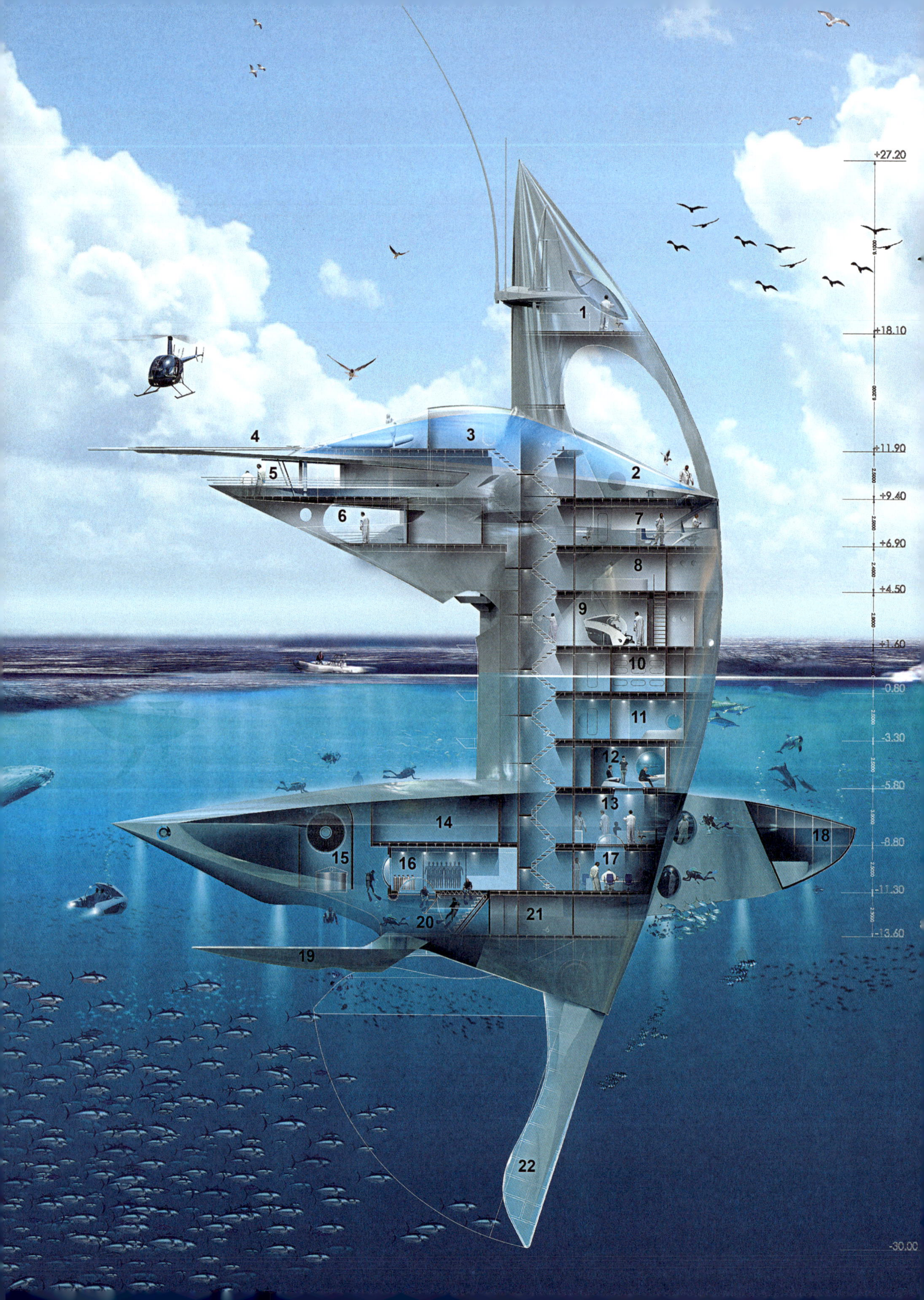
1
2
3
4
5
6
7
8
9
10
11
12
13
14
15
16
17
18
19
20
21
22
+27.20
+18.10
+11.90
+9.40
+6.90
+4.50
+1.60
-0.60
-3.30
-5.80
-8.80
-11.30
-13.60
-30.00

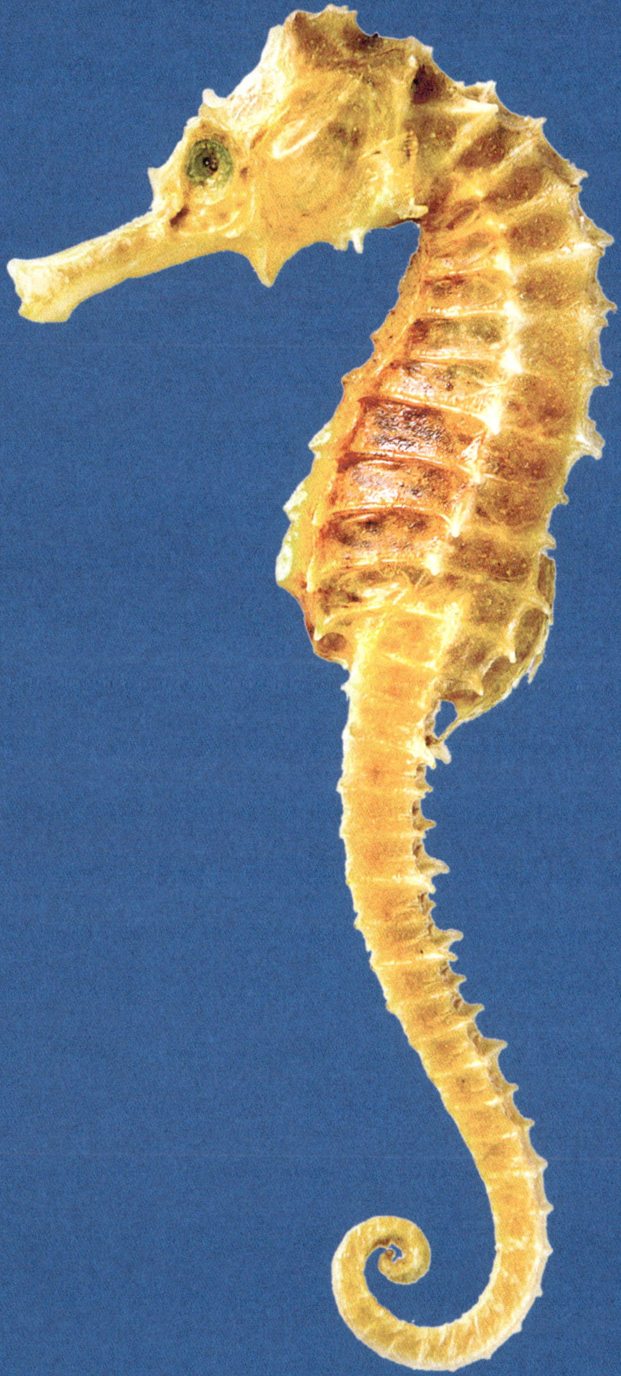

LEFT
Sectional view of the SeaOrbiter

Dried seahorse skeleton

makes them ideal models for marine habitats. Coral-inspired architecture is often modular and able to withstand currents and the shifting conditions of the ocean. Researchers are exploring how these structures can offer solutions for buildings capable of adapting in real time to environmental changes while preserving local biodiversity.

These biomimetic materials provide a new pathway for designing durable and robust structures.

Leonardo da Vinci: Pioneer of Biomimicry

Leonardo da Vinci, undoubtedly one of the greatest geniuses in human history, regarded nature as the ultimate model. According to him, "nature is the master of art", an idea that resonates powerfully today in the field of biomimicry. Leonardo understood that nature holds solutions infinitely more sophisticated than those conceived by humans. Through his observations, he not only anticipated numerous scientific discoveries but also the idea that humans could draw inspiration from natural structures to reimagine their constructions.

Leonardo's studies of marine creatures and how they function and adapt offer solutions to the challenges of life under water. His drawings of fish and marine creatures are not merely biological studies but concept sketches for inventions inspired by their forms and natural mechanisms.

This approach, now called biomimicry, is increasingly inspiring modern coastal architecture and the design of floating cities and underwater habitats. A vision that is reflected today in research on how to create human structures that respect the marine environment while functioning effectively.

It is fascinating to note that even in his time, the sea was already perceived as a wellspring of knowledge.

The Ocean's Impact on Human Imagination

While the ocean has inspired science and technology, it has also fuelled the collective imagination for centuries. From Jules Verne's *Twenty Thousand Leagues Under the Sea* (1871) to the utopias of modern architects, the idea of living on or under water has fascinated us. Verne anticipated maritime technologies and imagined futuristic marine creatures, but, above all, he envisioned the sea as a space for life and civilisation. Today, this approach could be linked to marine biomimicry, where floating and underwater structures are designed to integrate harmoniously and sustainably into their environment.

These floating cities and underwater homes are no longer pure science fiction; thanks to advances in biomimicry, they are inspiring projects ranging from underwater stations to floating villages and homes designed to adapt to changes in depth.

Projects for floating cities, inspired by natural phenomena like coral reefs and marine organisms, could offer a sustainable, integrated, and environmentally friendly living environment.

RIGHT
Abyssal Explorer and its inspiration, a squid

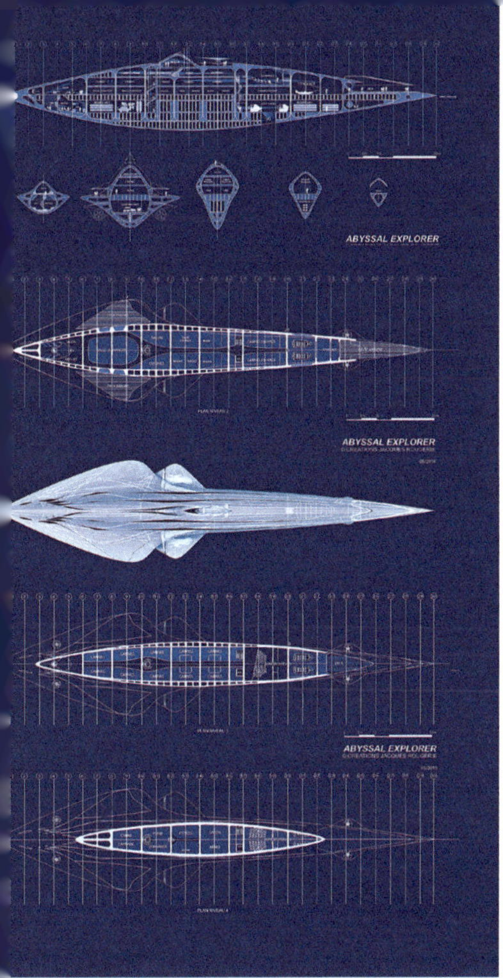
ABYSSAL EXPLORER
ABYSSAL EXPLORER
ABYSSAL EXPLORER
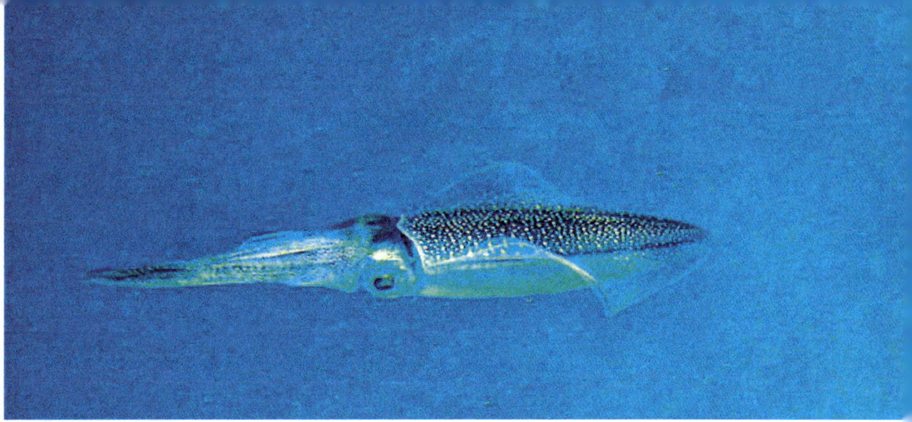
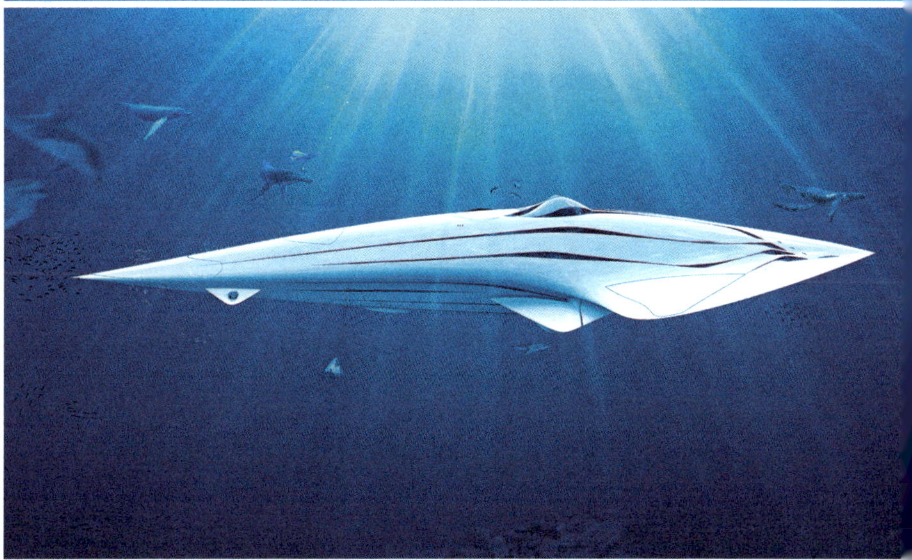
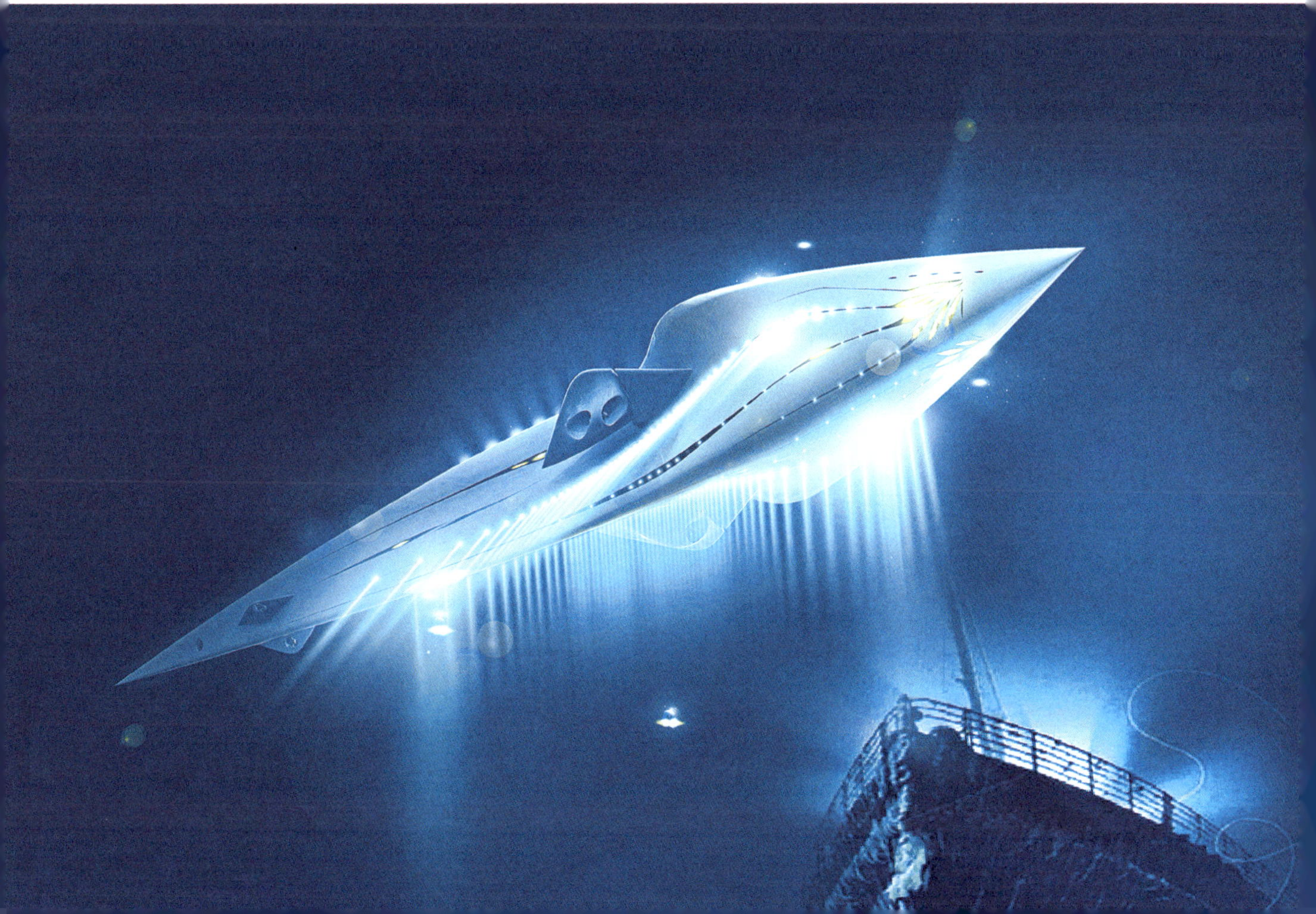

A Personal Exploration of Floating and Underwater Biomimetic Architecture

Guided by this philosophy and inspired by Leonardo da Vinci's biomimetic genius, I have conducted research with a multidisciplinary team into various bio-inspired structures, including coastal, marine and submarine studies. These initial inquiries and creations were documented in my book *Habiter la mer* (*Inhabiting the Sea*, 1978), which includes, among other things, a brief futuristic vision of life in an underwater village:

"No sudden movements, I slip under a transparent bubble of air, with its jellyfish-inspired shape, one of many that are dotted along the 'streets' of my underwater village, allowing me to catch my breath.

In the main street, 'Chemin de Glaukos', children play with their pet octopuses, while I move with complete freedom, equipped only with contact lenses, a monofin, and a thin white suit made of 'fibraleau', a material unknown a decade ago.

A 'Nautipousse' glides silently by, powered by hydraulic energy. These mechanical squids with undulating skirts, ridden by *Mérien* aquanauts [inhabitants of this underwater world], propel themselves through long, successive pulsations.

I emerge from the pocket of air where I had taken refuge and now head underwater towards a steep street, awash with a profusion of cascading air fountains, a luminous rain rising towards the 'liquid sky'.

Underwater houses cling to the rocks with their fibreglass legs and gaze at me with their bulging, semi-spherical window eyes.

In the background, in this constantly moving universe, the homes suspended between two waters by tension cables create an illusion of extreme lightness, as if poised to come alive and join this life, following the aquatic animals that inspire them. Some, round-bellied under taut skin, adorned with carmine-purple anemones and blue-green algae swaying gently, feature 'terraces', platforms without railings where one can perch without vertigo at the edge of the void".

This research into biomimicry has since led me, with a passion and daring, to imagine, design, and construct bio-inspired vehicles, as well as floating and subaquatic habitats, in which I have had the privilege of living underwater on multiple occasions and for extended periods.

I am, therefore, an inhabitant of the underwater world, a 'Mérien', a child of the water, a child of a new world, that of Poseidon and Nemo, as described in my book *From 20,000 Leagues Under the Sea to SeaOrbiter* (2000).

Technological Innovations Inspired by the Sea

In *Life's Devices* (2003), Steven Vogel explores how the natural principles of marine organisms influence current technological innovations: for example, ship hulls shaped like fish or maritime structures that are more efficient, resilient, and eco-friendly.

Innovations inspired by corals, shellfish and other marine organisms could give rise to floating buildings and underwater research stations capable of withstanding the ocean's fluctuations while preserving its ecological balance. These projects focus on energy efficiency, resilience to extreme maritime conditions, and the harmonious integration of these habitats with marine ecosystems, using bio-inspired materials that minimise their ecological impact.

The Psychological and Physiological Challenges of Underwater Life

Living in symbiosis with water does not just involve architectural and technological challenges, it also requires profound psychological and physiological adaptation. The underwater world, with its ebb and flow, constant changes, and sensory challenges, profoundly alters the perception of space and time. The process of diving, weightlessness and multisensory immersion necessitate rethinking the ergonomics of spaces and the requirements of inhabitants to ensure their comfort and well-being.

The idea of a future in which humanity lives in aquatic environments is gaining traction. Inspired by nature, innovative architecture could enable the construction of floating cities, underwater homes, laboratories, and multifunctional buildings in complete harmony with the sea. These modular and dynamic habitats would adapt to the ocean's changing conditions.

This evolutionary approach to architecture would offer sustainable, ecological solutions that respect both the planet and the needs of future generations, while maintaining a balance with marine ecosystems.

Throughout humanity's evolution, those who have sought, like today's Mériens, to live in symbiosis with the ocean have found their answers in its waves, its energy and its biodiversity: where the beauty of the world to come resides.

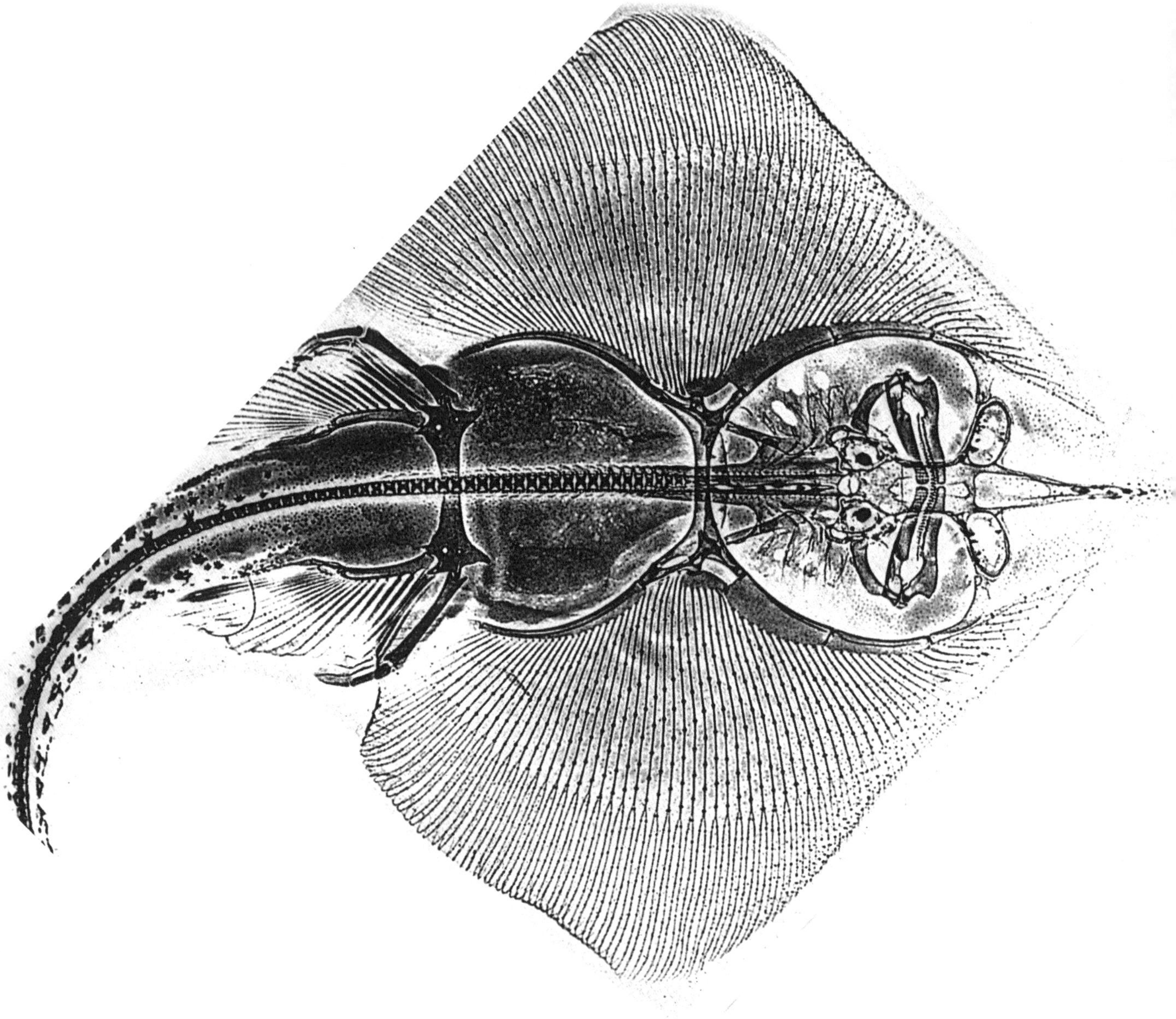

Manta ray skeleton

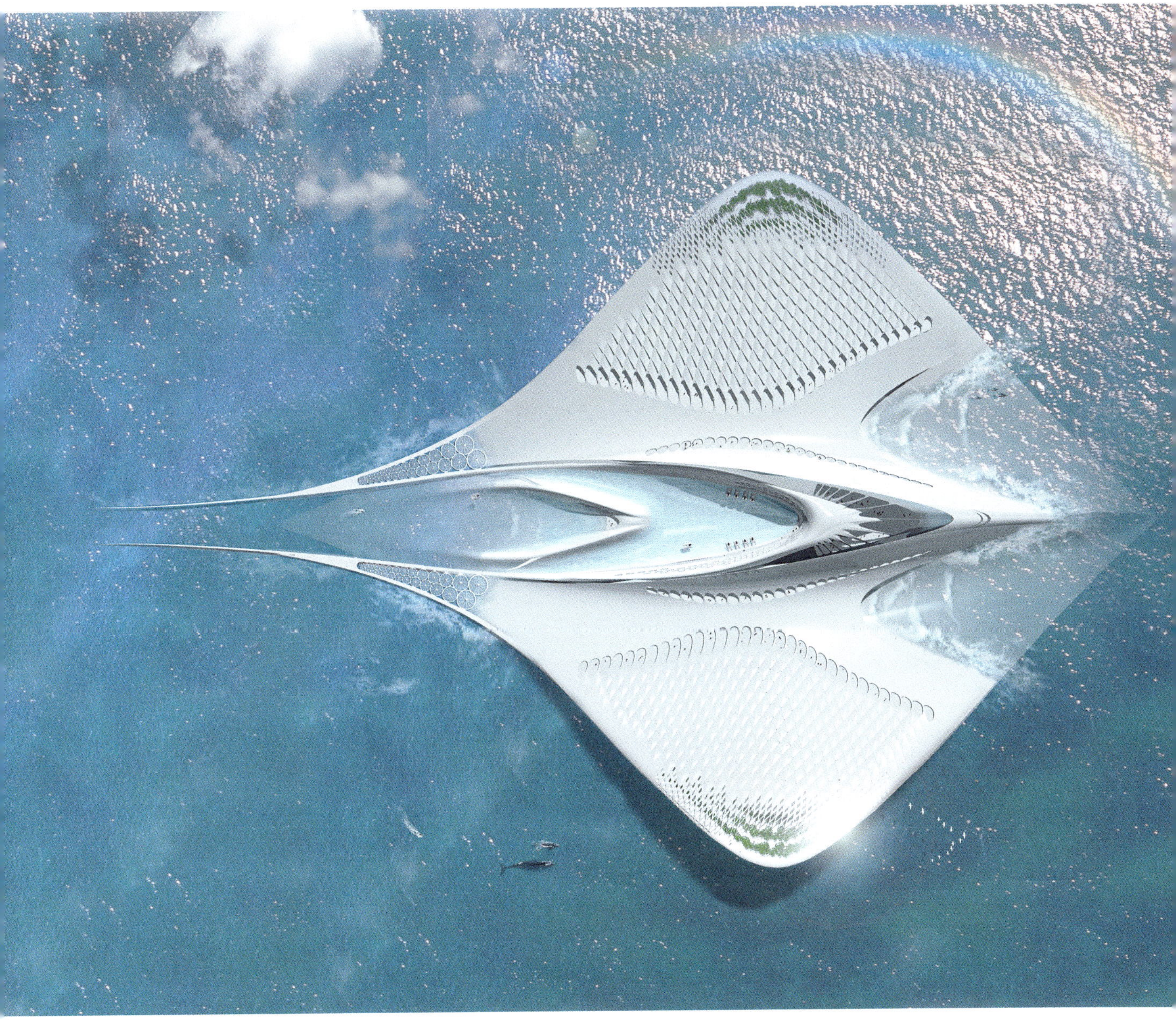

Cité des Mériens

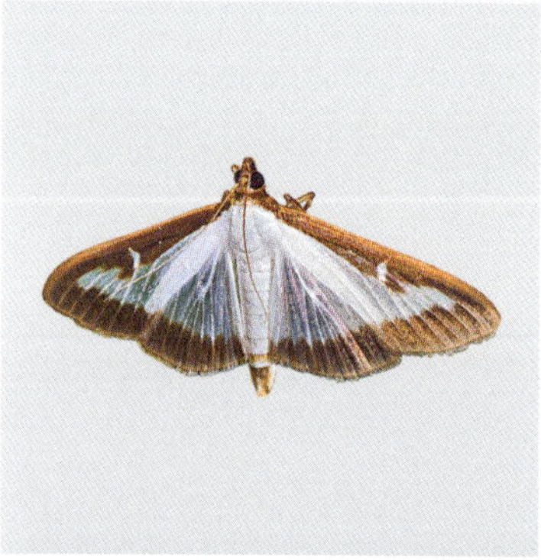

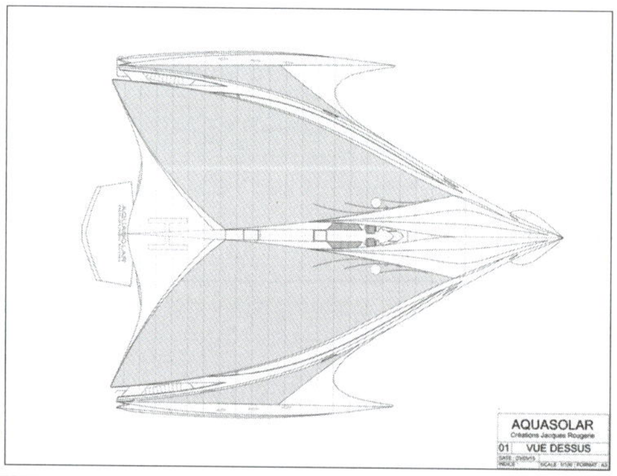

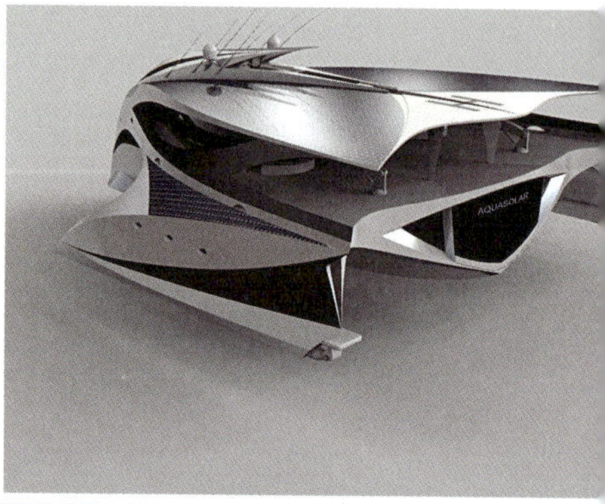

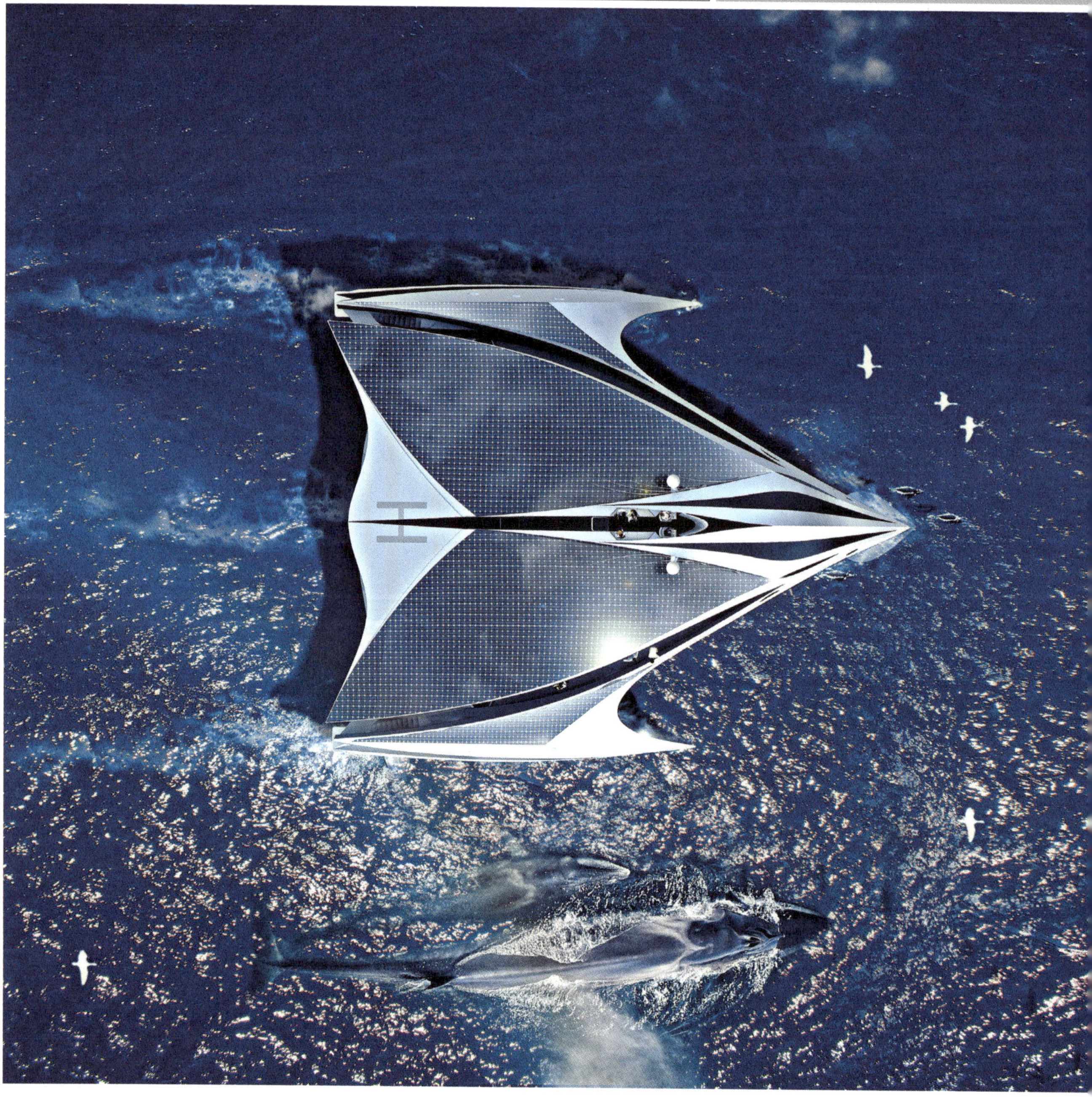

Aquasolar and its inspiration, a box tree borer

Bibliography

Benyus, Janine M. *Biomimicry: Innovation Inspired by Nature*. New York: HarperCollins, 2002.

Lange, T. *Biomimetic Architecture: Nature Inspired Innovation in Building Design*. Hoboken, NJ: Wiley-Blackwell, 2017.

Roberts, Callum. *The Ocean of Life: The Fate of Man and the Sea*. London: Penguin, 2012.

Rougerie, Jacques. *Habiter la mer*. Paris: Éditions Maritimes et d'Outre-Mer, 1978.

Rougerie, Jacques. *From Twenty Thousand Leagues Under the Sea to SeaOrbiter*. Paris: Democratic Books Eds, 2010.

Verne, Jules. *Twenty Thousand Leagues Under the Sea*. Paris: Pierre-Jules Hetzel, 1871.

Vogel, Steven. *Life's Devices: The Physical World of Animals and Plants*. Princeton, NJ: Princeton University Press, 2003.

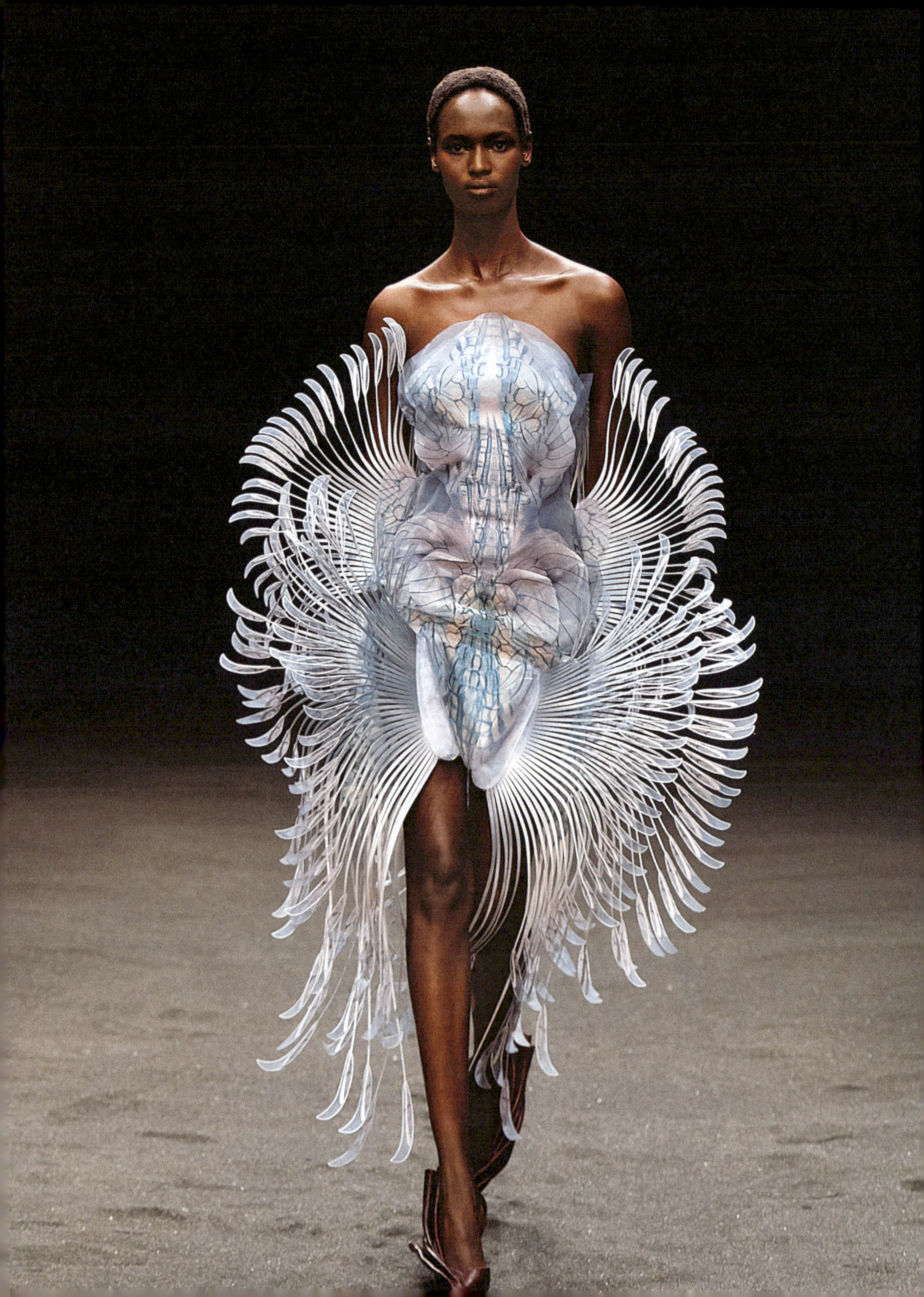

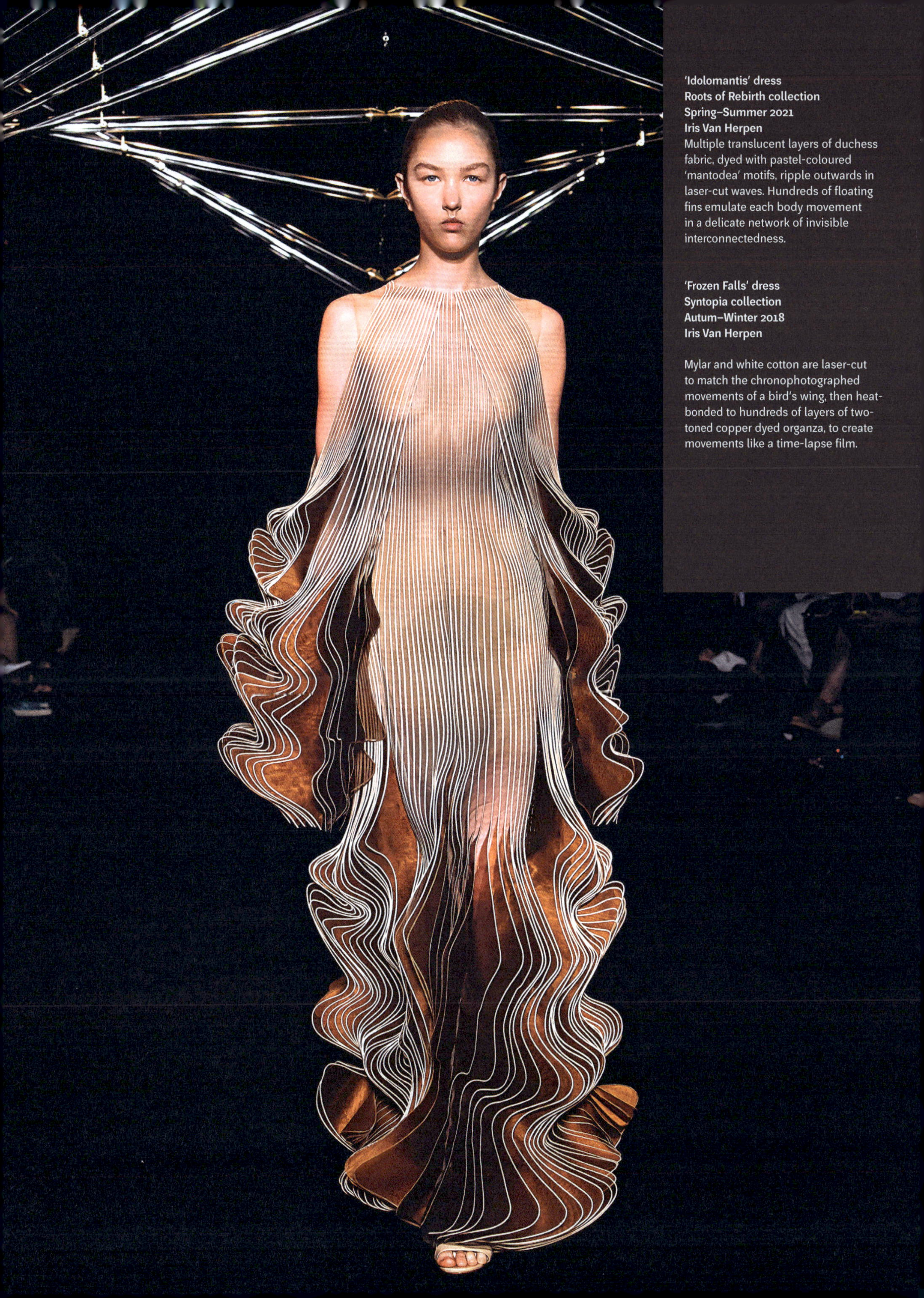

'Idolomantis' dress
Roots of Rebirth collection
Spring–Summer 2021
Iris Van Herpen
Multiple translucent layers of duchess fabric, dyed with pastel-coloured 'mantodea' motifs, ripple outwards in laser-cut waves. Hundreds of floating fins emulate each body movement in a delicate network of invisible interconnectedness.

'Frozen Falls' dress
Syntopia collection
Autum–Winter 2018
Iris Van Herpen

Mylar and white cotton are laser-cut to match the chronophotographed movements of a bird's wing, then heat-bonded to hundreds of layers of two-toned copper dyed organza, to create movements like a time-lapse film.

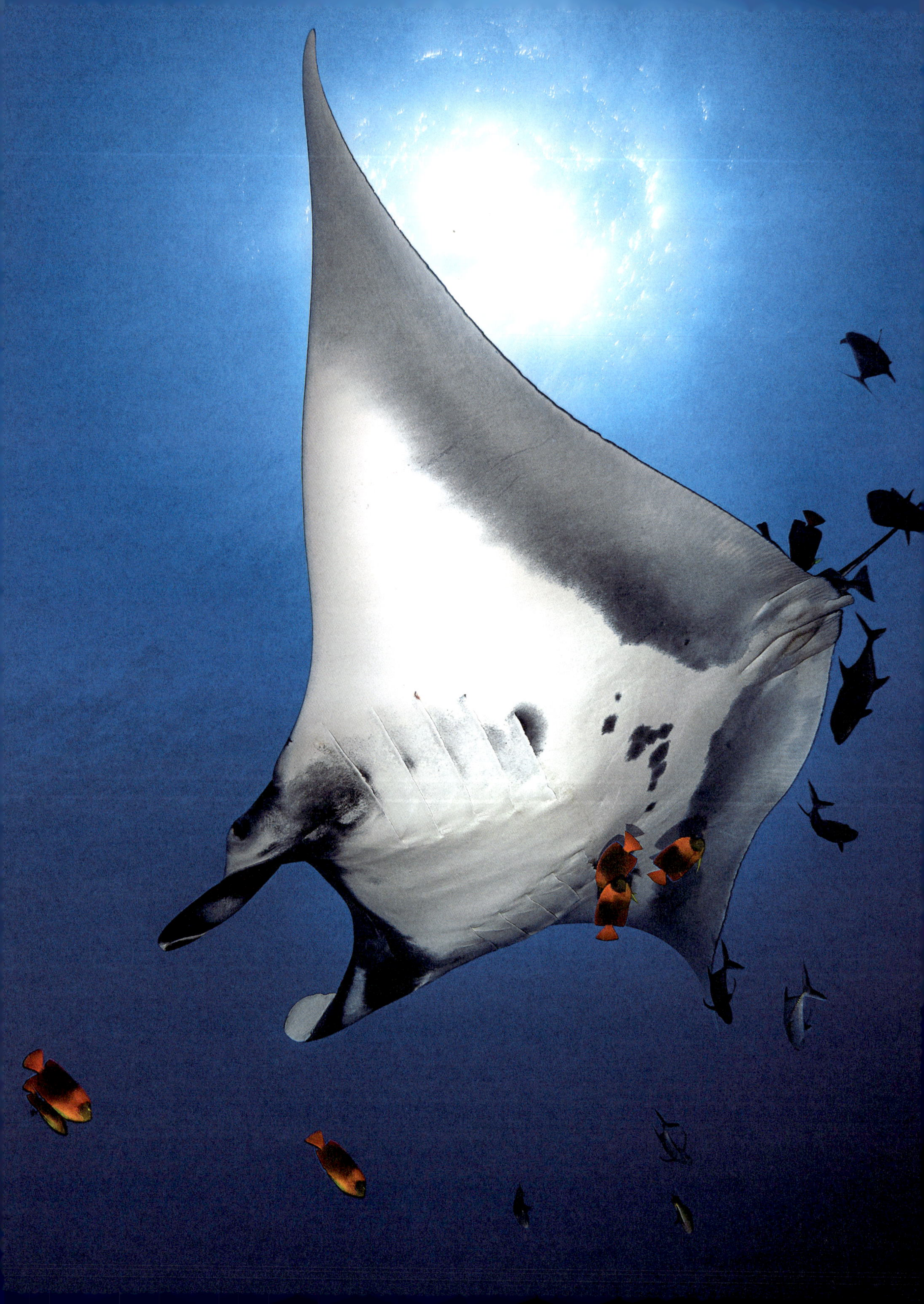

MANTA RAYS

ALEXANDER NEUWAHL
AND POLYTECHNIC UNIVERSITY OF MILAN

From childhood, Leonardo da Vinci was fascinated by nature and the solutions it provides to animals to fully exploit their environments. His reflections were rooted in analogical thinking. During his studies, he frequently employed this approach, drawing analogies between air and water, the functions of animals and machines, humans and automata.

While pure imitation has clear limitations in terms of innovation, analogy allows one to move beyond this by venturing into abstraction.

Leonardo's approach finds echoes today in different fields of research and technology, such as bio-inspired engineering, particularly in mechanics. This discipline combines the principles of mechanical engineering with the observation and emulation of biological systems in nature. It enables the development of innovative, highly efficient solutions inspired by the structures, movements and mechanisms refined over millions of years of evolution of living organisms.

By leveraging biomechanical principles observed in natural organisms, bio-inspiration can improve the design and performance of devices and machines. Here are some simple examples:

Structural efficiency: bones and natural structures often feature optimised geometrical configurations that minimise weight while maximising strength. This principle is applied in the aeronautical and automotive industries.
Adaptability and flexibility: many living organisms have structures that adapt continuously to their environments, inspiring the development of smart materials and robotic devices.
Optimised movements and mechanisms: the study of birds in flight, fish swimming, and insect locomotion informs the design of bio-inspired robots and drones.
Multifunctional materials: biological tissues are frequently lightweight and self-repairing or durable, inspiring the creation of new composite and biomimetic materials.

Bio-inspired engineering has applications across numerous fields, contributing to the development of increasingly advanced and sustainable technologies. Examples include:
Prosthetics and medical devices: the emulation of human bone structures and tissues facilitates the creation of more functional, body-compatible biomechanical implants.

LEFT
Manta ray, Socorro, Mexico

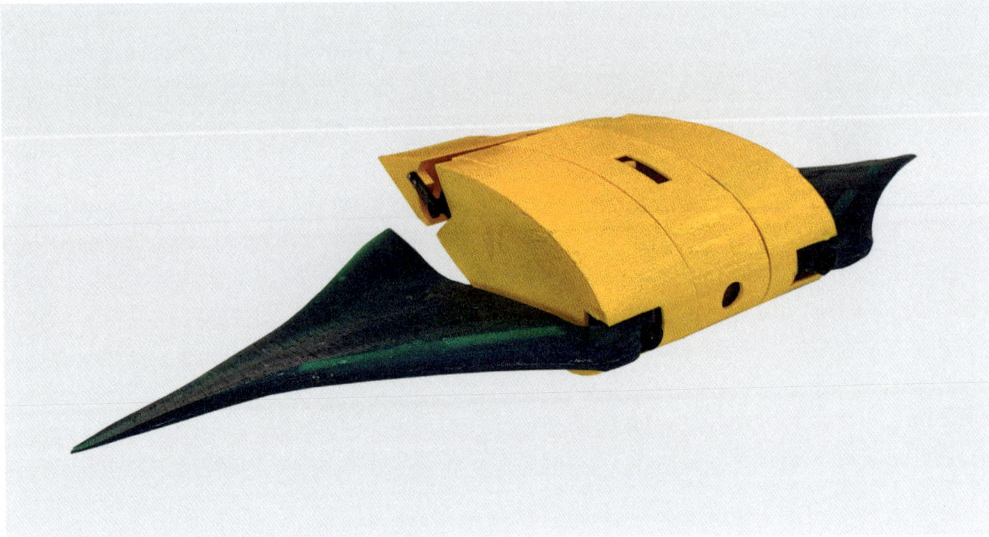

Fig. 1 . Small manta ray robot produced by Milan Polytechnic

Bio-inspired robotics: robots that emulate snakes enable exploration of challenging environments, while insectoid robots support environmental monitoring.

Aerodynamics and transport: the study of bird wings and fish fins informs the design of more efficient aircraft and underwater vehicles.

Bio-inspired materials: spider silk inspires ultra-light, high-strength fibres, while sharkskin guides the development of low-friction surfaces for marine applications.

A bio-inspired approach to mechanical engineering offers numerous advantages: enhanced energy efficiency, improved durability and innovative solutions, often unattainable through conventional methods. However, replicating biological mechanisms and employing advanced simulation and manufacturing techniques presents significant challenges.

With this in mind, the Polytechnic University of Milan has developed a prototype underwater robot inspired by the movement of manta rays [fig. 1].

These animals generate a wave with their broad fins, which propagates from head to tail, pushing water backwards and ensuring efficient propulsion through the regularity of their movements. This mode of locomotion provides advantages in efficiency, manoeuvrability, and silence, making manta ray-inspired robots particularly suitable for underwater exploration and marine environmental monitoring.

The robot was inspired by the cownose ray, characterised by a diamond-shaped body and large triangular fins. The main challenge lay in the faithful reproduction of the fin movement. Several solutions were considered. The simplest involves controlling each fin with a single actuator, relying on the fin's passive deformation to generate the propulsive wave. A more complex variant uses two motors: one controls vertical movement, the other rotation. The combination of these movements produces the wave that propagates along the fin. The most advanced solution manipulates the fin using three independent ribs, each driven by a mechanism to achieve the

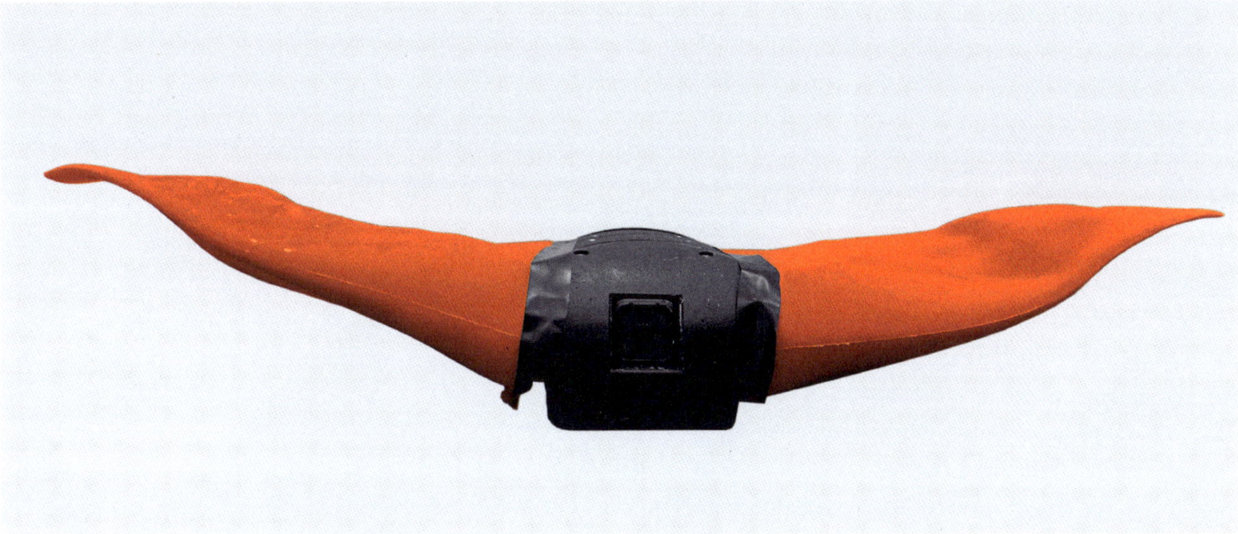

Big manta ray robot produced by Milan Polytechnic

desired curvature, creating a wave that propagates in the direction of movement.

The first solution was adopted for this robot: each fin is driven by a servomotor positioned at the robot's front, allowing easy replacement. Two caudal fins control pitch and ensure stability during lateral fin movement.

The central, watertight section houses the electronic components: a battery, switch, USB connector, camera, button, two LEDs, four servomotors, an inertial measurement unit, a camera, an SD card module, a Wi-Fi module, and an ammeter. The robot's electronic control board is an Arduino Due, offering high computational power.

The central section employs a NACA 0020 airfoil profile to minimise water resistance. The fins, made of silicone rubber with reinforced edges, interact with the water to generate thrust. Replicating this complex interaction required simplified modelling to ensure optimal fin deformation during movement.

The fin's vibration modes were analysed using simulation software. The fin's underwater behaviour was subsequently tested in a tank, ensuring that the movement generated sufficient thrust. This nature-inspired robot propels itself through passive fin deformation, achieved via interaction with water. This technique is distinguished by its remarkable efficiency and simplicity of control. Developments are underway to refine the robot's movement control and fin design.

Another project at the Polytechnic University of Milan, also inspired by the manta ray, tackles the issue of microplastics, a major threat to ecosystems.

The primary source of microplastics is the washing of synthetic textiles. Several strategies are under consideration to tackle this issue: prevention, mitigation and collection.

The Polytechnic's project develops a bio-inspired approach to separate microplastics from water, harnessing vortices generated by specific filter structures [fig. 2]. The system directly emulates the gill-based water filtration used by manta rays to extract plankton, their primary food source [fig. 3].

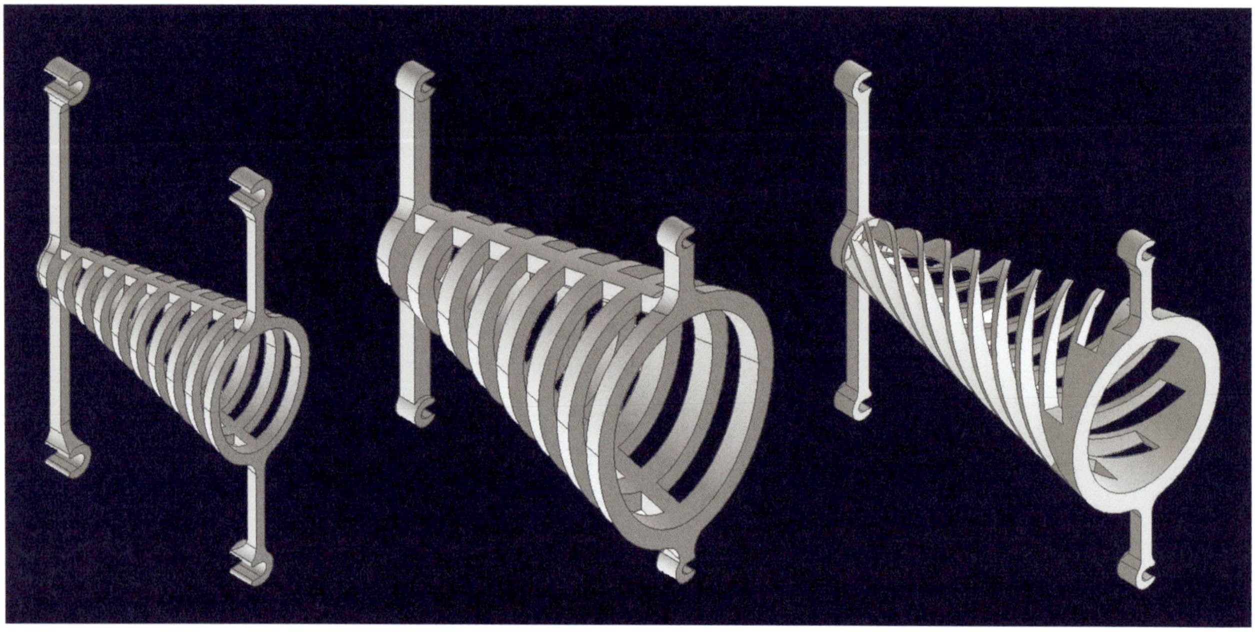

Fig. 2. Technical drawings of filtration systems designed by Milan Polytechnic

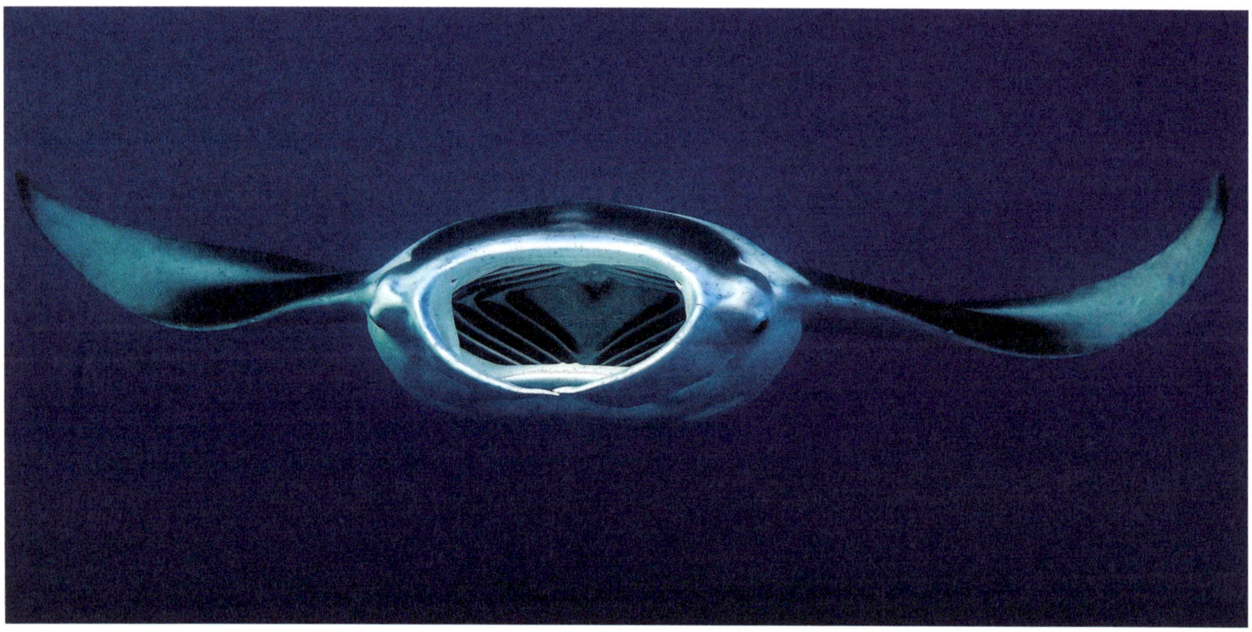

Fig. 3. Manta ray with its mouth open, showing its filtration system

Various approaches were examined:

Direct filtration: captures particles through perforations of different size.

Cross-flow filtration: diverts water-carrying particles of varying sizes to a collection zone.

Vortex filtration: concentrates particles at the centre through vortices generated by internal elements.

Interception: captures particles via contact with adhesive surfaces.

The results of these studies, conducted under different flow conditions using 3D-printed filter prototypes, were evaluated through digital imaging to determine their effectiveness.

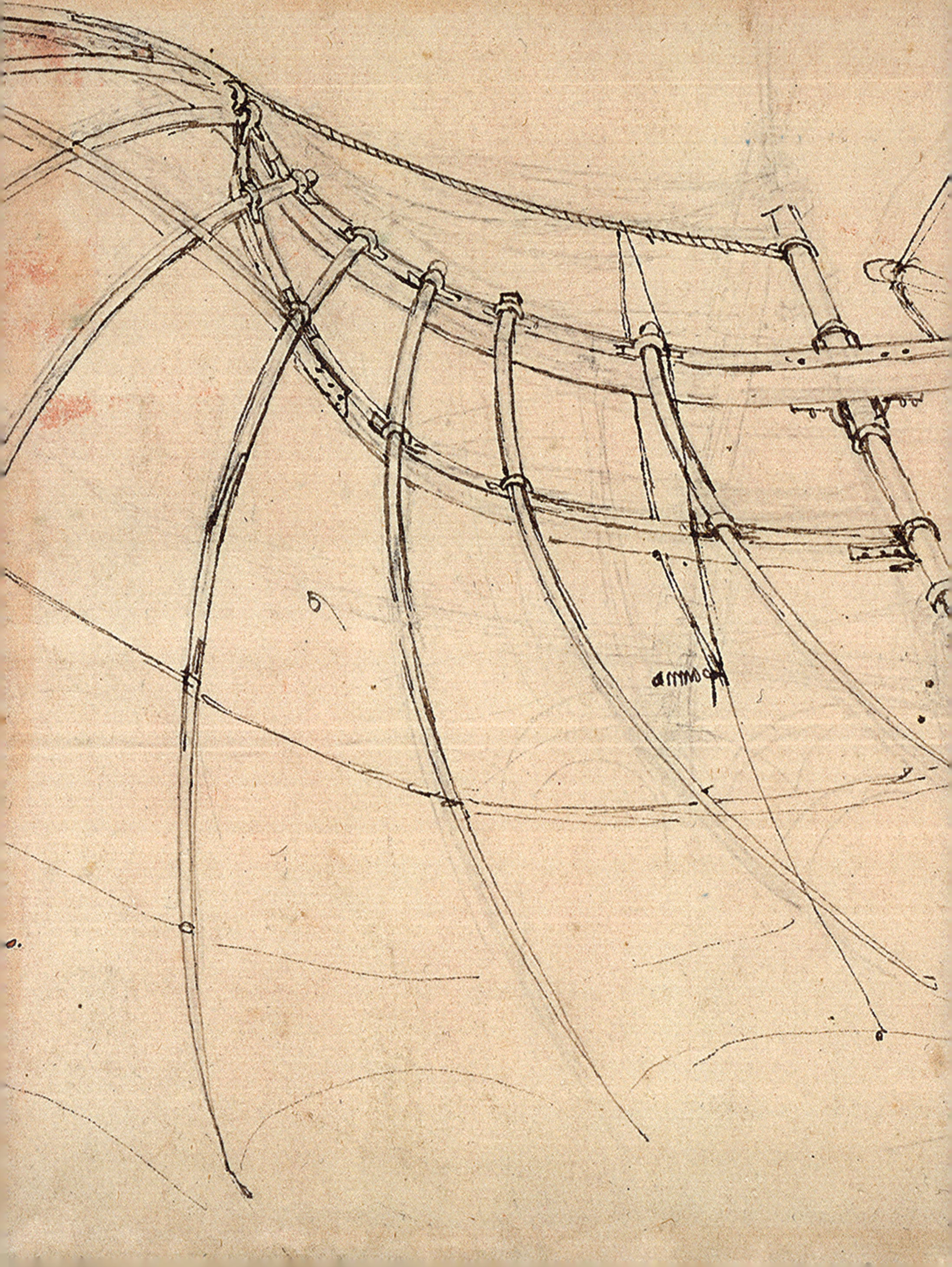

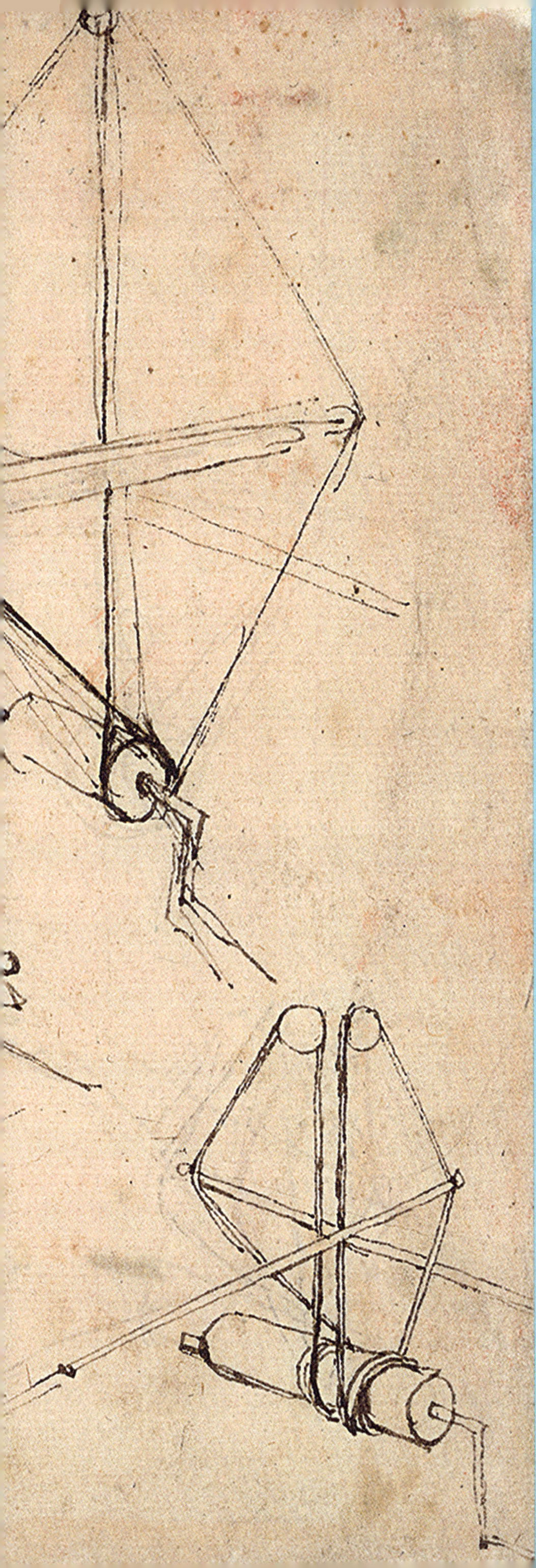

Flying Creatures and Biomimicry

Chapter III

Se l'alia e la coda sarà troppo sopra vento abbassi la metà dell'alia opposita e riceverà dentro la percussione del vento e 'l moto e ssi verrà a rizzarsi.

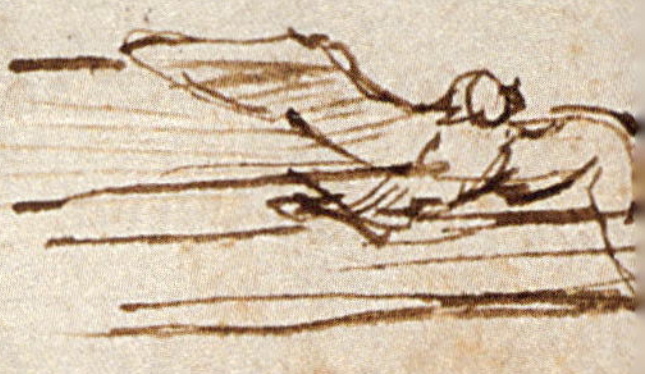

E sse l'alia e lla coda fussi sotto vento alzi la [illegible] opposita e rizzerassi a tanto moto [illegible] alla [illegible] sarà [illegible] obbliquo [illegible] [illegible] [illegible] opposito.

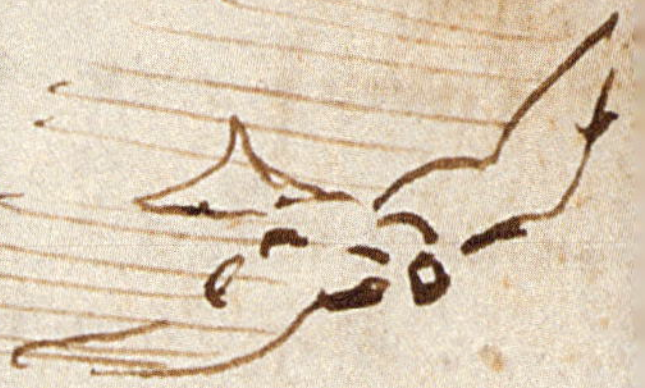

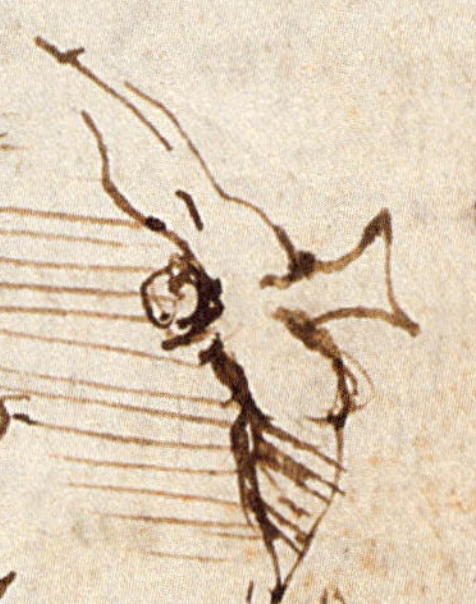

Se l'alia e 'l petto sarà sopra a vento abbassi il [illegible] dell'alia opposita la quale fia percossa dal detto vento e rigi[illegible] [illegible] e [illegible] l'uccello.

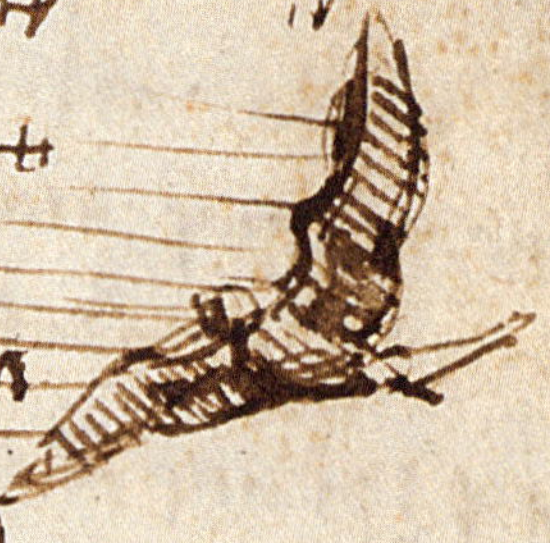

[illegible] l'alia e lla [illegible] sarà sotto vento alto [illegible] alzare l'alia opposita e [illegible] [illegible] [illegible].

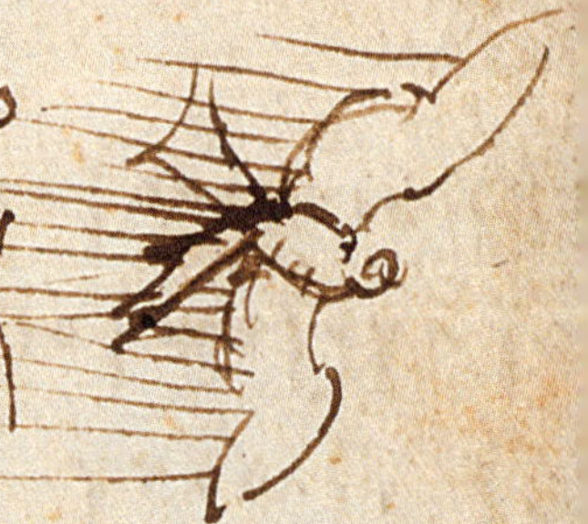

[illegible] l'uccello sarà [illegible] sopra vento alto [illegible] [illegible] sotto vento [illegible] [illegible] [illegible].

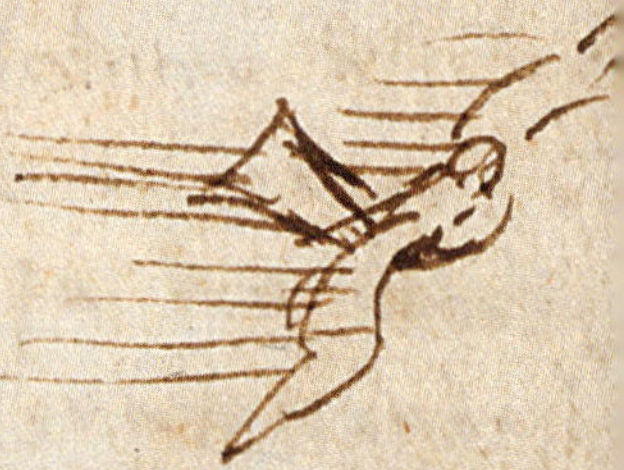

[illegible] l'uccello [illegible] sotto [illegible] [illegible] sopra [illegible] [illegible].

THE WORKS OF LEONARDO DA VINCI AT THE ROYAL LIBRARY OF TURIN

Enrica Pagella

> Man has been called a lesser world by the ancients, and indeed the term is rightly applied, for just as man is composed of earth, water, air and fire, so too is the body of the earth. If man has bones to support his flesh, so the world has the rocks which are the supports of the earth; if man has within him a pool of blood wherein the lungs as he breathes expand and contract, so the body of the earth has its ocean, which also rises and falls every six hours with the breathing of the world. (*Codex Atlanticus*, f. 55v)

In this passage, Leonardo da Vinci evokes the ancient idea that macrocosm and microcosm are intimately linked and exist in harmony. As is often the case in his writings, he compares the human body and the terrestrial body, asserting that "movement is the cause of all life" (*Manuscript H*, f. 141r). This organic and dynamic vision suggests a fundamental connection between man and nature, foreshadowing a form of ecology where humanity coexists harmoniously with the world around it. Thus, Leonardo da Vinci paves the way for new reflections on the destiny of man and the universe, particularly relevant in the Anthropocene era.

Leonardo da Vinci explored art and nature, anatomy and proportions, engineering, physical sciences, mathematics, and poetry. These themes run through the thirteen autograph folios held at the Royal Library of Turin, dating from 1480 to 1515, and the *Codice sul volo degli Uccelli*, written in 1505 and 1506.

The most famous drawing in Turin, also one of Leonardo's best-known works after the *Mona Lisa* and *Vitruvian Man*, is his *Self-Portrait* (D.C. 15573). Despite a century of studies and publications, the mystery of this solemn face remains unsolved: some see it as a true portrait of an aged Leonardo, others as a recurring facial type in his works, akin to the apostles in *The Last Supper* in Milan.

Another masterpiece in Turin, the *Face of a Maiden* (D.C. 15572), dated 1483–85, is linked to the *Virgin of the Rocks* in the Louvre. The depth of her gaze reflects Leonardo's investigations into the soul and vital forces. Fascinated by how organs respond to external stimuli and internal humours, he grappled with the visual and perceptual faculties of individuals.

PREVIOUS PAGE
Leonardo da Vinci, *Codex Atlanticus*, 1480, pen and ink, f. 858r, Veneranda Biblioteca Ambrosiana

LEFT
Fig. 1. Leonardo da Vinci, *Codice sul volo degli uccelli*, "Studies of flying birds", c. 1505-1506, f. 8r, Biblioteca Reale, inv. Cod. Varia 95

A folio once thought to be a portrait of Cesare Borgia (D.C. 15573) shows a man's face from three angles, exploring the capacity of drawing to express movement. *Head of a Man in Profile Crowned with Laurel* (D.C. 15575), executed in red chalk and inspired by a classical model, is now interpreted as a reflection on medicine and the depths of the human soul.

Leonardo's studies on proportions are documented in Turin by a frontal image of a face accompanied by explanatory notes (D.C. 1574-76). This is one of the artist's many attempts at measurement. Unlike Albrecht Dürer, he never formalised a treatise, although his research moved beyond the abstract theories of Vitruvius, also cherished by Lorenzo Ghiberti, favouring a relativism rooted in experimentation and nature.

The Royal Library also holds six folios devoted to the musculature of horses and of man. The earliest, possibly a study of legs (D.C. 15578), bears on its verso a sketch and a short text on the vanity of carnal pleasures and the true light of knowledge: "O wretched mortals, open your eyes."

The other folios (D.C. 15577, 15630, 15579, 15580, 15582), created during preparations for the monument to Francesco Sforza in Milan and the development of *The Battle of Anghiari* in Florence, reflect Leonardo's quest to depict the movement of bodies, though these works remained unfinished, either because of external circumstances or the overly ambitious scope of his vision.

In the spring of 1505, Leonardo was in Florence and resumed his studies on human flight. This theme united his most accomplished reflections on anatomy, technology and mathematics.

His walks in the hills of Fiesole give rise to the notebook known today as the *Codice sul volo degli uccelli* (*Codex on the Flight of Birds*), a small booklet of eighteen folios that the artist had already used for various sketches in red chalk and pen.

Leonardo nurtured the idea of writing an actual treatise in four books. His plan was clear: first, to understand the mechanics of flight in nature, then to study flight in different animal species, and finally to recreate the process of flight using physical and mechanical sciences.

During his years as an apprentice in Verrocchio's studio, where he worked on ephemeral devices for festivals and celebrations, he laid the foundations for his research into flight.

It was in Milan that the dream of flight became a matter of great importance. In the 1480s, Leonardo focused his attention on reproducing flapping-wing flight, using equipment designed to harness and strengthen human muscle power. This led to his 'ornithopters', devices with large artificial wings powered by pedals, levers and springs. At a later moment, Leonardo became aware of the importance of wind, both as a propulsive force and as a danger to the stability of flight.

His Florentine period marked a return to his study of nature. Observation of the animal world became essential to understanding the physical laws of wind movement and its action on bodies in the air [fig. 1].

In the first part of the notebook, Leonardo analysed the articulation of wings and proposed mechanical models that imitated their movements [fig. 2].

In addition to the relationship between wingspan and air pressure, he explored the rotation of human joints and their angles of inclination. He then addressed the question of gliding flight and the challenges related to controlling direction and balance, particularly in response to the thrusts of air masses.

The final section of the notebook is a theoretical examination of the equilibrium of bodies, anticipating the concepts of static physics. In it, Leonardo discusses the notions of weight, resistance, lift and thrust, concepts later developed by modern science. Each demonstration is an

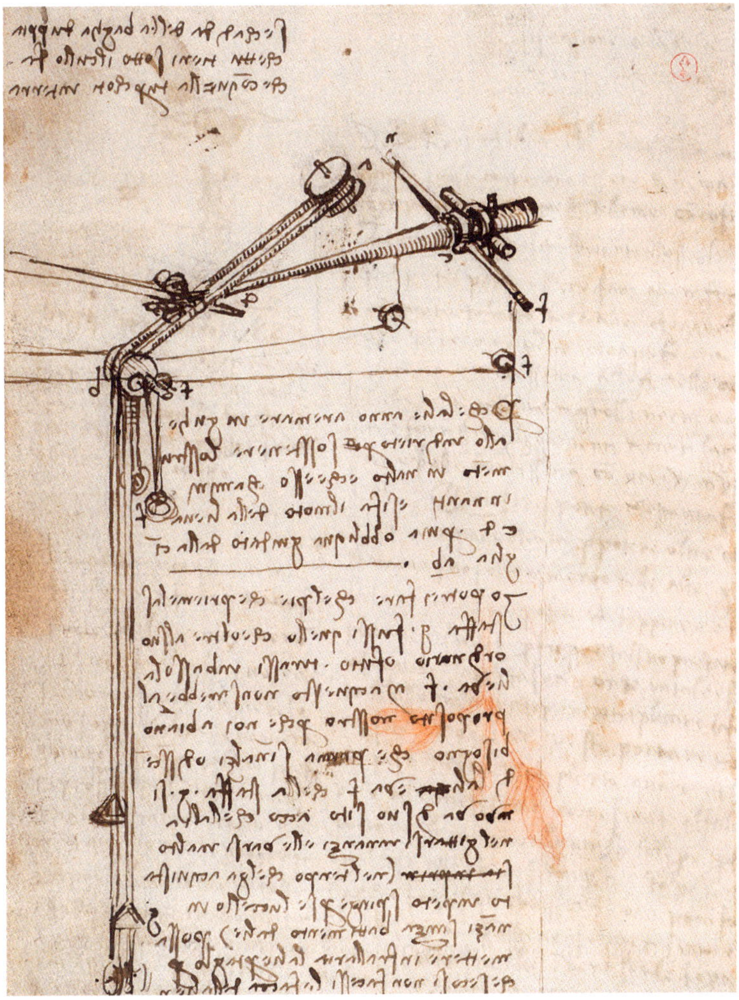

Fig. 2. Leonardo da Vinci, *Codice sul volo degli uccelli*, "Wing rotation device", c. 1505-1506, f. 16v, Biblioteca Reale, inv. Cod. Varia 95

attempt to reconstruct in words his observations, which are all the more astonishing since they are carried out at a distance and on bodies in constant motion. Leonardo pursued the same goal with his drawings: using pen and ink, he reproduced the different postures of birds, using crosshatching to symbolise the currents of air, whose "vivifying" vibration was to capture the imagination of Paul Valéry in his day.

The text, which describes flight manoeuvres and the various parts of wings, plumage and tail, is interspersed with passages in which Leonardo seems to be addressing either himself or the potential pilot of his flying machine, to which he always referred as a "bird". Other notes refer to the mechanical wing projects he had been working on many years earlier:

> Remember that your bird [flying machine] must imitate none but the bat, for its membranes serve as a framework, or rather as connections to the framework, that is to say they are the masters of the wings. (15r)

Leonardo also kept in mind the diversity and complexity of nature, as the wing is not a simple compact surface but a set of elements whose characteristics vary across animal species:

> Therefore, you who study the flight of birds, let not your calculations rest solely on the measure of their wings, but observe also the differing qualities of wings in all creatures of the air. (8v)

The *Turin Codex* represents the culmination of Leonardo's reflections on biomimicry. His famous prophecy about the flying machine, written on the inside back cover, reveals the scholar's awareness and pride in what he achieved, as he envisions in the sky the triumph of a bird-man.

> Upon the ridge of Mount Ceceri, the great bird shall take its first flight, filling all writings with its fame, and bringing eternal glory to the nest where it was born.

We do not know whether, during these months, Leonardo moved from the theory of flight to practice. It is, however, certain that he must have felt very close to a truth capable of transforming a myth into reality for the first time. In his notebook, he records several indications of manoeuvres and equipment designed for experimentation. He discusses and affirms the legitimacy of this endeavour, comparing the strength of man with that of birds. It is here that the form of the artificial bird, tethered to the ground by cables, emerges, accompanied by advice for crafting a safety harness for the pilot, a kind of airbag made of bags fastened together:

> Bags such that, when falling from a height of six *braccia*, a man will be protected from injury, whether he falls into water or onto land. And these bags, linked like a rosary, wind around his body. (16r)

The large drawing of this wing with a tether [fig. 3], faithfully reproducing the anatomy of a natural wing, takes into account the characteristics of the construction materials. These must be as close as possible to living materials, carefully avoiding the use of iron. Leonardo thus envisages leather "joints" and silk "sinews".

He uses the remaining blank spaces of his notebook to add comments and new reflections. On the inside back cover, which is the inside front cover in the reading order intended by the artist, he sketches the façade of a grand residence and, alongside it, a dam for a watercourse and two drawings concerning piles and a gear. As for the inside front cover, the inside back cover for Leonardo, it contains instructions for striking medals.

Mention should also be made of several marginal notes, particularly the famous description of a childhood memory that prompted Freud's psychoanalytic interpretation, and the enigmatic passage occupying a section of folio 13r:

> In summer, snow will be brought to hot places, gathered from the lofty mountain heights, and let fall during festivals over the piazzas.

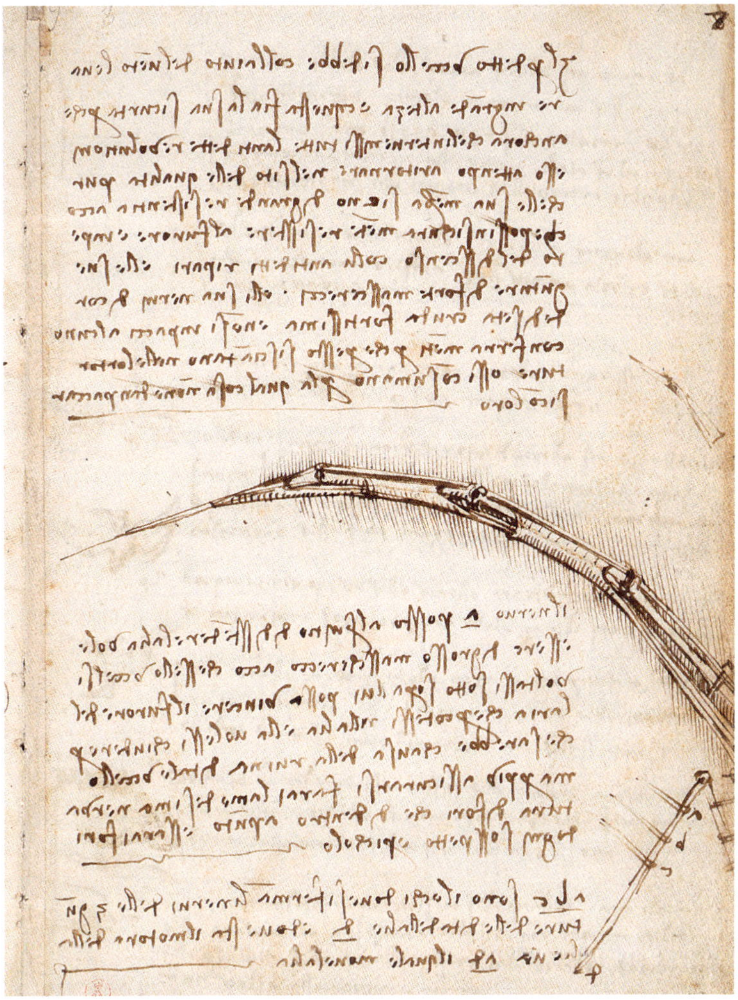

Fig. 3. Leonardo da Vinci, *Codice sul volo degli uccelli*, "Figure of the single tie-rod wing", c. 1505-1506, f. 7r, Biblioteca Reale, inv. Cod. Varia 95

This text appears unrelated to the main content of the page, which describes a bird hovering motionless in the air, its wings spread, thanks to the balance of gravitational forces. It has therefore been suggested that it might be interpreted as a riddle alluding to the melting of snow that feeds rivers and spouting fountains in summer. However, another reading, proposed several years ago by the historian Luigi Firpo, cannot be entirely dismissed. Considering the difficulty of preserving ice at that time, he attributes to Leonardo the idea of a gliding bird tasked with transporting snow from the mountain heights to the cities, enabling the staging of natural snowfall over the piazzas.

Leonardo concludes with a reflection on truth and falsehood, highlighting the humility of experience over grandiose speeches. Though written in small characters in the margins, it encapsulates the spirit of the manuscript:

> The proportion of falsehood to truth is as darkness to light. Truth is so noble that even when it concerns the humblest subject, it far outshines mere uncertainties and lies, transcending even the most sublime discourses. [...]

> But you, who live on dreams, delight more in sophistical debates and grand uncertainties than in modest subjects grounded in natural certainty.

Mention of "modest subjects grounded in natural certainty" brings us to the last, tiny folio in the Royal Library of Turin, featuring sketches of a *Cerambyx* beetle and a dragonfly (D.C. 15581). Of remarkable finesse, it testifies to the life Leonardo infused into his works, renewing the splendid Lombard tradition of the *Tacuina Sanitatis* [fig. 4].

Nature and experience, truth and humility together provide a timeless warning that resonates across the centuries.

Essential Bibliography

Da Vinci, Leonardo. *Il codice sul volo degli uccelli nella Biblioteca Reale di Torino*, Augusto Marinoni (ed.). Florence: Giunti, 1976.

Giacobello Bernard, Giovanna (ed.). *Leonardo da Vinci. Capolavori in mostra*, exh. cat., Turin, Biblioteca Reale, 10 February – 19 March 2006. Milan: Hoepli, 2006.

Laurenza, Domenico. *Leonardo. Il Volo*. Florence: Giunti, 2004.

O'Grody, Jeannine A. (ed.). *Leonardo da Vinci. Drawings from the Biblioteca Reale in Turin*, exh. cat., Birmingham Museum of Art, 28 September – 9 November 2008; Fine Arts Museums of San Francisco, 15 November 2008 – 4 January 2009. Birmingham, AL: Birmingham Museum of Art, 2008.

Pagella, Enrica, Paolo Di Teodoro, Francesco, SALVI, Paola. *Leonardo da Vinci. Disegnare il futuro*, exh. cat., Turin, Musei Reali, 16 April – 14 July 2019. Cinisello Balsamo: Silvana, 2019.

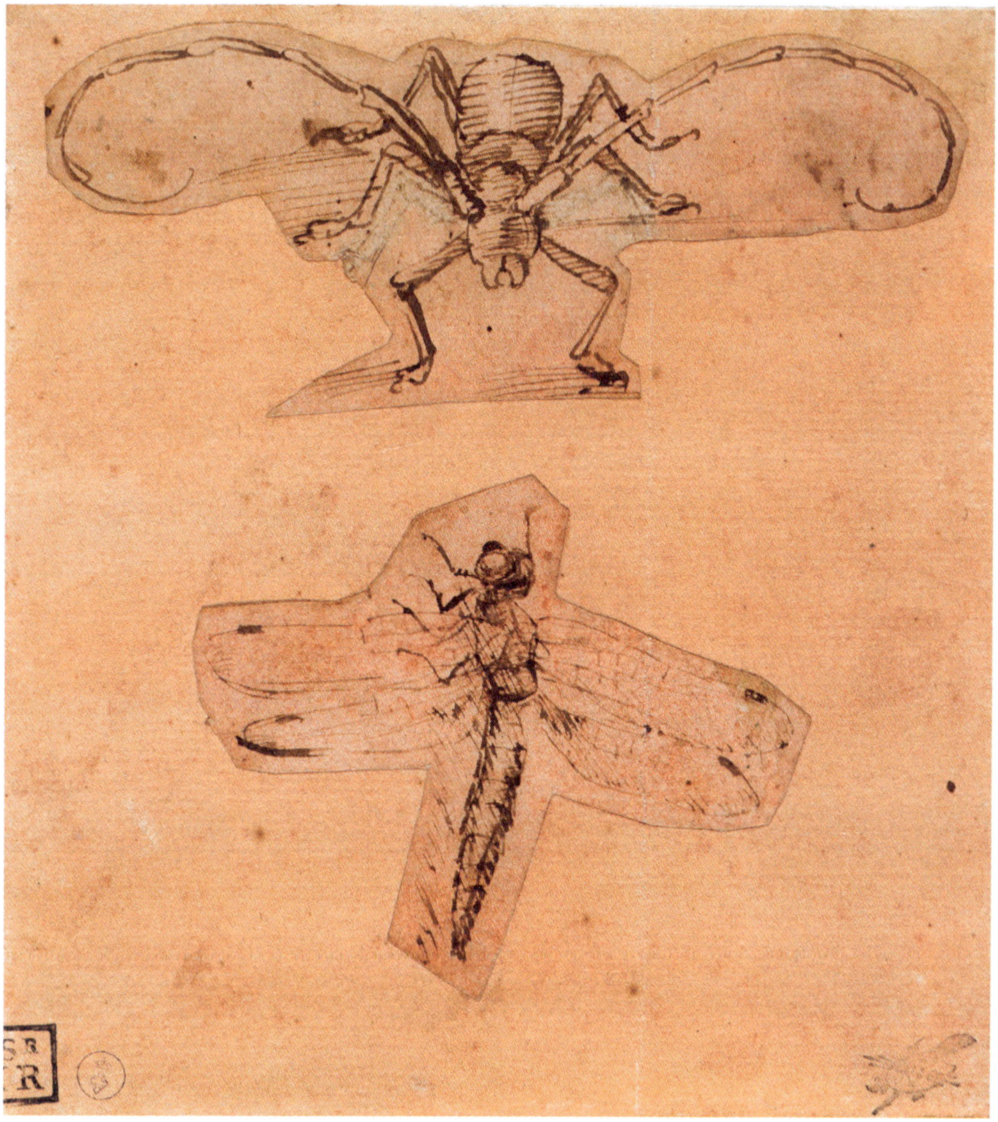

Fig. 4. Leonardo da Vinci, *Studies of insects*, top, *cerambyx* (c. 1480-1490), bottom, dragonfly (c. 1505-1506), Biblioteca Reale, inv. D.C. 15580

References

The letters A, H, K, and G refer to the codices of Leonardo da Vinci at the Institut de France. Other citations without letters come from the *Codex on the Flight of Birds* in Turin. For the reference to Paul Valéry, see *Introduction à la méthode de Léonard de Vinci* (Paris: Gallimard, 1957 [1st ed. 1894]), p. 36.

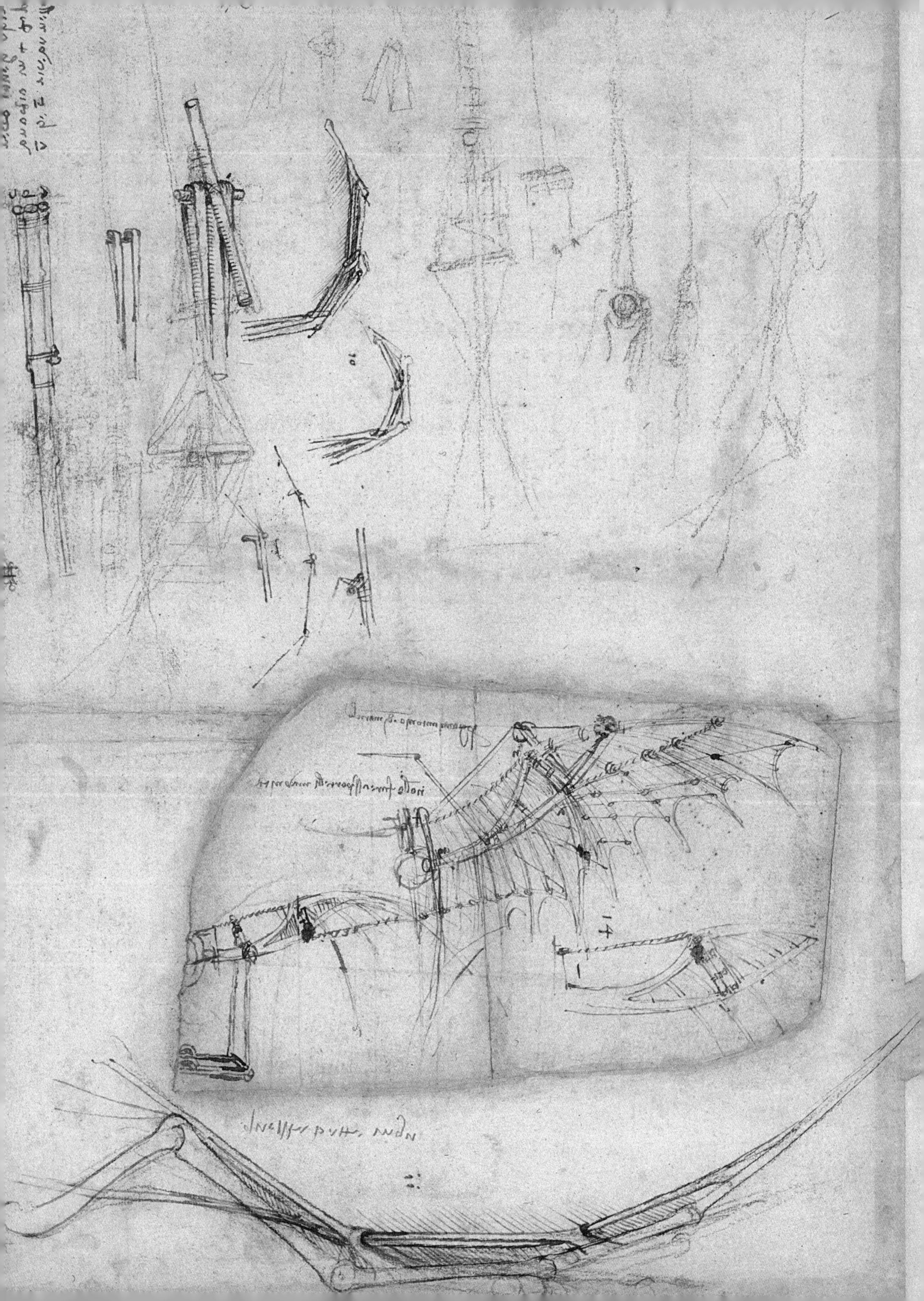

BIOMIMETIC INSPIRATION IN STUDIES ON FLYING MACHINES

ANDREA BERNARDONI

Human flight has always captured our imagination. The myth of Icarus in ancient times offered an early, imaginative attempt to equip man with artificial wings. During the Renaissance, religious ceremonies and theatrical performances presented organisers and designers with the technical challenge of depicting flight and the ascent of angels, which they sought to recreate by the use of machines, captivating the audience's imagination. The goal was not to imitate the flight of birds but to replicate the flapping motion of their wings by using a combination of screws, pulleys, gears and cranks. It was within this context of theatrical set design that Leonardo da Vinci's earliest drawings of flying machines seem to have been created. His biomimetic inspiration is immediately evident in the wing design from the *Codex Atlanticus* (f. 858r, 860r) and in the pictorial rendering of the wings of the Archangel Gabriel in Leonardo's *Annunciation* at the Uffizi Gallery in Florence: both meticulously reproduce the plumage of a bird of prey.

Leonardo's studies of flying machines developed along two parallel lines: on the one hand, he examined the structure and morphology of wings to determine the most efficient and effective model; on the other, he studied systems to move them and achieve a flapping speed sufficient to lift and keep the machines he envisioned airborne. It is curious to note that these two lines of research did not result in a design of a complete machine that integrated both wings and a propulsion system.

His biomimetic inspiration is most clearly evident in his studies of wings, starting with his earliest drawings that featured models inspired by such bird species as kites and falcons (*Codex Atlanticus*, f. 70r, 846r, 853r). Leonardo also appears to have been fascinated by bats' wings, having been intrigued by the uniqueness of their structure, which lacks feathers but features an elastic membrane better suited to the 'decomposed' flight required for hunting nocturnal insects (*Manuscript B*, f. 89v, cod., vol. 15v). In *Manuscript F*, folio. 41v, he explicitly writes: "Dissect the bat and adhere closely to its structure; from this, craft the design of the instrument" (flying machine). For Leonardo, bats' wings, being the most versatile, were the most effective.

LEFT
Fig. 1. Leonardo da Vinci, *Codex Atlanticus*, 1478-1518, pen and ink, f. 854r, Veneranda Biblioteca Ambrosiana

When designing a flying machine, one must address the challenge of reopening the wing: as its closure propels the device skyward, its opening negates that effect. Birds overcome this by altering the geometry of their wings between these two phases, sometimes tilting them vertically or thinning their feathers to reduce the surface area exposed to resistance. By observing birds, Leonardo developed several mechanical solutions, the most effective of which, at least at first glance, appears to be the 'flapped' wing. This technique relies on the opening and closing of a series of flaps: during the downstroke, the air beneath the wing compresses, closing the flaps and pushing them toward the structure; during the upstroke, the flaps open, allowing air to pass through.

Folio 74r of *Manuscript B* also specifies the materials to be used in constructing the wing: the supporting structure should be made of fir wood, and the sails of fustian, onto which feathers should be glued to provide greater resistance to airflow. The rear part of the wing, where the flaps are located, should be made of taffeta or paper. On folio 854r of the *Codex Atlanticus* [fig. 1], Leonardo wrote: "For Gianni Antonio di Mariolo / do not make a perforated wing but a solid one". Written as instructions for the craftsman building the wing model, this note demonstrates Leonardo's active involvement in experimenting with flying machines. It refers to a reconsideration of the flapped wing in favour of a model with fixed sails mounted on a wing with a foldable outer section. The biomorphic inspiration of this semi-rigid wing is further emphasised when combined, for example, with the nacelle drawn in *Manuscript B*, folio 74v. In this wing control system, pedals control the opening and closing movements. The opening occurs with the wings tilted vertically to reduce air resistance from above, replicating the movements Leonardo observed in birds.

The search for the most efficient mechanical system led Leonardo to extend his observations to insects. He focused on specimens such as the antlion, butterfly (*Manuscript G*, f. 64v, 65r, 92r), and dragonfly (*Codex Atlanticus*, f. 1051v, *Manuscript B*, f. 100v), which possess two pairs of wings. It was the flapping of the dragonfly's wings that particularly captured his attention: "When one pair moves upwards (upstroke), the other moves downwards (downstroke). The dragonfly flies with four wings: when the forewings rise, the hindwings lower. But each pair of wings must be capable of lifting the insect's entire weight". This alternating motion ensures continuous lift and stability, a principle Leonardo sought to replicate in his designs for flying machines. Although this solution is logically sound, the problem of controlling a flying machine remained. An additional pair of wings doubles the weight to be lifted and significantly complicates the mechanics of the transmission system; to such an extent that Leonardo was forced to abandon the idea of a pilot lying prone in the machine, operating solely with pedals, and instead proposed a vertical nacelle with pedals and cranks in the centre, which he deemed necessary to generate enough power to drive the wings. To refine this design, he immersed himself in biomechanical studies, arriving at a mechanism that simultaneously engaged the operator's arms, legs and back. This transformed the pilot from a mere controller into the machine's 'engine', while still incorporating space for at least one passenger (*Manuscript B*, f. 80r) [fig. 2]. Despite being meticulously designed, Leonardo ultimately abandoned the apparatus when he recognised this concept was unworkable.

This setback, however, did not deter him. Leonardo turned his attention back to the flight of birds, examining winds, updraughts, and how birds exploit them to glide for extended periods, sometimes even gaining altitude without flapping their wings (*Codex Atlanticus*, f. 845r; Vol Ucc.,

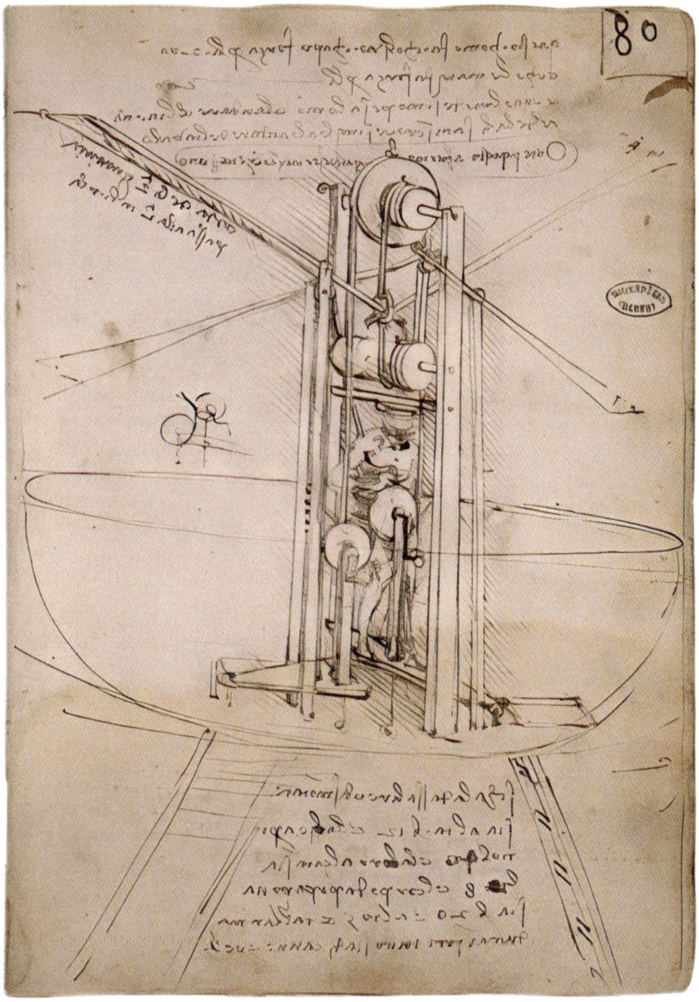

Fig. 2. Leonardo da Vinci, *Manuscript B.*, c. 1487-1489, 24.3 × 18.7 cm, f. 80r, Bibliothèque de l'Institut de France, Ms 2173

f. 8r-8v). He also studied the behaviour of windborne objects, such as leaves falling from trees, their paths guided by the stems acting as rudders. These falling leaves highlighted the material properties of air, demonstrating that, like water, it was alive with currents capable of supporting and carrying heavy objects. Inspired by this, Leonardo conceived machines with rigid wings designed to harness these natural forces to move them (*Codex Atlanticus*, f. 70br, 846v).

One of his earliest projects consisted of a sail mounted on a rigid structure shaped like a leaf, controlled by a system of cords to adjust its angle to the wind to harness air currents more effectively (*Madrid Codex I*, f. 64r) [fig. 3]. It is interesting to note that Leonardo envisioned it advancing with its tapered end forward, with the apex acting as a rudder, similar to leaves. The radial structure of a thistle seed, on the other hand, appears to have inspired another singular invention, the 'flying sphere', sketched on the same folio as a glider. This enormous structure consists of three concentric circles, each 12 metres in diameter, fitted with sails. Though capable of reacting to air currents from any direction, it would spin unpredictably. It was essentially a thought experiment

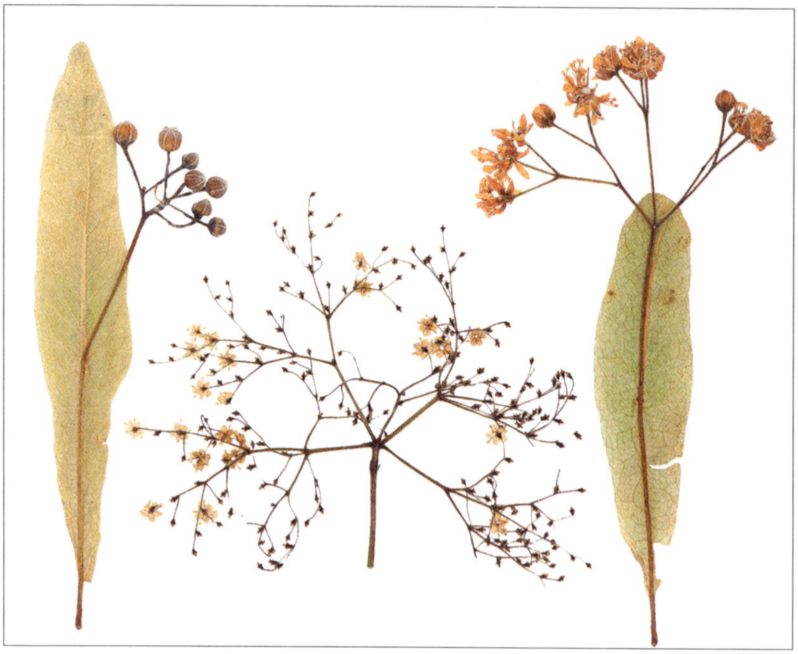

Linden bracts, 2016

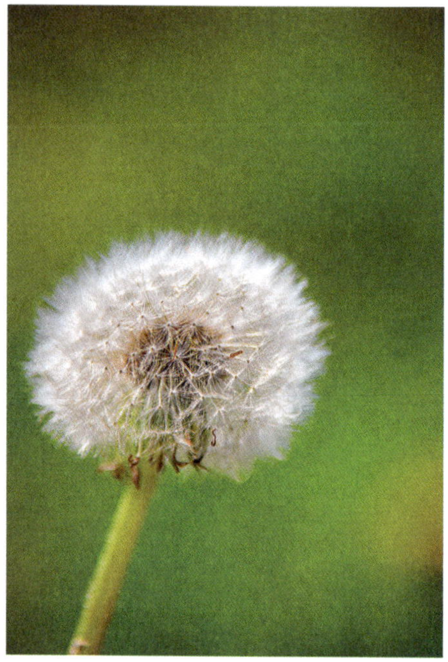

Dandelion flower, 2021

to test a gimbal-like suspension or 'Cardan joint', with a basket for the occupant at the sphere's core ensuring the person remained upright regardless of the sphere's rotations.

Leonardo did not limit himself to observations; he also engaged in the study of wings through the anatomical dissection of birds, seeking to understand their structure and to construct physical models to test joint movements (*Codex Atlanticus*, f. 844r). Although his research on flight was ultimately unsuccessful and there is no evidence of actual experimentation with his flying machines, his work precisely reflects the method he followed, now known as biomimicry.

Bibliography

Bernardoni, Andrea. *Leonardo ingegnere*. Rome: Carocci, 2020.

Giacomelli, Roberto. *Gli Studi di Leonardo da Vinci sul Volo*. Rome: Bardi, 1936.

Laurenza, Domenico, "Gli studi leonardiani sul volo: spunti per una riconsiderazione", in Frosini, Fabio. *Tutte le opere non son per istancarmi: raccolta di scritti per i settant'anni di Carlo Pedretti*. Rome: Edizioni Associate, 1998, pp. 189-202.

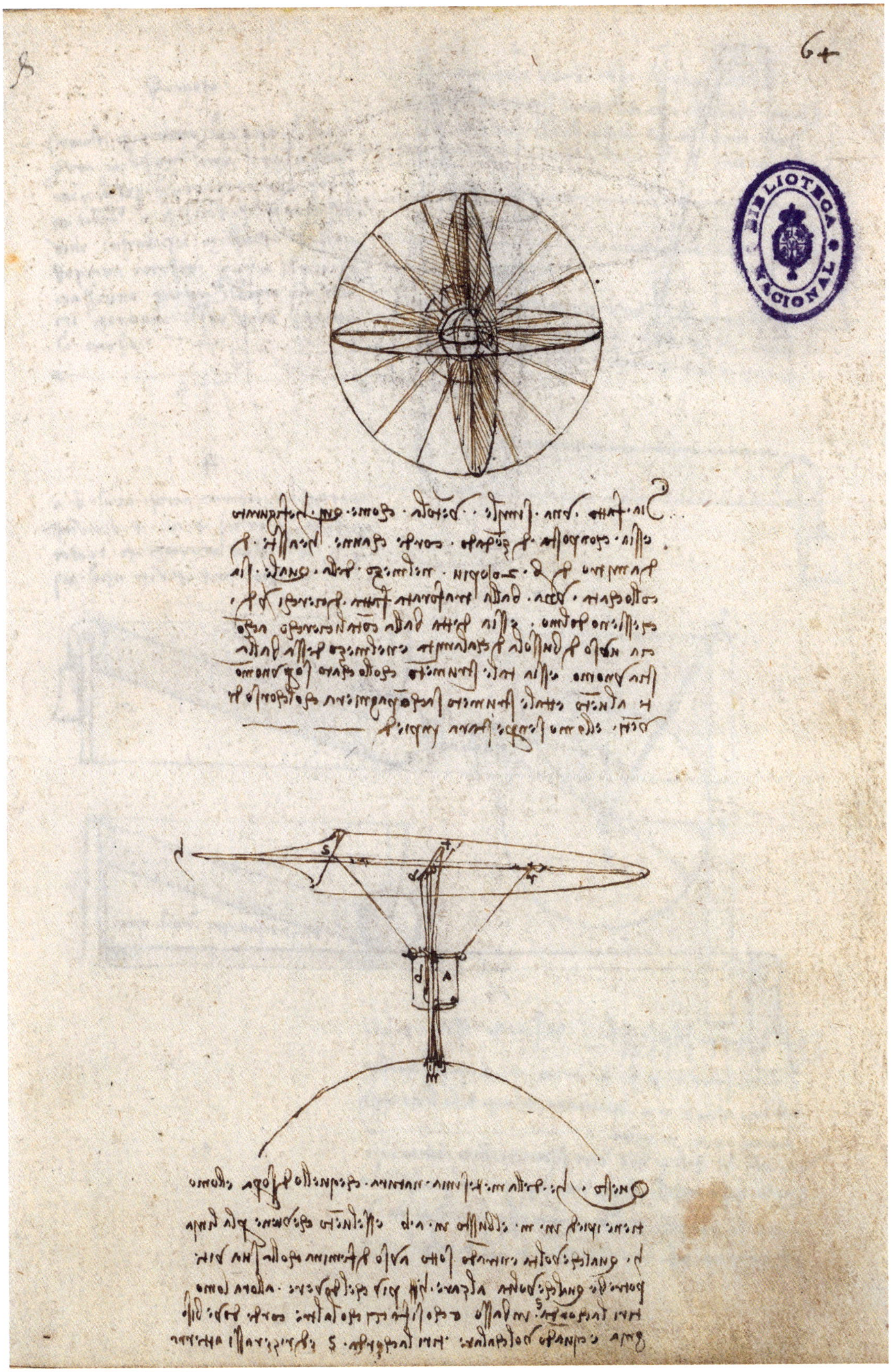

Fig. 3. Leonardo da Vinci, *Codex Madrid*, f. 64r, Biblioteca Nacional de España, Mss/8936

INSECTES

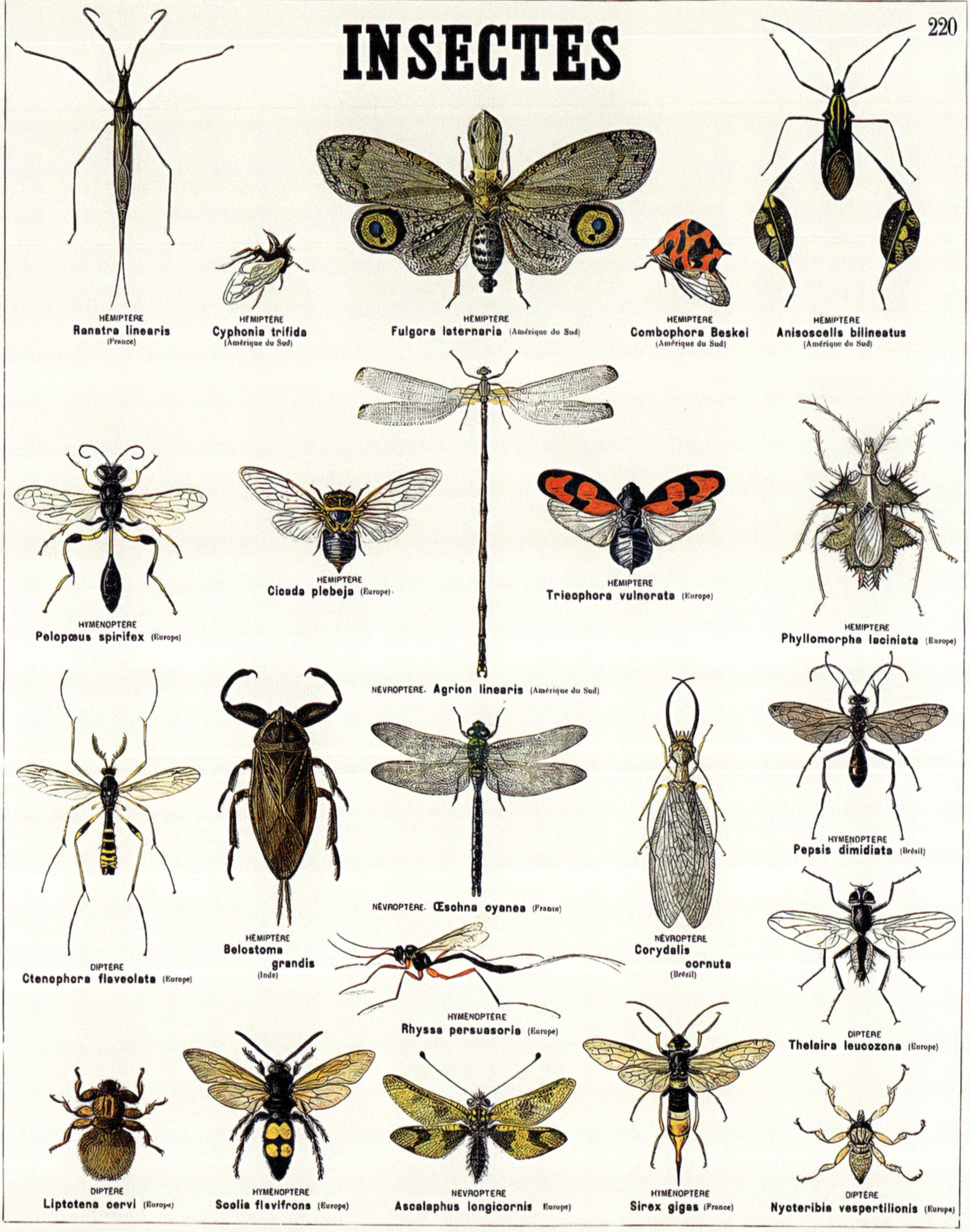

HÉMIPTÈRE
Ranatra linearis (France)
HÉMIPTÈRE
Cyphonia trifida (Amérique du Sud)
HÉMIPTÈRE
Fulgora laternaria (Amérique du Sud)
HÉMIPTÈRE
Combophora Beskei (Amérique du Sud)
HÉMIPTÈRE
Anisoscelis bilineatus (Amérique du Sud)
HYMÉNOPTÈRE
Pelopœus spirifex (Europe)
HÉMIPTÈRE
Cicada plebeja (Europe)
HÉMIPTÈRE
Triecphora vulnerata (Europe)
HÉMIPTÈRE
Phyllomorpha laciniata (Europe)
NÉVROPTÈRE. Agrion linearis (Amérique du Sud)
HYMÉNOPTÈRE
Pepsis dimidiata (Brésil)
NÉVROPTÈRE. Œschna cyanea (France)
HÉMIPTÈRE
Belostoma grandis (Inde)
NÉVROPTÈRE
Corydalis cornuta (Brésil)
DIPTÈRE
Ctenophora flaveolata (Europe)
HYMÉNOPTÈRE
Rhyssa persuasoria (Europe)
DIPTÈRE
Thelaira leucozona (Europe)
DIPTÈRE
Liptotena cervi (Europe)
HYMÉNOPTÈRE
Scolia flavifrons (Europe)
NÉVROPTÈRE
Ascalaphus longicornis (Europe)
HYMÉNOPTÈRE
Sirex gigas (France)
DIPTÈRE
Nycteribia vespertilionis (Europe)

WHEN INSECTS INSPIRE THE ROBOTS OF THE FUTURE

Julien Serres

Drawing inspiration from nature to solve complex problems is an idea far older than one might think. Imitating living organisms has been a common research approach, from Leonardo da Vinci to the present day. It was only in the 1950s, however, that biomimicry emerged as a distinct scientific discipline. It encourages humanity to draw from the multiple sources of inspiration offered by nature: forms, materials, energy and information management, as well as sustainable synergies and ecosystems. These are solutions refined over millions of years of evolution. Nature represents a veritable trove of knowledge that we must first understand and then replicate to address the complex challenges facing our societies. Biorobotics aims to understand animal behaviour through robots that mimic their perception and locomotion systems (Viollet et al., 2020). Its results, often counterintuitive to experts, lead to innovations from which drones, autonomous vehicles, and intelligent machines must draw inspiration if they are to achieve the agility and resilience of a moving animal.

Perceiving the Environment through the Eye of an Insect

The European CurvACE project marked a major breakthrough with the first miniature artificial eye that challenges the limits of perception. It is both reprogrammable and capable of detecting motion and measuring the scrolling speeds of visual contrasts across five decades of brightness (Floreano et al., 2013), from moonlight to a bright sunny day.

This cylindrical masterpiece [fig. 1], weighing 1.75 grams with a volume of 2.2 cm3, is studded with 630 optical facets, providing a panoramic field of view spanning 180° horizontally and 60° vertically, with a diameter of just 15 mm and a power consumption of only a few milliwatts.

LEFT
Deyrolle 'Insects' educational board

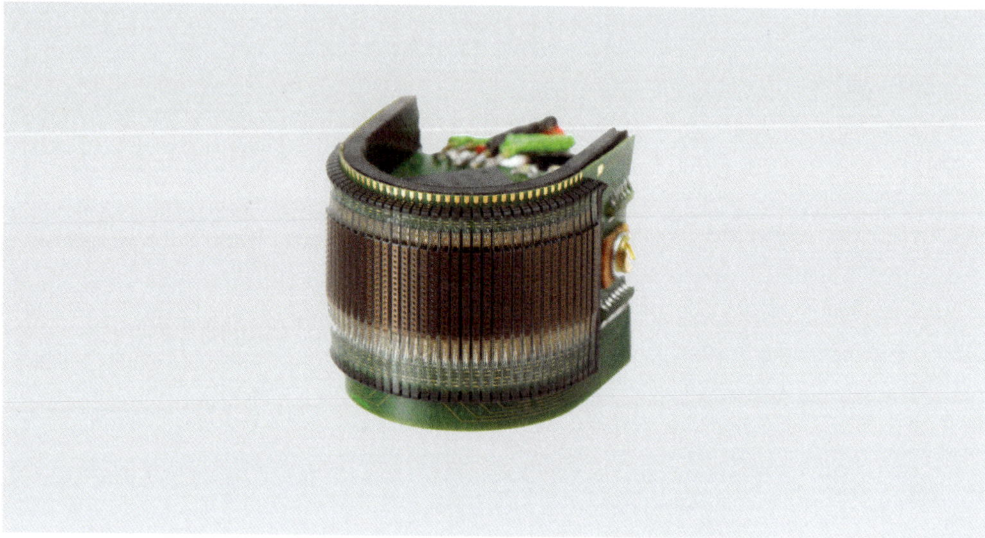

Fig. 1. First functional curved compound eye produced as part of the European CurvACE project

The first 80-gram rotary-wing micro-aircraft, equipped with a pair of CurvACE sensors and named BeeRotor, was able to navigate uneven terrain. These sensors, weighing only a few milligrams, could have numerous applications in the micro-aircraft of tomorrow (Serres et al., 2017).

Folding and Unfolding like a Bird

The quadrotor drone, named Quad-Morphing [fig. 2], was inspired by bird flight and has the unique ability to fold and unfold mid-flight to reduce its wingspan (Rivière and Viollet, 2018). This ability to change shape in flight addresses the challenge of avoiding obstacles in cluttered environments. To achieve this, a central servomotor rotates pairs of propellers to align them, thereby reducing the aircraft's wingspan.

To orchestrate this transformation, the drone detects a narrow passage using a high-speed camera (120 frames per second), then the onboard computer initiates a ballistic trajectory through the narrow space. Once the manoeuvre is complete, it methodically unfolds on the other side to restore its flight attitude. Using this operational mode, the drone successfully halves its wingspan to pass through a tiny doorway at a speed of 2.5 metres per second, much like a bird in flight; the transformation takes only 250 milliseconds. This rapid modification inevitably leads to a loss of stability due to the change in the drone's shape. This type of reconfigurable morphology is particularly suitable for exploration in indoor or confined environments.

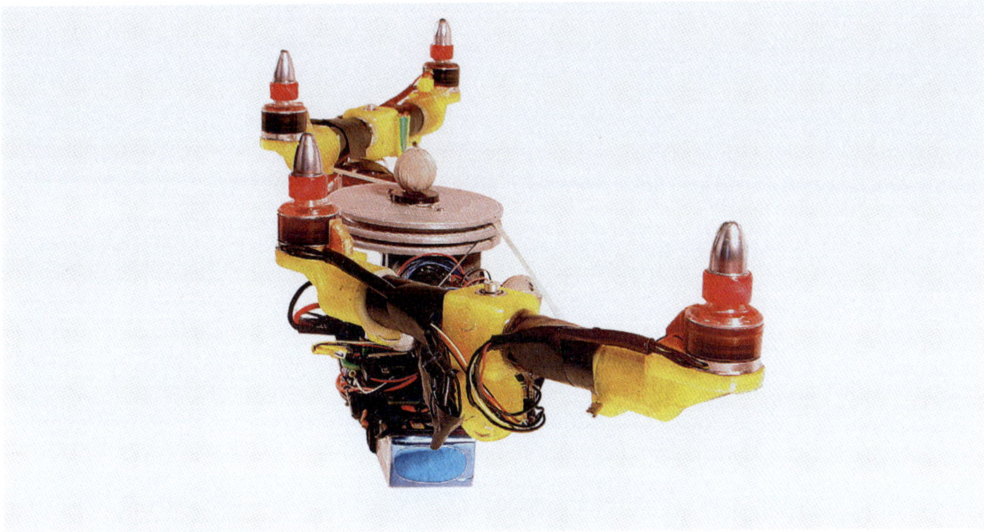

Fig. 2. A bio-inspired quadcopter drone, Quad-Morphing, inspired by birds to overcome narrow spaces

Navigating Without Geolocation Devices like an Insect

The undisputed champions of the ant world are the desert ants *Cataglyphis*. They can travel up to 1 kilometre to find food and return to their nest in less than 30 minutes over terrain that can reach temperatures of over 50° C.

The AntBot robot [fig. 3] is equipped with two visual sensors inspired by these ants (Dupeyroux et al., 2020; Viollet et al., 2020). The first is an optical compass consisting of two ultraviolet-sensitive photoreceptors topped with polarising filters. By rotating these filters, it is possible to scan the sky and determine the robot's heading to within 0.5°. The second sensor is an artificial retina composed of 12 photoreceptors that adapt to changes in light levels, similar to the CurvACE artificial compound eye, and faces the ground.

This small biomimetic retina measures the optical flow of the ground, providing a reliable estimate of the distance travelled. This is calculated by combining step counting and optical flow, much like desert ants do. Tested under various cloud cover conditions, the AntBot robot repositioned itself with an error of just 7 centimetres, a value nearly 100 times lower than that of a geolocation device after a 15-metre journey (Dupeyroux et al., 2020; Viollet et al., 2020). In the face of satellite jamming, this navigation method could be integrated into autonomous and intelligent vehicles.

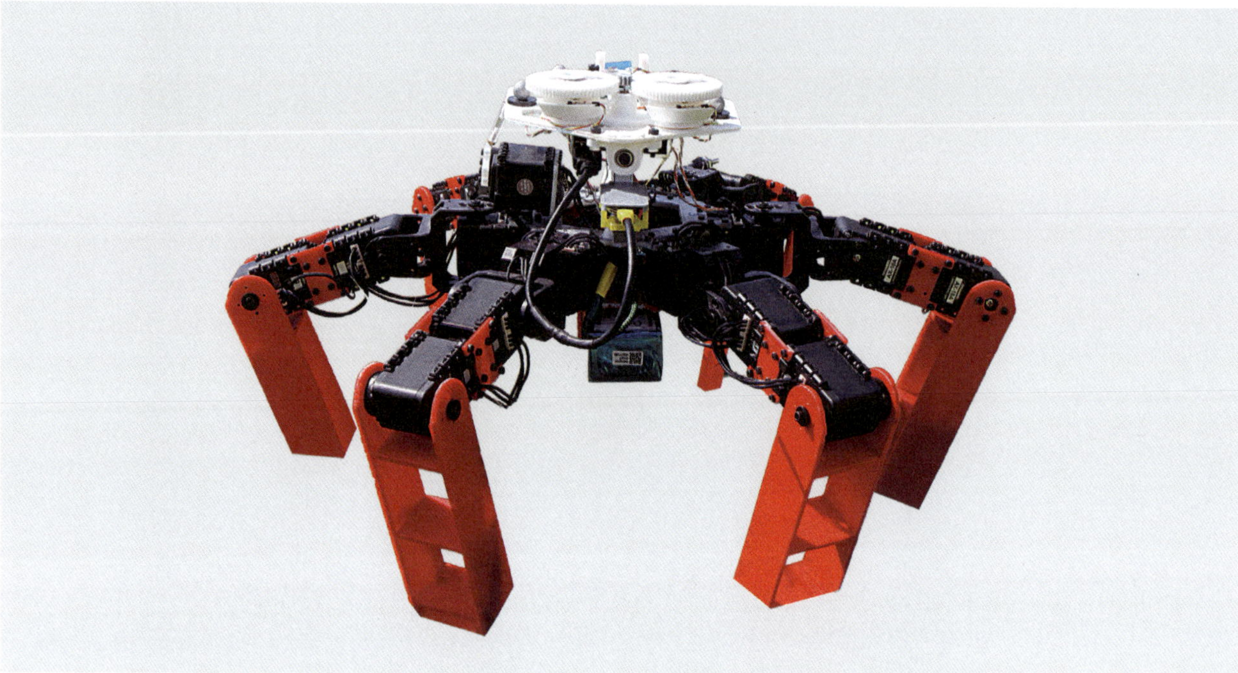

Fig. 3. Photo of the AntBot hexapod robot, whose optical compass is inspired by the desert ant

Walking and Carrying Loads like an Ant

Unlike the AntBot robot, which is based on a skeleton powered by 'hobby grade' servomotors, the Pohod15Leg prototype [fig. 4] is exoskeletal like insects, and its anatomy is modelled on the legs of the *Cataglyphis* desert ant.

Pohod15Leg weighs 420 grams, meaning a complete hexapod robot would weigh 2.5 kilograms (the same weight as AntBot). The two limbs were compared using the MiMiC-ANT test bench [fig. 4], specially built in the laboratory to evaluate different robotic legs with a walking frequency of 0.3 Hz (i.e., a walking cycle of 3 seconds).

This frequency is close to that of the *Barbarus* ant when carrying loads of up to 15 times its body weight (whereas human weightlifters can lift about twice their body weight).

Cataglyphis, on the other hand, is a sprinting ant with a walking cycle as short as 25 milliseconds (40 Hz). For comparison, Olympic sprinters achieve cycles of 250 milliseconds (i.e., 4 steps per second, 4 Hz). Using the MiMiC-ANT test bench, researchers demonstrated that an AntBot leg had three times the energy efficiency of the leg of the Pohod15Leg, but the latter heated up less quickly, making it 'more resilient' in high heat. Moreover, AntBot's energy consumption at rest represented 33% of its energy consumption while walking, whereas Pohod15Leg consumed nothing at rest. These results show that ants still have much to teach us about mimicking their locomotion in extreme conditions.

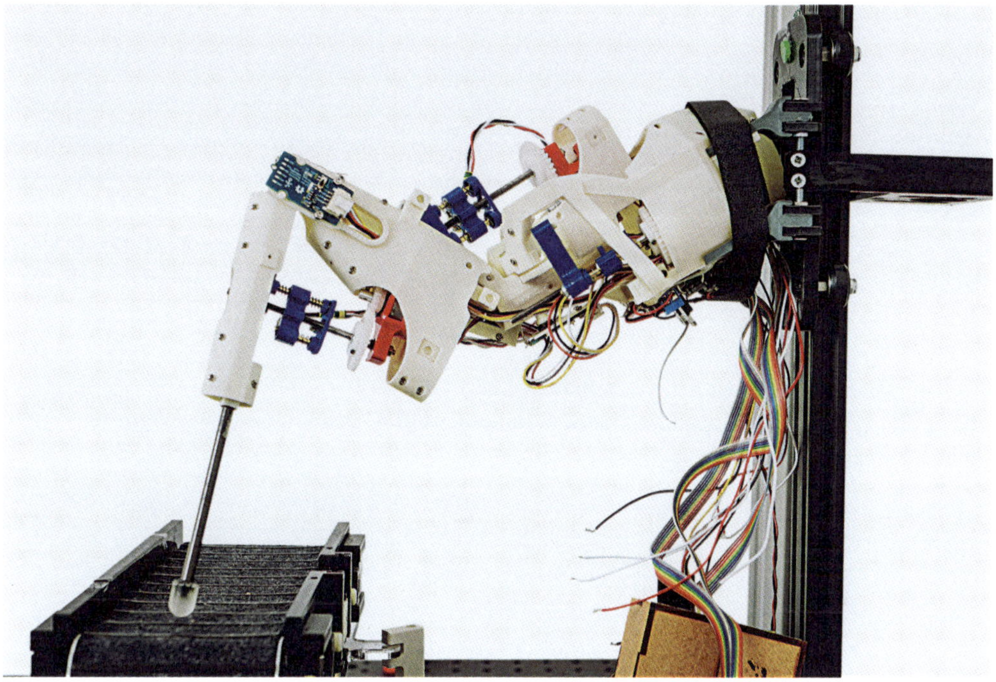

Fig. 4. Photo of the Pohod15Leg bionic leg, inspired by the desert ant, installed on an evaluation conveyor belt called MiMiC-ANT

Bibliography

Dupeyroux, Julien, Serres, Julien, and Viollet, Stéphane. "AntBot: un robot qui s'oriente comme une fourmi – Applications à la navigation à vue sans GPS ni magnétomètre", Ref. IN236, *Éditions Techniques de l'Ingénieur* (2020). DOI: https://doi.org/10.51257/a-v1-in236, HAL: https://amu.hal.science/hal-02500157.

Dupeyroux, Julien, Serres, Julien, and Viollet, Stéphane. "Le robot fourmi AntBot. Conception et réalisation d'un robot bio-inspiré". *Techniques & Culture. Revue semestrielle d'anthropologie des techniques*, 73 (2020), 128-41. DOI: https://doi.org/10.4000/tc.13557, HAL: https://amu.hal.science/hal-02892659.

Floreano, Dario, Pericet-Camara, Ramon, Viollet, Stéphane, Ruffier, Franck, Brückner, Andreas, Leitel, Robert, Buss, Wolfgang, Menouni, Mohsine, Expert, Fabien, Juston, Raphaël, Dobrzynski, Michal Karol, L'Eplattenier, Geraud, Recktenwald, Fabian, Mallot, Hanspeter, A., and Franceschini, Nicolas. "Miniature Curved Artificial Compound Eyes". *Proceedings of the National Academy of Sciences*, 110(23) (2013), 9267-72. DOI: https://doi.org/10.1073/pnas.1219068110.

Manecy, Augustin, Rivière, Valentin, and Viollet, Stéphane. "Agile Robotic Fliers: A Morphing-Based Approach". *Soft Robotics* 5⑤ (2018), 541-53. DOI: https://doi.org/10.1089/soro.2017.0120, HAL: https://amu.hal.science/hal-01803737.

Ruffier, Franck, Serres, Julien, and Viollet, Stéphane. "Microdrones bio-inspirés - Doter nos futurs robots aériens de l'agilité des insectes". *Éditions Techniques de l'Ingénieur* (2017), Ref. S7717 V1. DOI: https://doi.org/10.51257/a-v1-s7717, HAL: https://amu.hal.science/hal-01574508.

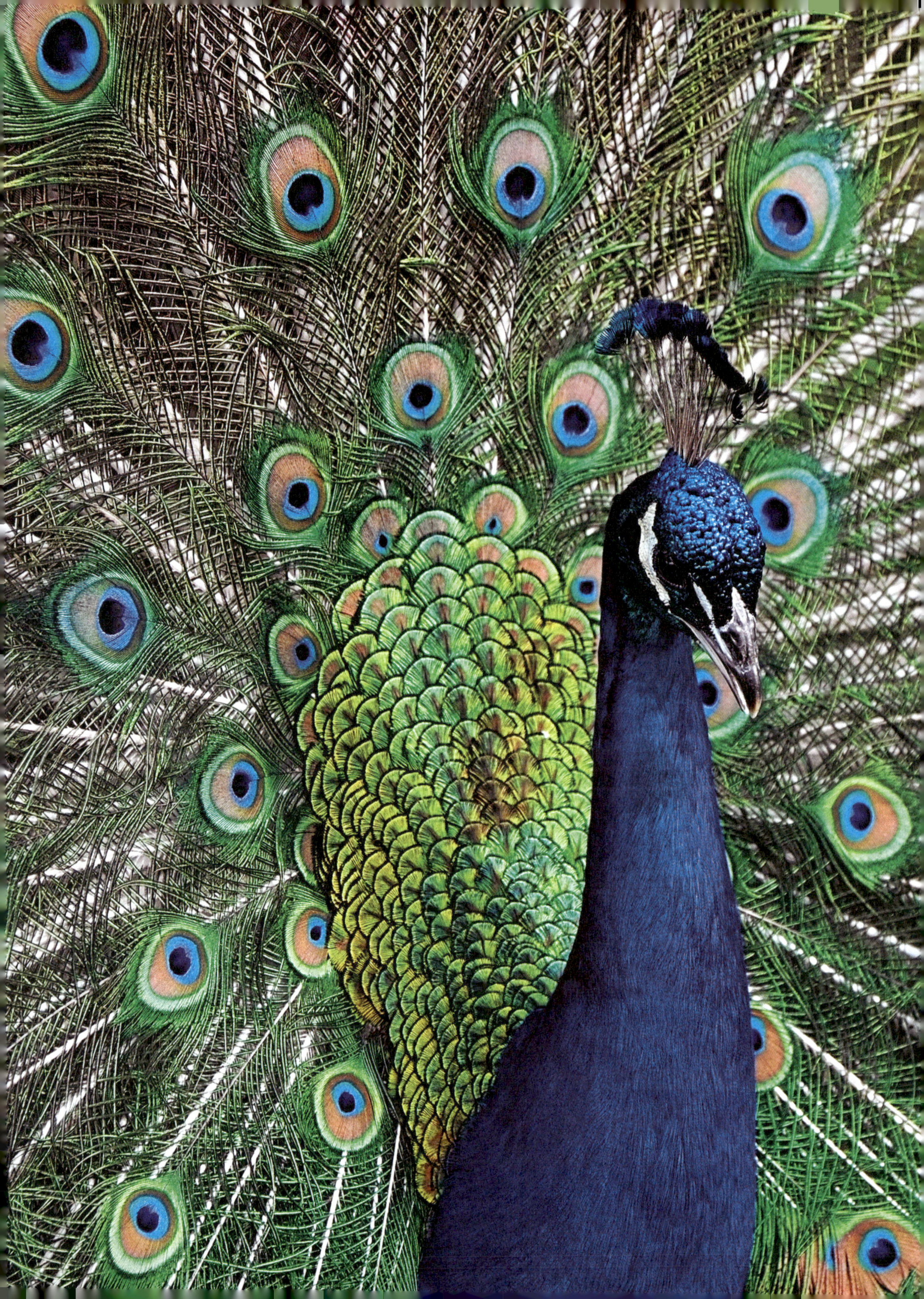

HOW CAN WE IMITATE THE COLOURFUL WONDERS OF NATURE?

VINOD KUMAR SARANATHAN

Leonardo da Vinci is well known for his studies on the flight of birds, whether on swifts or birds of prey. Yet, his insights into the theory of their coloration are perhaps less widely known. The iridescent hues of peacocks [fig. 1] and on the necks of pigeons and ducks captivated him. In his Notebooks, he writes in the section 'On the Colours in the Feathers of Certain Birds' (Windsor, RL 19150r):

> In many birds, in various parts of the world, the most brilliant colours appear in their feathers as they move, as we see in the feathers of peacocks or on the necks of ducks or pigeons. Similarly, we observe colours on the surface of ancient glass found underground and on the roots of turnips kept for some time at the bottom of wells or other stagnant waters, that each root is encircled by a range of colours resembling those of the rainbow. These colours can also be seen when oil is spread on water, and in the solar rays reflected from the surface of a diamond or beryl. Through the angular facet of a beryl, every dark object against a background of the atmosphere or any other pale surface is surrounded by these rainbow colours between the atmosphere and the dark body; and in many other circumstances which I will not mention, as these suffice for my purpose.

As far as we can judge, Leonardo da Vinci was the first – long before Newton, Michelson, Rayleigh, and Raman – to correctly compare the 'vivid' colours of birds to similar colours in the physical world, such as oil slicks or gemstones.

In nature, colours are typically produced by pigments or dyes. However, in animals, this is not the case for blues and greens. These hues are instead of structural origin, arising from the interference of light with submicron structures (measuring a few hundred nanometres, roughly 500 times smaller than the width of an average human hair). Never fading, these colours are omnipresent and play a crucial role in the lives of fauna [fig. 2 and 3]. The result of millions of years of evolution, they serve purposes ranging from camouflage to courtship and communication with other species (CUTHILL et al., 2017; SARANATHAN et al., 2021; SARANATHAN and JALAIS, 2024).

LEFT
Fig. 1. Peacock, 2009

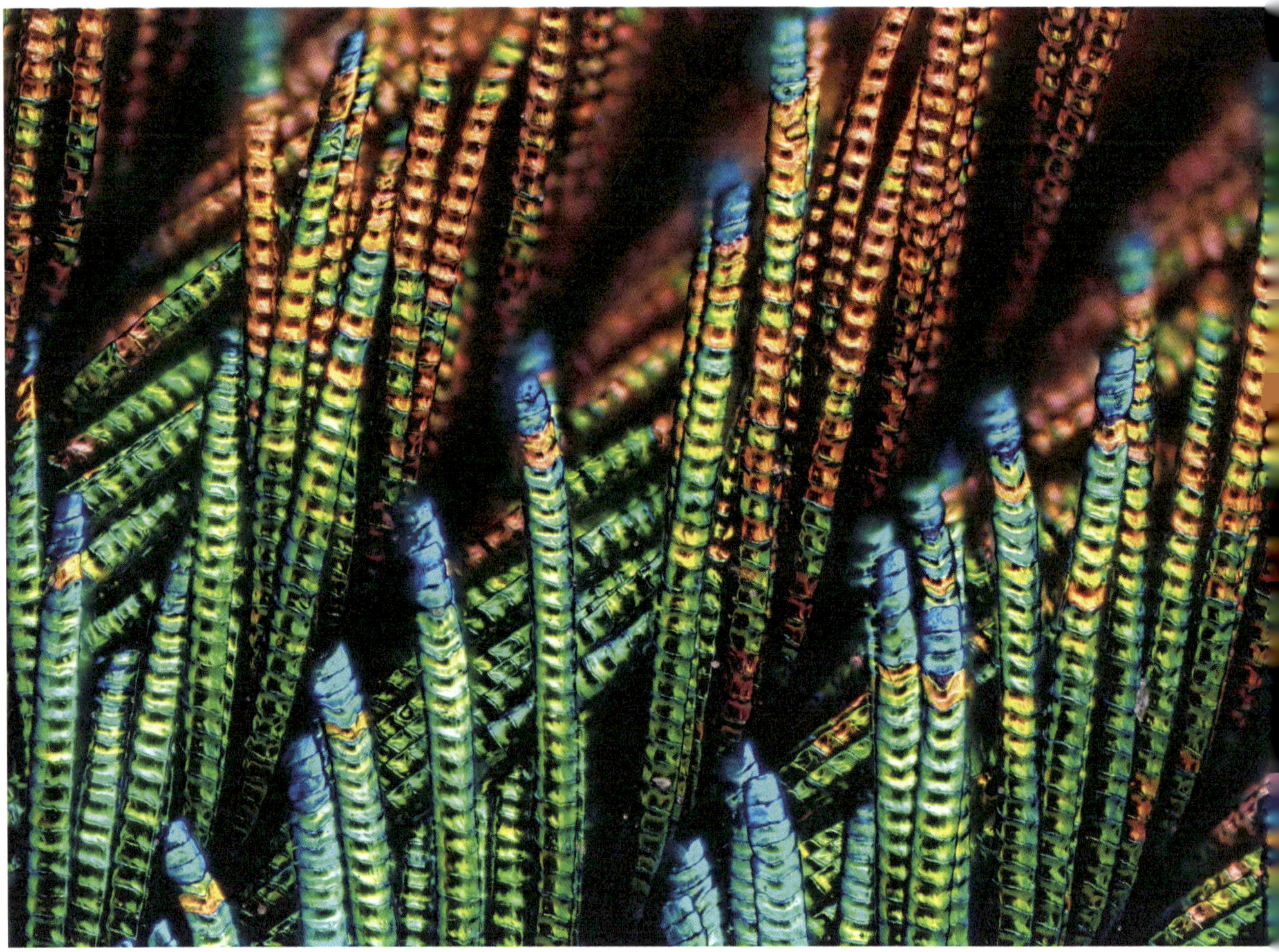

Fig. 2. Light microscope images of the barbules (branches of a branch) of the iridescent feathers of a peacock

From high-speed trains inspired by the kingfisher's beak to adhesives inspired by geckos, physicists and engineers are increasingly turning to nature to find solutions to contemporary technological problems, following the approach pioneered by the father of biomimicry, Leonardo da Vinci.

The modern and accepted definition of biomimicry is the interdisciplinary approach of taking nature as a model for the sustainable design of products, processes and systems (ISO 18458:2015). And if there is one domain that relies neither on simple nor sustainable processes, it is the synthesis of coloured materials.

The chemical synthesis of dyes is neither simple nor sustainable. Traditionally costly, it involves heavy metals or toxic polychlorinated components and uses large quantities of solvents and organic acids. This process not only generates toxic by-products but also produces colours that lack vibrancy and fade over time. For example, titanium dioxide, referred to by the innocuous euphemism E171, was recently banned in Europe as a food additive as it may be carcinogenic. It remains, however, one of the most important pigments in terms of industrial production and is widely used in paints, inks, pharmaceuticals, cosmetic and textile coatings, and rubber. To date, there is no safe and sustainable alternative.

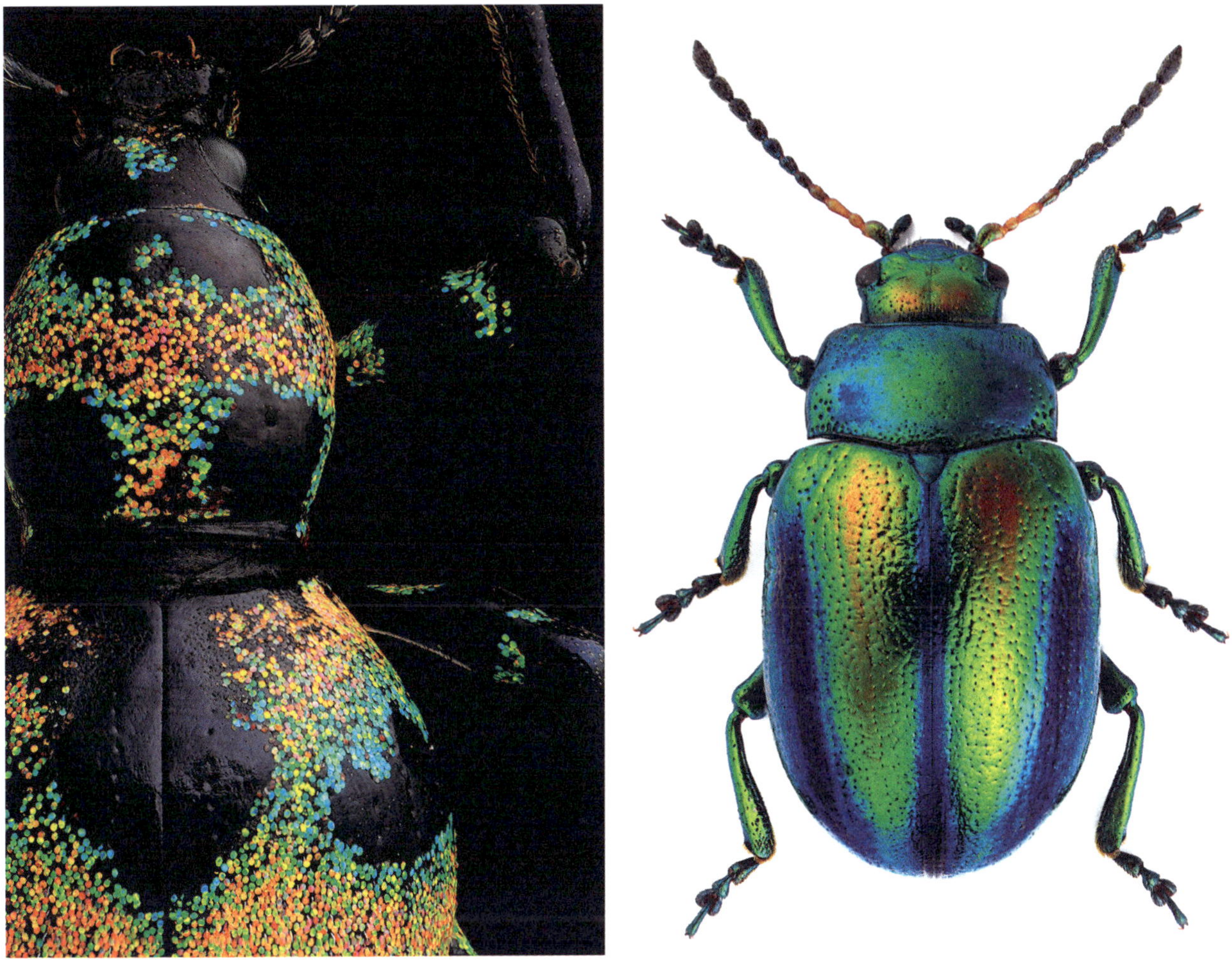

Fig. 3. Philippine weevil scales (*Pachyrrhynchus orbifer*, left), and lacewing cuticle (*Chrysolina fastuosa*; right), showing the different ways of producing the iridescent structural colours of the insects

With existing technologies, it is easy to synthesise materials at wavelength scales much smaller or much larger than a few hundred nanometres, but it is exceedingly difficult to produce photonic materials that reflect visible colours – that is, materials that interact with and control the flow of light within the spectrum visible to the human eye. This is where nature far surpasses our species.

Animals easily produce such photonic nanostructures that operate in the visible spectrum, which is difficult for humans to access. They achieve this by using the physical properties of the biological materials that make up their integument (skin, feathers, scales, etc.), through a form of self-assembly. This is essentially a fundamental physical process whereby a mixture undergoes demixing or separation (the same process occurs when a salad dressing separates or beer goes flat, for example); in the case of animals, this process is controlled and halted before complete separation occurs [fig. 4].

With over a million documented species, insects constitute the most abundant, colourful, and prolific animal group in the world. It is, therefore, unsurprising that they exhibit an unparalleled diversity of photonic nanostructures, which have evolved multiple times across different families.

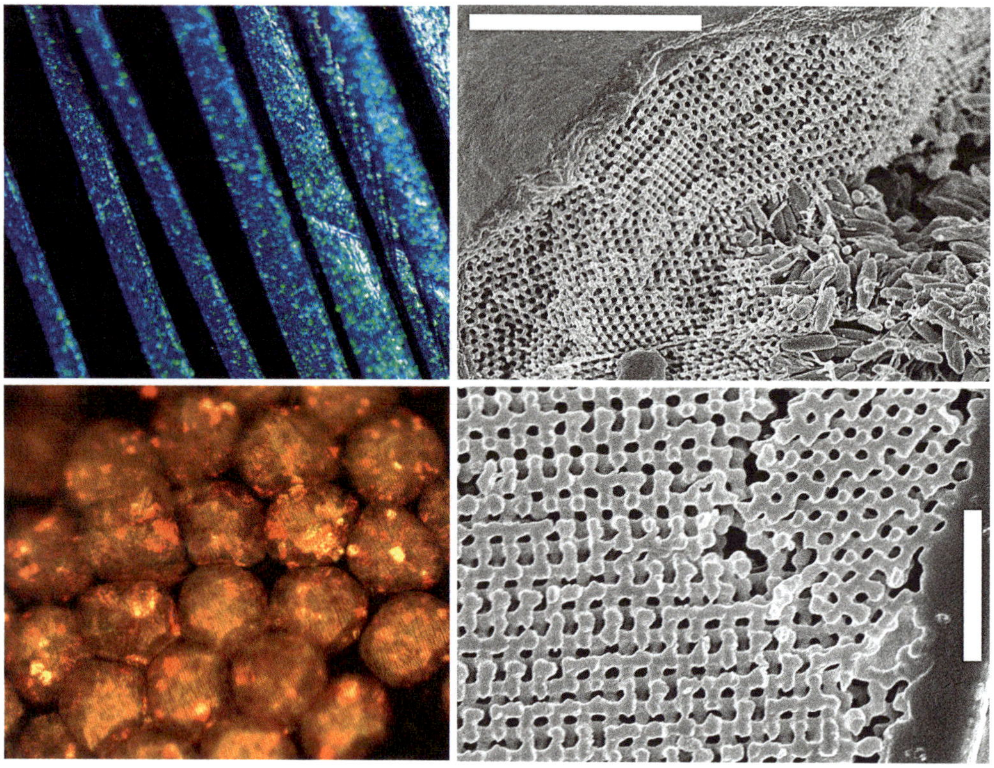

Fig. 4. Optical microscope and scanning electron microscope zoom images of photonic crystals producing iridescent colours in the blue barbs on the feathers of a blue-winged verdinid (top) and in the red scales on the wings of a Eupholus weevil (bottom)

Given their short generation times and ease of breeding, insects represent the ideal system for studying how nature is capable of producing these complex nanostructures. Despite the staggering variety of insects, only a small number currently serve as 'model organisms' in this field, and these are often not very colourful (e.g., fruit flies, silkworm moths, brush-footed butterflies, bumblebees, mealworms, etc.).

To understand how insects produce structural colours, a multidisciplinary approach combining engineering and materials science with experimental and computational biology is required. This will help answer fundamental questions about how animals develop nanostructures that function in multiple contexts. For a circular economy, it is possible and necessary to push this approach further and repurpose natural waste for additive manufacturing. For example, chitosan – a material chemically similar to chitin, which forms the exoskeletons of insects and crustaceans – is produced from shrimp industry waste. With millions of tonnes of this waste generated annually, chitosan is an ideal candidate for recycling. Recently, researchers have demonstrated that large-area films, mimicking the multicoloured appearance of many beetles, can be created from chitosan [fig. 5] (Kompa et al., 2024)

By exploring how insects produce and modify their structural colours, we could revolutionise industries like cosmetics and textiles, and more advanced applications like sensors, optical fibres, photovoltaics, and catalysis. This offers a new biomimetic and sustainable pathway for synthesising functional materials using biopolymers.

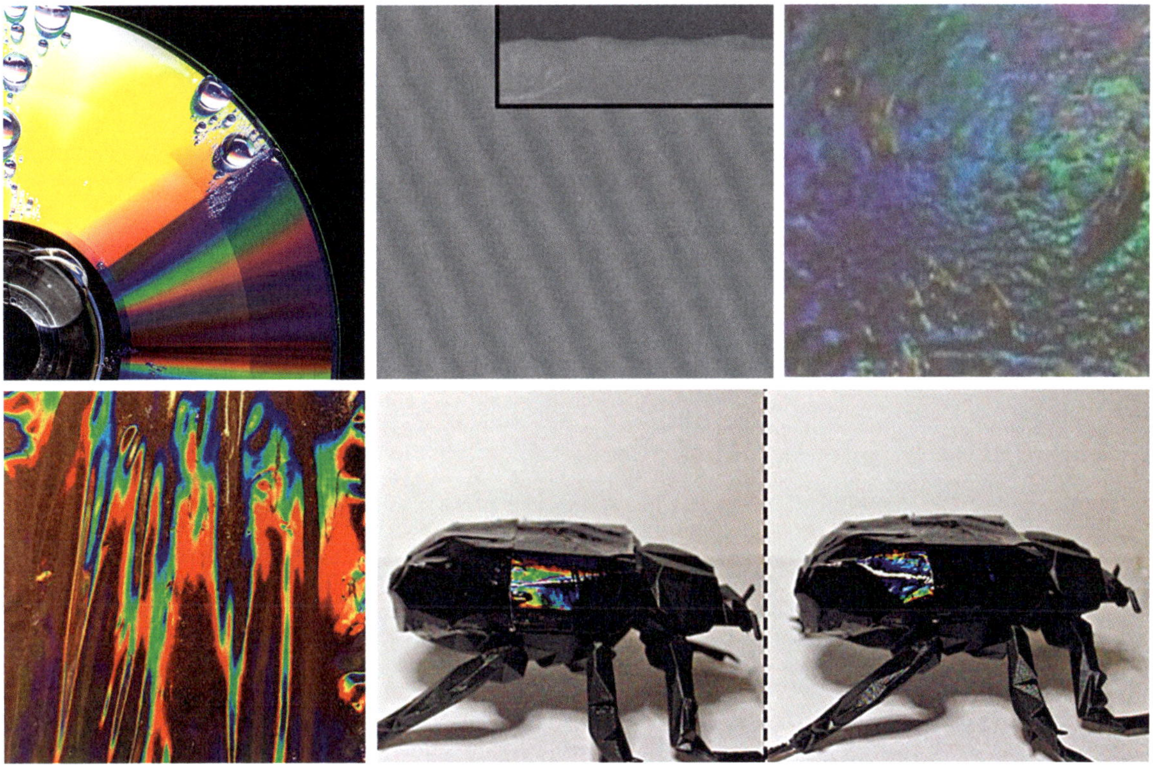

Fig. 5. Diffraction grating of a compact disc (top left) and scanning electron microscope images of a transparent chitosan film with a striated surface structure prepared using a negative casting (top centre) and its corresponding visual appearance (top right)
Chitosan film iridescent over a large area on a dark background (bottom left) and wrapped around a 3D printed beetle from two different angles (bottom centre and right)

Bibliography

Cuthill, Innes C. et al. "The Biology of Colour". *Science* 357 (2017): eaan0221.

Da Vinci, Leonardo. *Notebooks*. Paris: Gallimard, 2019.

Kompa, Akshayakumar et al., "Large-Scale Artificial Production of Coleoptera Cuticle Iridescence and its Use in Conformal Biodegradable Coatings". *Advanced Engineering Materials* 26 (2024): 2301713. Saranathan, Vinod Kumar et al. "Evolution of Single Gyroid Photonic Crystals in Bird Feathers". *PNAS* 118 (2021): e2101357118.

Saranathan, Vinod Kumar, Jalais, Annu. "The Colour Blue: from Pigments to Self-Assembly". *Photoniques* 124 (2024): 49–53.

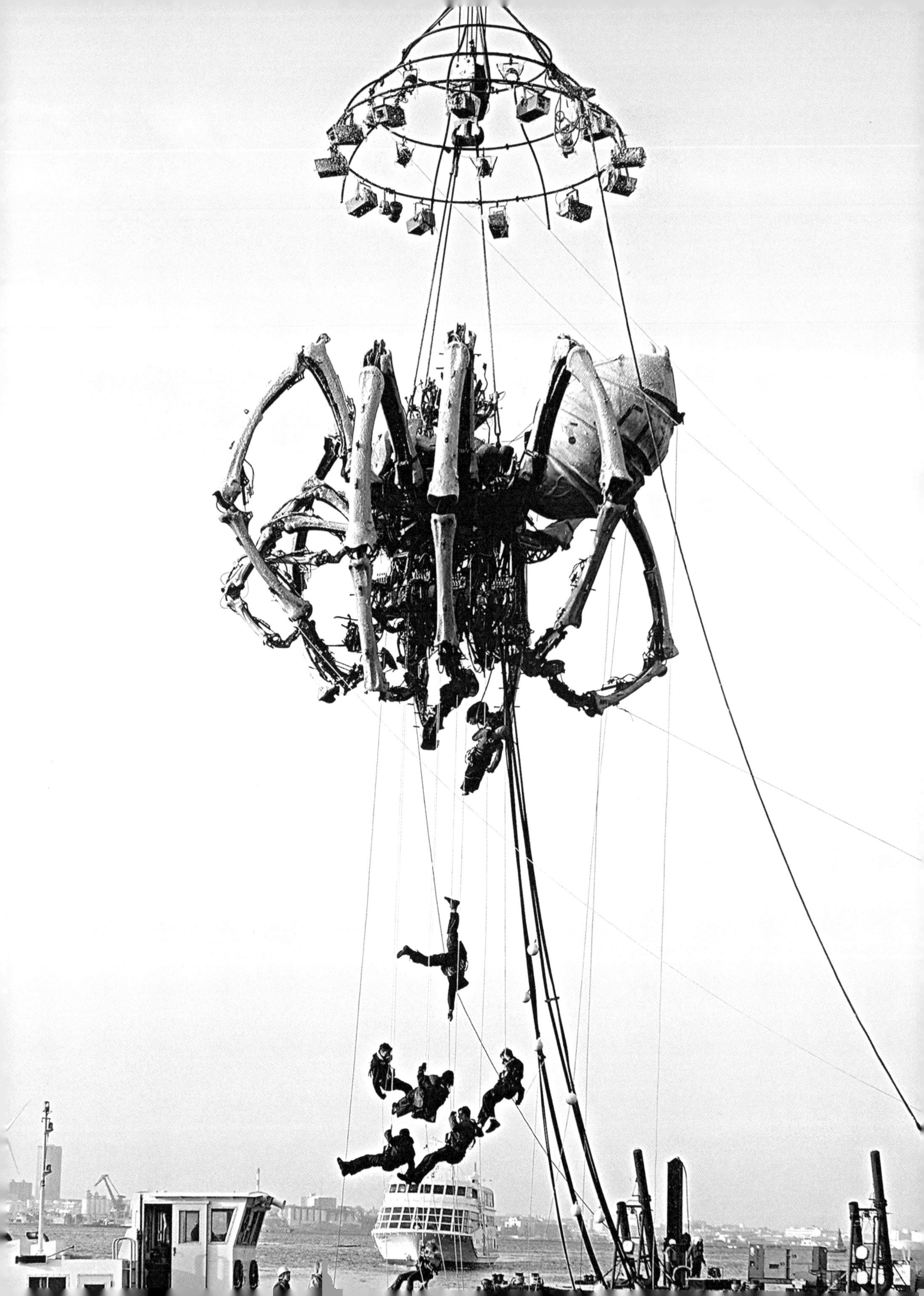

INTERVIEW WITH FRANÇOIS DELAROZIERE ABOUT COMPAGNIE LA MACHINE

Pascal Brioist

A draughtsman with a masterful touch, François Delaroziere is renowned worldwide. His animated machines have travelled far and wide, to China and Canada, Britain and France. In Nantes and Toulouse, his fertile imagination reflects that of a poetic artist influenced by his passionate observation of nature, living beings and movement.

When was Compagnie La Machine established?

Compagnie La Machine was officially established in 1999 in Tournefeuille, in the suburbs of Toulouse, though it had existed as an association for five or six years before that. Today, it is based at L'Usine, a national street arts centre in Tournefeuille, and in a fairly large workshop and design office on Nantes's Île de Nantes. We've also opened La Halle de La Machine, a stable for our mechanical creatures, which houses all the machines we have created for our shows: our Minotaur, giant spiders, and over a hundred smaller machines. The public can see them in motion during our permanent show 'La Grande Impro'.

The two sites in Toulouse and Nantes have radically transformed the urban landscapes of these cities. Can you explain this phenomenon?

Our machines make their appearance in the heart of towns and neighbourhoods with the aims of altering how public spaces are viewed and turning them into playgrounds of wonder and delight.

LEFT
The Giant Spider, Yokohama, 2009

The city becomes a vast theatre in which these giant, living machines roam. Urban architecture is transformed into a stage set. With music, special effects, costumes and actors, the procession of these machines reshapes how we experience the space and creates an emotionally powerful spectacle. Scenographer Marcel Freydefont envisioned the concept of 'infused theatre' in the city as a way to bring a new dimension to urban life and redefine our relationship with performance and theatre.

What inspires you?

I read a lot of technical manuals, science books and biographies. Novels don't conjure mental images for me, so I rely on observing nature and studying pictures and behaviour. These days, the internet is a bit like the Tower of Babel for me, a huge library with a wealth of information. When I draw a chameleon, for example, I need to know in detail how its tongue works when it catches flies or insects. Online, I can find incredible images, generously shared by researchers.

You're fascinated by living beings.

Living beings and architecture, whether plant, animal or mineral in origin, captivate and inspire me. This is where I draw my inspiration. Since I focus on living beings and movement, I'm less interested in other artists' interpretations. I also like architecture with a coherent design philosophy, where the aesthetic flows from the visible interplay of structural forces and tensions.

Like Leonardo da Vinci, your machines take inspiration from flying creatures, aquatic animals, bipeds and quadrupeds. Could you tell us about a few of them?

Among the large-scale creations are the early designs from my Royal de Luxe collaborations. First, there was the 9.5-metre tall Human Giant that began life in Le Havre. It was suspended like a puppet from a support structure 14 metres high and 8 metres wide. With this structure occupying three traffic lanes, we had to remove roundabouts and traffic lights just to allow the giant to roam its host cities.

Then, there was a huge giraffe, 12 metres tall. The technical specifications were very precise: it had to be able to raise its eyes, move its eyelids and ears independently, open its mouth, stick out its tongue, sneeze, and even urinate and defecate. To mimic these naturalistic movements, I had to study giraffes very closely in the zoo. The result was a mechanical creature that grazed gracefully alongside the tallest plane trees in the cities. It was both amazing and deeply moving.

I have also created giant spiders, a Minotaur, an elephant, and several dragons.

Beyond these colossal machines, there are also those that produce sound and music. The *Cocotte à flûtes*, for example, is a standard pressure cooker with two musical instruments – recorders – grafted onto its lid. When filled with water and brought to the boil, the steam passing through the instruments produces whistling sounds.

We've even created machines that catapult bread.

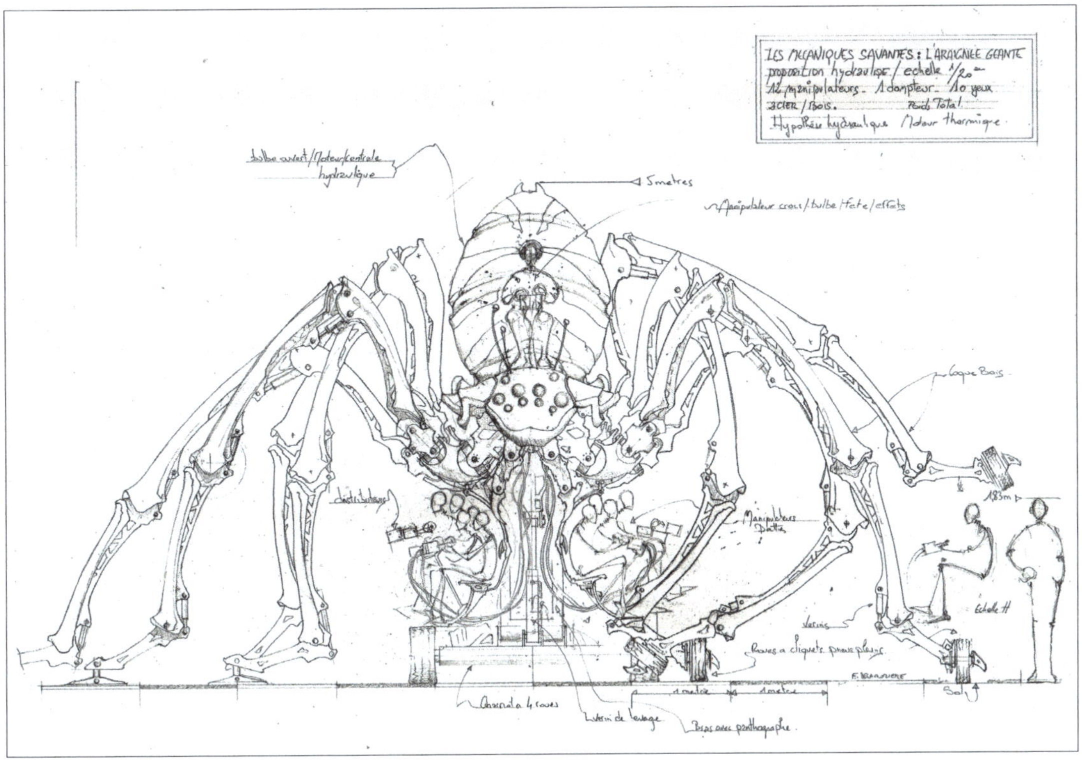

Drawing of the Giant Spider, 2007

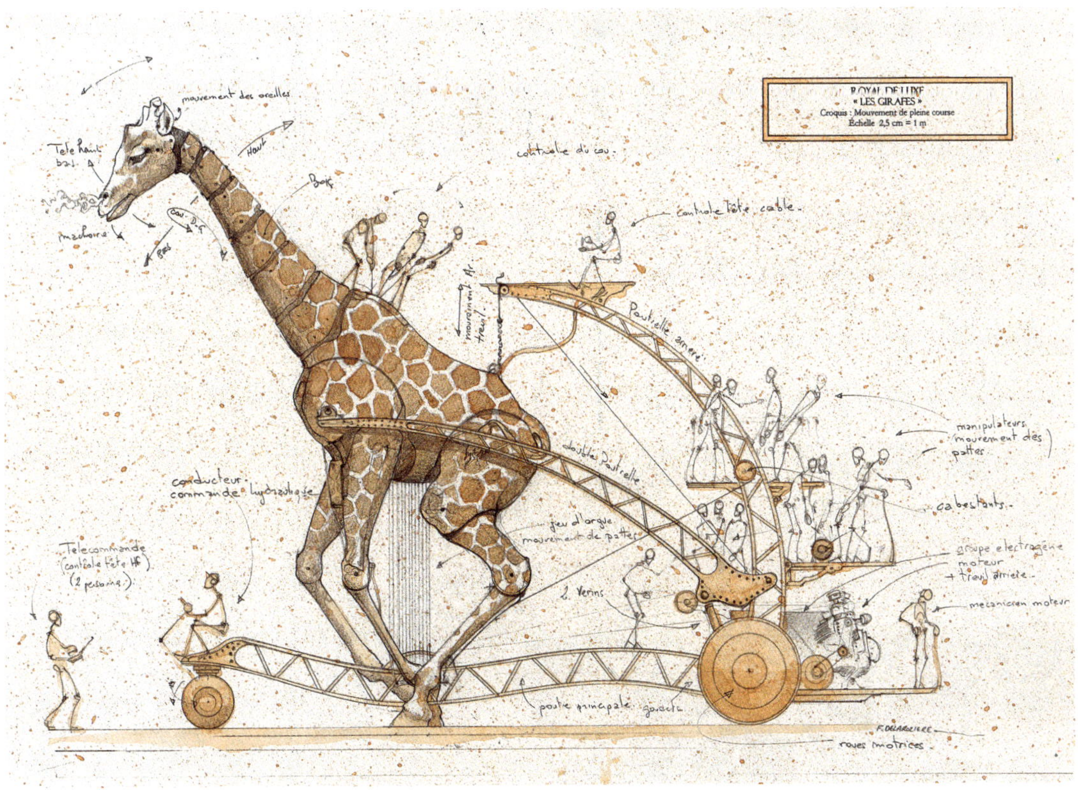

Drawing of the Giraffe, 1998

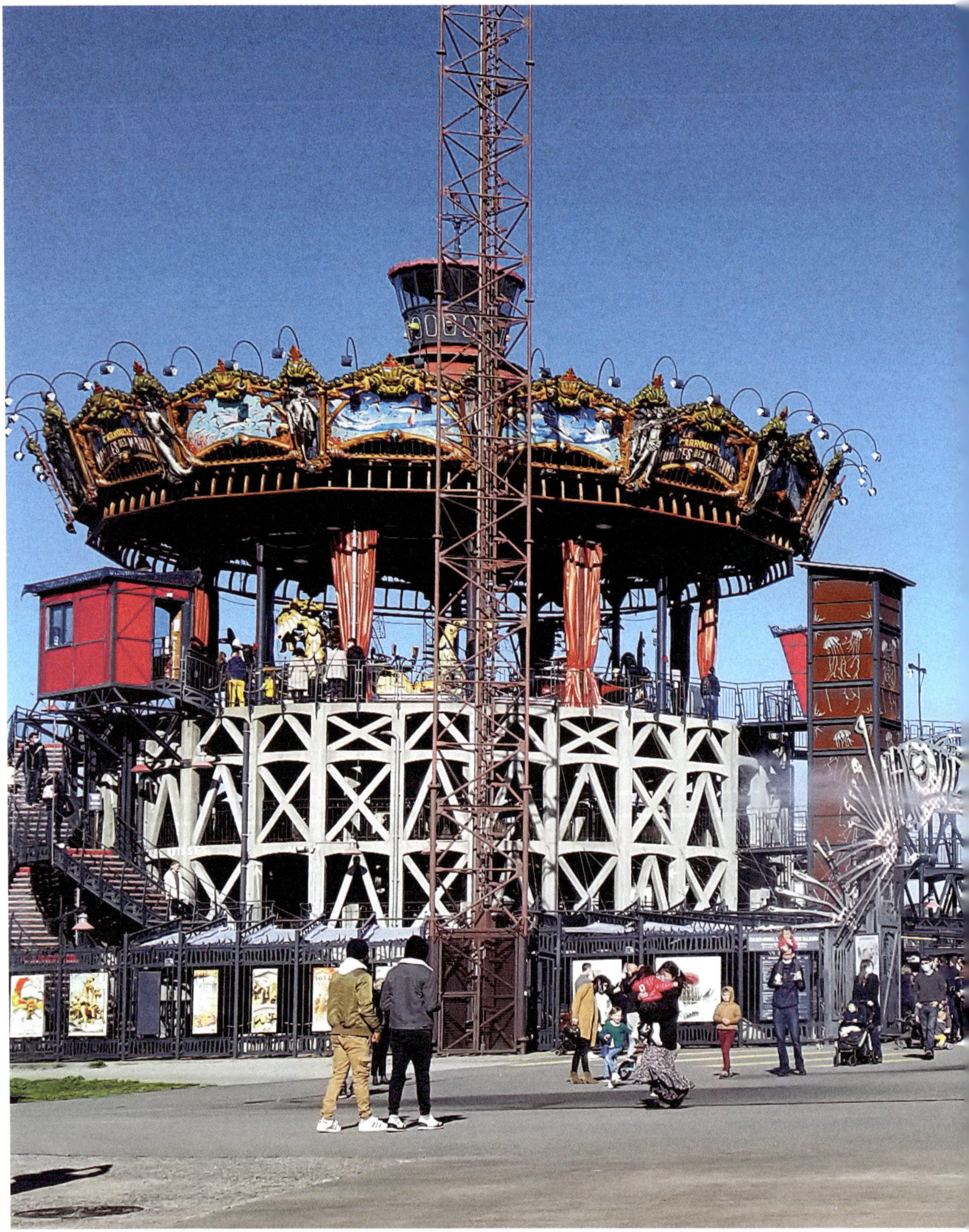

The Great Elephant and the Carousel of the Marine Worlds, 2007-2012

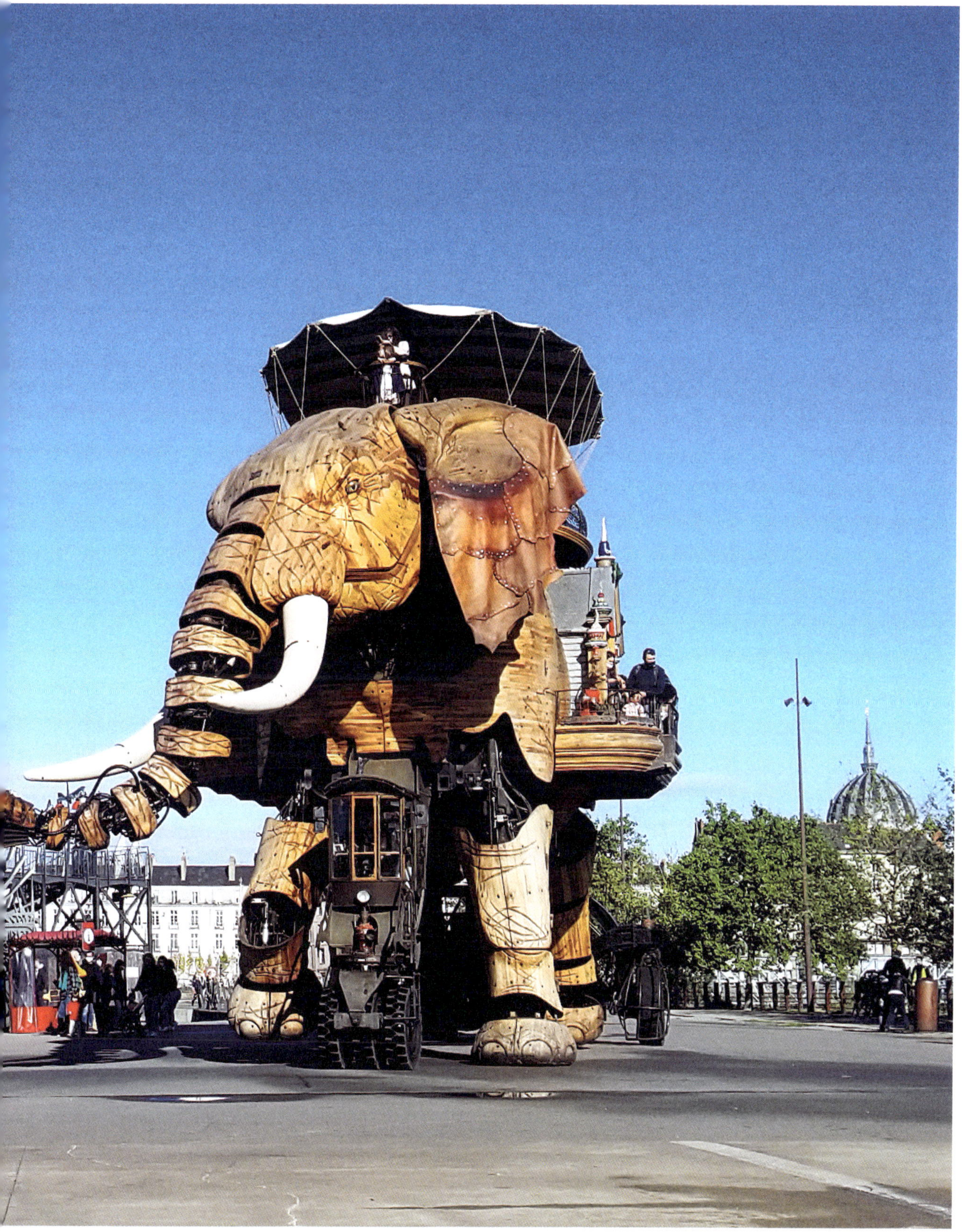

Could you describe some of the biomechanical systems in your machines?

Creating machines that feel alive means following nature's laws and replicating its mechanisms.

For the Giraffe's seven vertebrae, we fitted each with a vertical rotation axis (up-down) and a lateral one (side-to-side), mirroring nature. Hydraulic pistons replace muscles and tendons, pushing or pulling the vertebrae as needed to capture the fluid, sweeping range of a real giraffe's motion.

Is the gait difficult to replicate?

It's simple enough when manually controlled, but automating the process is far more complex.

To recreate the gait, we had to study nature carefully. Consider a giraffe at full gallop: almost fully airborne, with just one leg touching the ground at a time. I had to study that movement very carefully to break it down in order to recreate it for performances.

You've recreated flapping wings and birds in flight before, most notably in the magnificent *Heron Tree* project. Could you tell us more about this?

For the wings of a machine like the Heron, we had to contend with the same forces found in nature, like wind strength.

A storm with winds of 110-120 km/h exerts pressures of 100-150 kg/m2, so our wings need to be robust enough to withstand such forces while ensuring the feathers stay intact. The mechanisms are extraordinarily complex: they fold and unfold, with feathers rotating to harness air currents for lift. This means we have to observe and interpret the wings of real herons closely.

Like Clément Ader, we've also studied bat wings, which feature in our Dragons and a new and yet uncategorised lifeform. Their mechanics, similar to those of boat sails, are well understood, yet no less fascinating.

We've developed seven or eight wing prototypes, from herons and birds of prey to hummingbirds. The hummingbird presents particular challenges, as it can hover, fly backwards and move in a similar fashion to certain insects and dragonflies. We have to consider this range of possible movements, the shoulder rotation and flexibility, then integrate them all into the machine's mechanism, which already enables the wing deployment and feather mobility previously mentioned.

Working on numerous machines allows us to learn and refine with each iteration. As a result, the latest generation of flying creatures is now pretty sophisticated.

You've explored the insect world with the Giant Spider you took to Japan. Have you created other insects?

For our many carousel projects, we've built ants, praying mantises, various bugs, and all manner of rideable insects operated by controls of varying complexity. I've studied and created countless insects, notably for the Carré Sénart Carousel, where visitors can ride three giant buffaloes pulling a central platform like a plough, as a ring of a dozen insects operated by visitors circle around them, with cicadas and bees climbing the corner posts.

Like you, Leonardo da Vinci also designed theatrical machines in his day, in particular a mechanical lion and an animated suit of armour. What defines a truly successful theatrical machine?

The secret is movement that breathes life into them. It has to be coherent and credible, and to do that you have to be able to observe and draw inspiration from nature. To make a machine seem alive, you have to engineer the materials used and control the movements. Movement is an emotional language that stirs reactions in us. It can be manual, guided by hand; intricate, like clockwork or automation; or wholly digital, orchestrated into a fluid choreographic series of motions. Its strength lies in the dynamics: the rush of acceleration, the suspense of a pause. A mechanically blinking eyelid is lifeless; one that droops sleepily or snaps shut carries meaning. It is these subtle movements that make the eye truly come alive.

Your work also engages various senses – hearing, smell, even taste. The Dîner des petites Mécaniques (*Mechanical Engineering Dinner*) is a perfect example. You're also a storyteller.

What is creation? What defines humanity? It's our ability to weave narratives. Every performance stems from a story.

We invented money as a medium of exchange – an entirely imagined construct, as it doesn't exist naturally. From these agreed-upon rules, shared stories emerge, and once embraced, they become law, as is often the case with theatrical conventions. To imbue a gesture with intent, we first have to tell its story. This applies equally to machines: their character, history, origins and destiny need to be stated.

A project must be built upon stories. Take our Minotaur – its chest bears a gaping wound stitched with large copper staples. Legend has it that it fought a giant eagle that tried to tear its heart out.

Our machines leave the workshop with a story – they already have a history. These experiences are etched into their wooden bodies: eagle attacks, wounds, scratched shells. If you look at the Guardian of Darkness, you'll see her armour has been clawed in places.

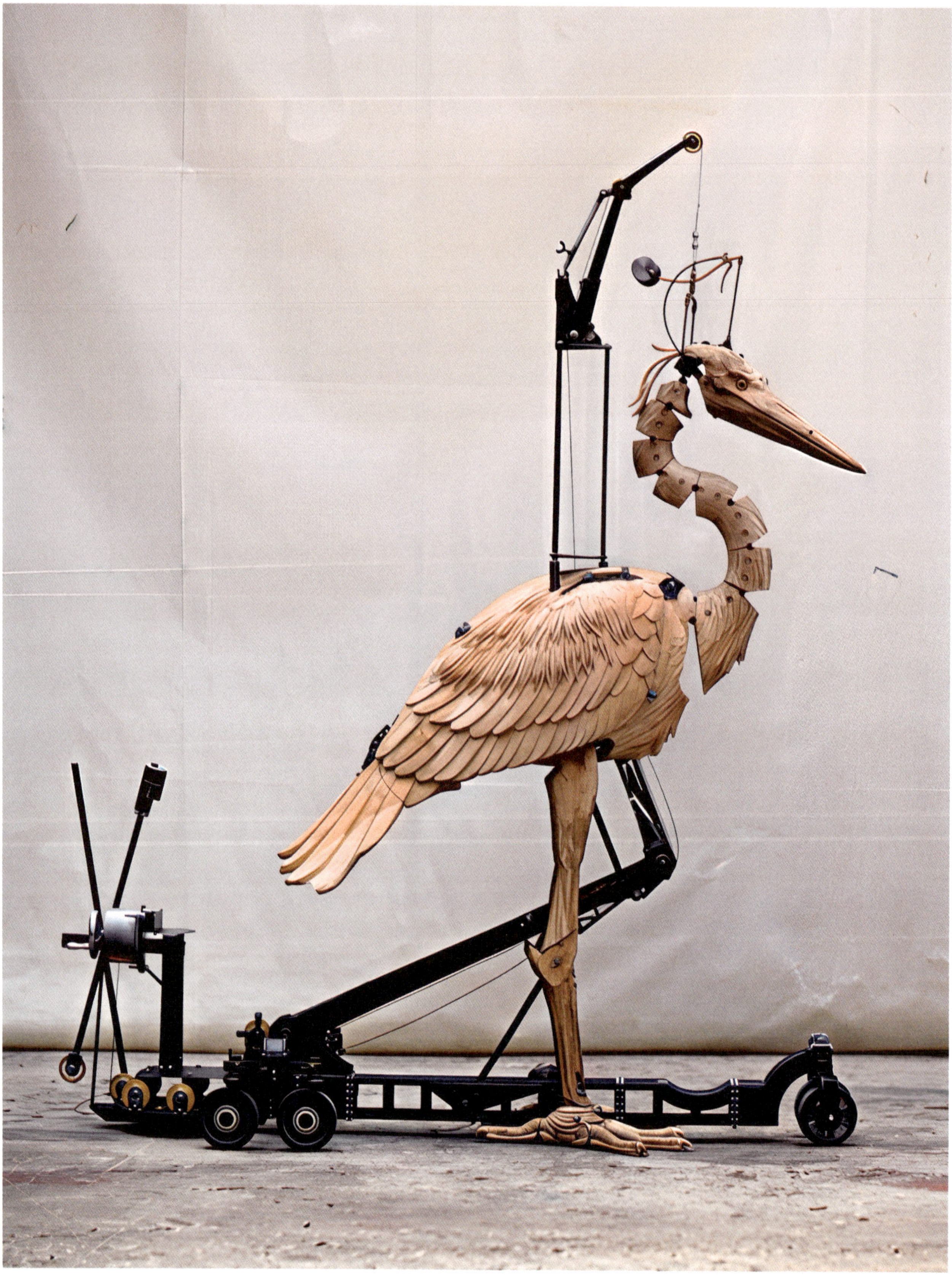

Model of the Heron Château

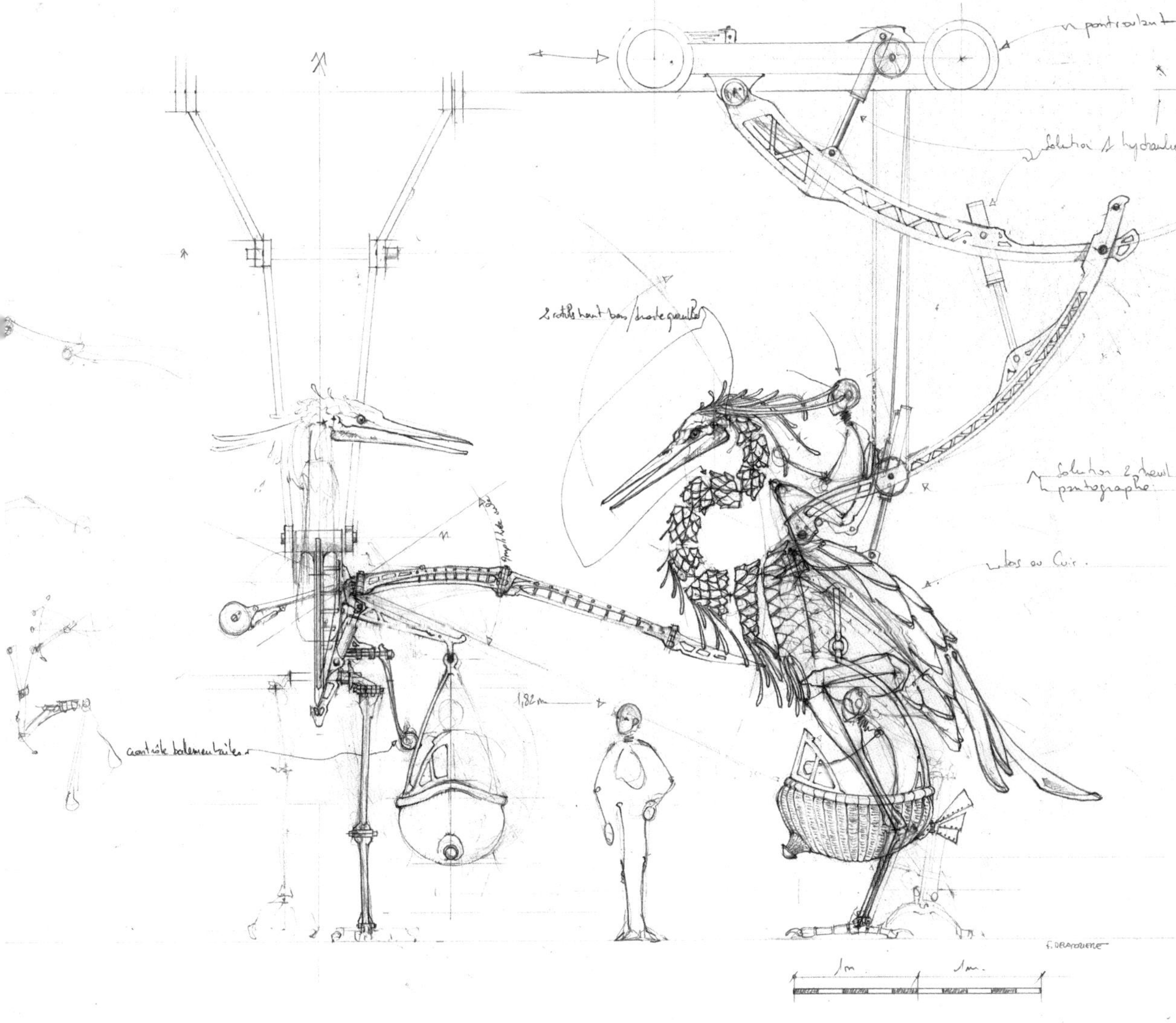

Drawing of the Heron, 2011

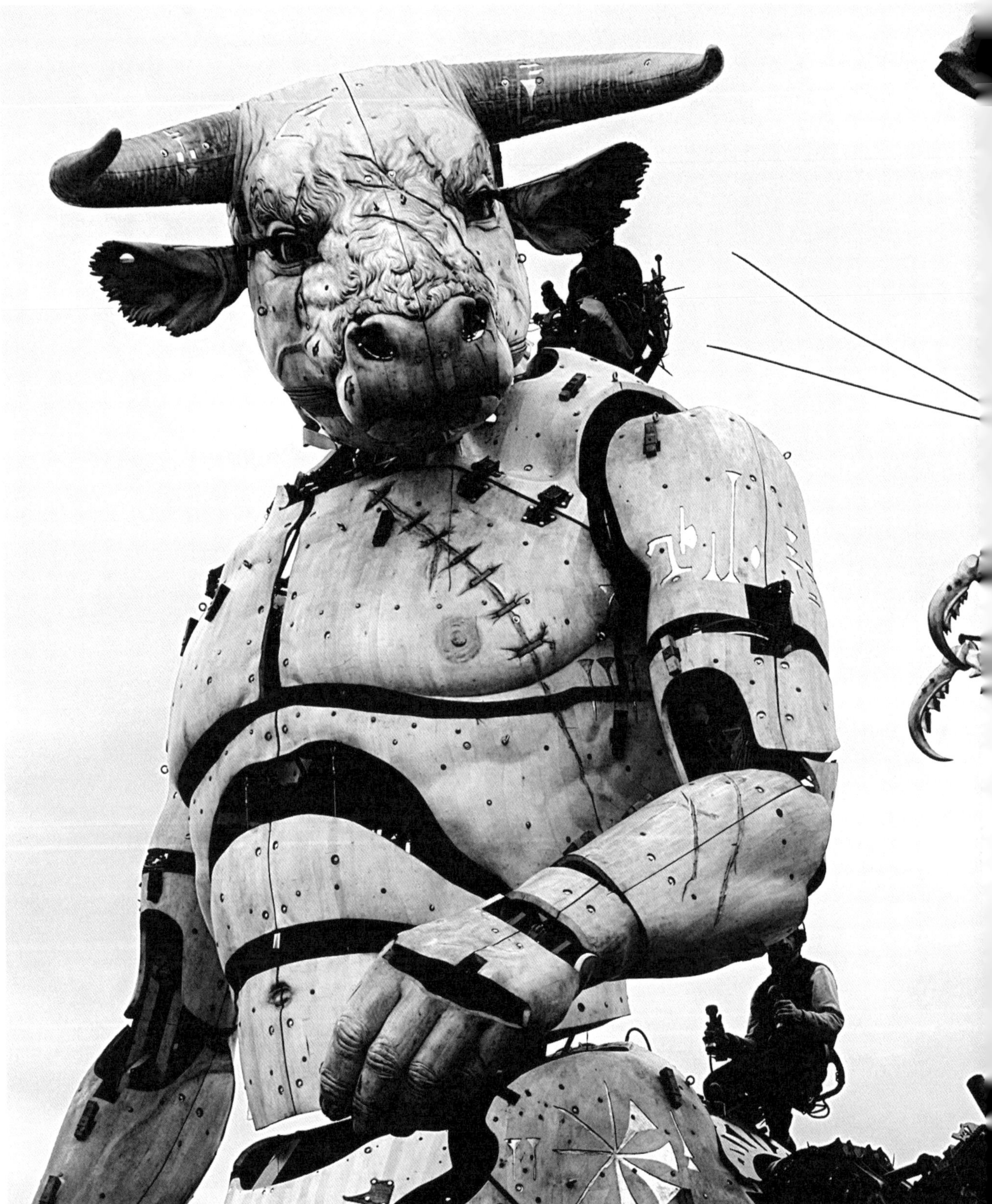

The Minotaur, Toulouse, 2018

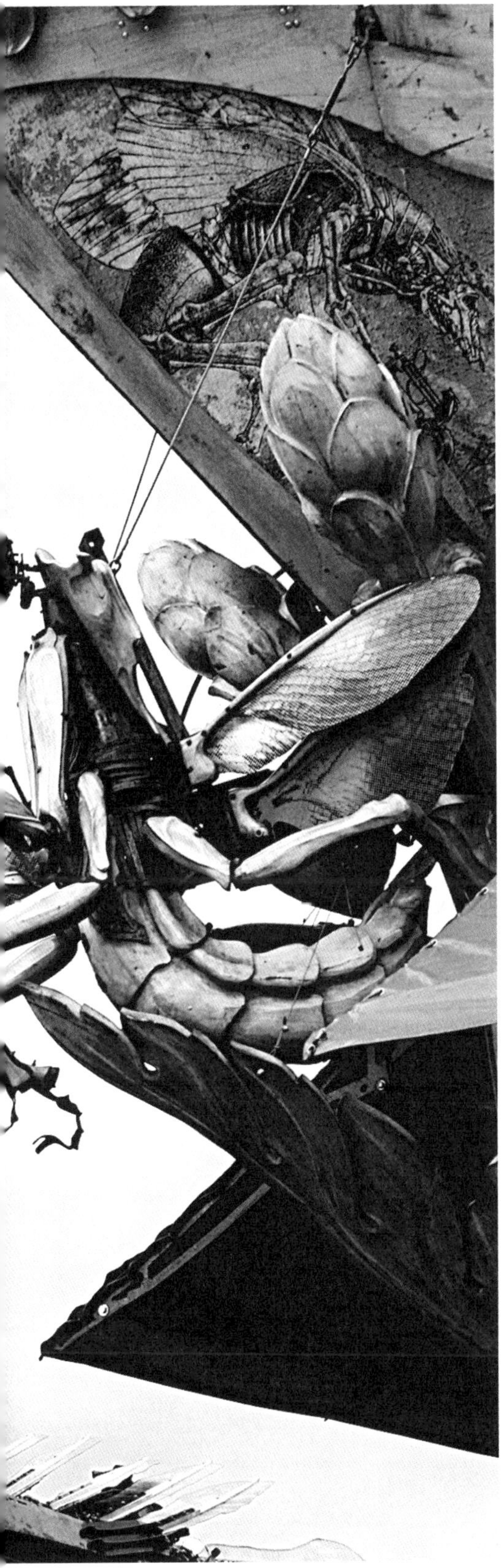

Where do your stories come from?

I create them. I love having control and then letting go, engaging with the entire creative chain: from the initial idea to the drawing, from scripting the performance to staging it, right through to the scenography and permanent exhibition of the machines.

What I enjoy in music, for example, is when an artist composes the score, writes the lyrics, and performs them on stage. I've nothing against revivals of classic works, especially in theatre, but they don't stir the deepest emotions in me. I love total expression. Leonardo da Vinci did everything from A to Z, and that's what I admire.

What are your upcoming projects?

We operate on rather extended timescales, so multiple projects are currently in the pipeline. We're conducting an ambitious feasibility study in the Hautes-Pyrénées region, while continuing work on a major commission for Calais, started in 2019, with its second phase to feature a spectacular public performance in November 2025. Additionally, we're preparing an exhibition at the newly restored Fort Risban. Several international projects are also taking shape, particularly in Mexico City.

Meanwhile, our drawings and scale models are on display at various venues, while several of our machines feature in the collections of the Natural History Museum and José Cabanis Library.

How has Leonardo inspired your work?

I discovered Leonardo da Vinci quite late. I knew his name, but I hadn't really delved into his world. As people kept talking to me about him and Jules Verne, I finally began to take an interest in them. I haven't read much Jules Verne and when I built the Great Elephant, I wasn't familiar with his steam-powered elephant machine. But as soon as I discovered Leonardo's work, I was fascinated, especially by his ingenious machinery and his drawings.

Viollet-le-Duc, with his sculptures inspired by nature, is also a source of inspiration for me. I'm also very interested in medieval engineering, because it's incredibly simple and powerful, especially when it comes to trebuchets and catapults.

Often, when I'm designing architecture, I go back to these different worlds. Leonardo da Vinci fascinates me because he observed living things. In decoding nature, I work in the same way. I'm fascinated by the body, both animal and human.

I think my sensitivity comes from my parents: my mother with her music and my father with his work with rough stone and wood. I was immersed in the language of materials, and therefore of nature, from a very early age. This is probably what connects me to Leonardo da Vinci.

RIGHT
The Giant, 2003

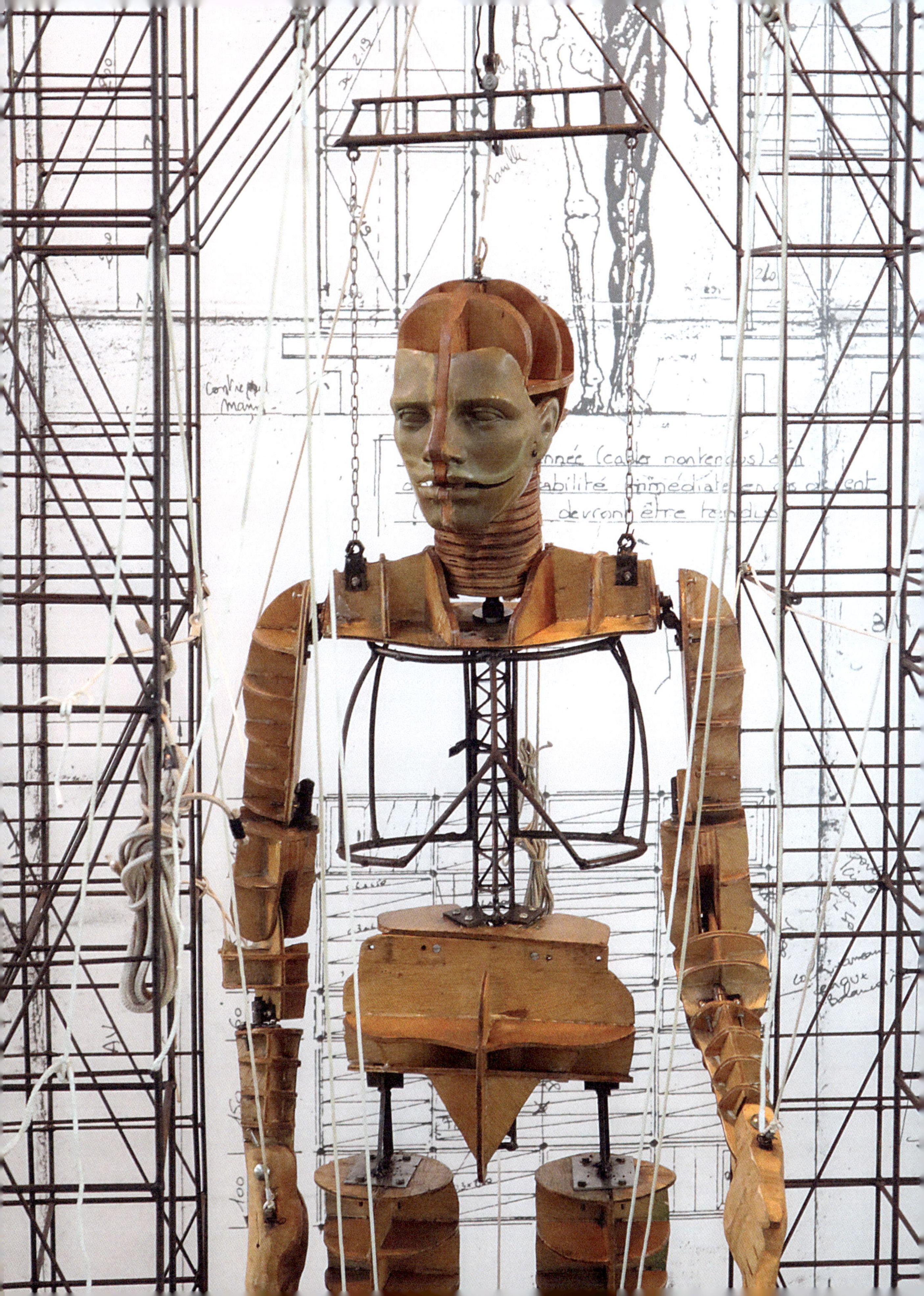

A WORK OF ART, A VISION: *STUDIES ON MECHANICAL FLIGHT AND OBSERVATIONS ON THE MOVEMENT OF WATER* BY LEONARDO DA VINCI

Leonardo da Vinci
Studies on mechanical flight and observations on the movement of water, folio 846v
c. 1490
Pen, ink, and red chalk on paper,
Codex Atlanticus, Biblioteca Ambrosiana, Milan

This folio, catalogued as 846v (formerly 309 verso-a), is a valuable testament to Leonardo da Vinci's investigations into the possibility of human flight and the natural dynamics of fluids. Comprising drawings executed in red chalk and pen and ink, it combines technical observation, anatomical exploration and physical speculation.

On the left side of the folio, three studies of mechanical wings, meticulously articulated, reveal Leonardo's focus on the structure and function of the supporting limb in birds. On the right, a system of straps, passing between the legs and around the torso, is designed to secure the apparatus to the body of the flying man, depicted standing. The design as a whole reflects an effort to simplify the flying machine, conceived here as an ornithopter with wings directly attached to the human anatomy.

The handwritten annotations, slightly later than the drawings, explore the movements of water, particularly its ascent through subterranean layers after descending from the heights. Leonardo questions the forces responsible for these invisible dynamics, within a perspective still influenced by Aristotelian physics. This type of reflection appears in several folios of the *Codex Atlanticus*, notably folios 468r, 101v, 1023v, and 70ii recto, where these issues are taken up again with formal variations.

Experts (Pedretti, Marinoni, Villata) agree that this folio is contemporaneous with folio 853, which it echoes in both graphic technique and content. The proposed chronology, around 1490 or slightly later (c. 1495 according to Carlo Pedretti), is based on stylistic analysis and the internal evolution of the ideas developed in these studies.

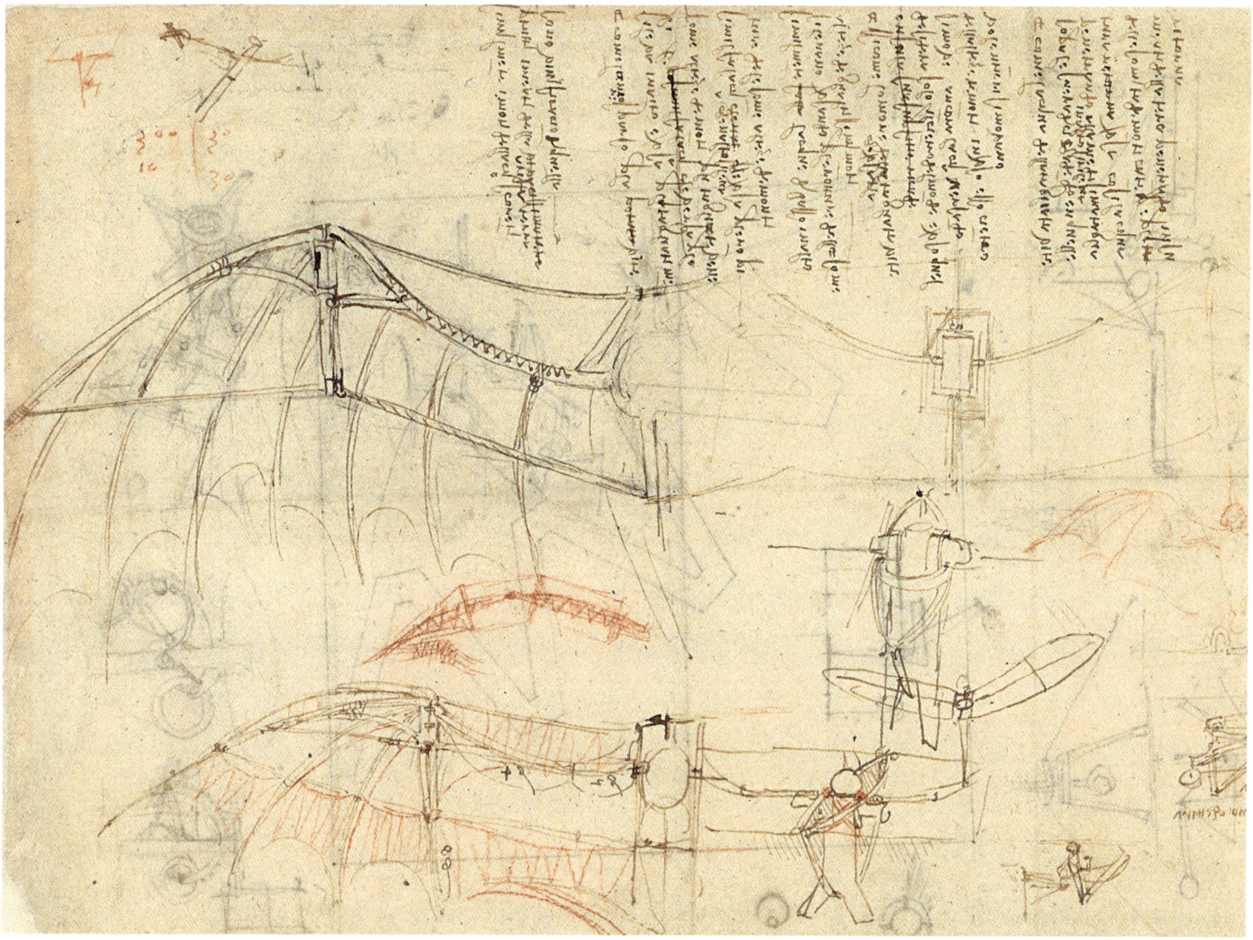

Leonardo da Vinci, *Codex Atlanticus*, 1478-1518, pen, ink and red chalk, f. 846v, Veneranda Biblioteca Ambrosiana

A Work of Art, A Vision: *The Rhinoceros* by Albrecht Dürer

Albrecht Dürer
The Rhinoceros
1515
Woodcut, 21 × 29.4 cm
4th edition (of 8), watermark: crowned shield with fleurs-de-lis and pendant letters "WR" (Meder no. 121)
Bartsch 136; Meder 273.4; Hollstein 273d
Galerie Martinez D.

On 20 May 1515, an Indian rhinoceros arrived in Lisbon, the first live specimen seen in Western Europe since Antiquity. Presented to King Manuel I of Portugal by Sultan of Gujarat Muzafar II of Cambay, the pachyderm immediately captivated the attention of scholars and merchants. It was the subject of handwritten descriptions and sketches by numerous witnesses who observed and drew it at the port. One such sketch was sent to Nuremberg by the printer Valentin Ferdinand and reached Albrecht Dürer (1471–1528), who, despite not having seen the rhinoceros himself, used it as the basis for a woodcut.

Created in 1515, *The Rhinoceros* is one of Dürer's most iconic works and a foundational image in the history of animal representation. Eschewing naturalism, the artist devised a stylised and ornamental vision, exploiting the graphic potential of the woodcut. He emphasised compartmentalised volumes, joints, and scale-like patterns, adding imaginary elements: a second horn on the back, legs covered in reptilian scales, and a profile suggesting fantastical armour. As Erwin Panofsky noted, Dürer transformed the rhinoceros into a "stylised combination of scales, laminae, and shells" (*The Life and Art of Albrecht Dürer*, 2012), blending indirect observation, medieval texts and imagination.

The print's success was immediate. By 1516, a copy had appeared in Martin Waldseemüller's *Carta Marina*. It was subsequently widely reproduced in naturalist works of the 16th and 17th centuries, notably in Conrad Gessner's *Historia Animalium* (1551) and Edward Topsell's *History of Four-Footed Beasts and Serpents* (1607). By the 17th century, eight editions of the print had been produced, and, until the second half of the 18th century, this imaginary depiction of the rhinoceros remained a standard iconographic model, even in scientific treatises, despite being based on no direct observation.

Blending observation, tradition and invention, *The Rhinoceros* encapsulates the challenges faced of representing animals in the Renaissance and powerfully embodies the evocative potential of the print as a vehicle for knowledge, narratives and forms.

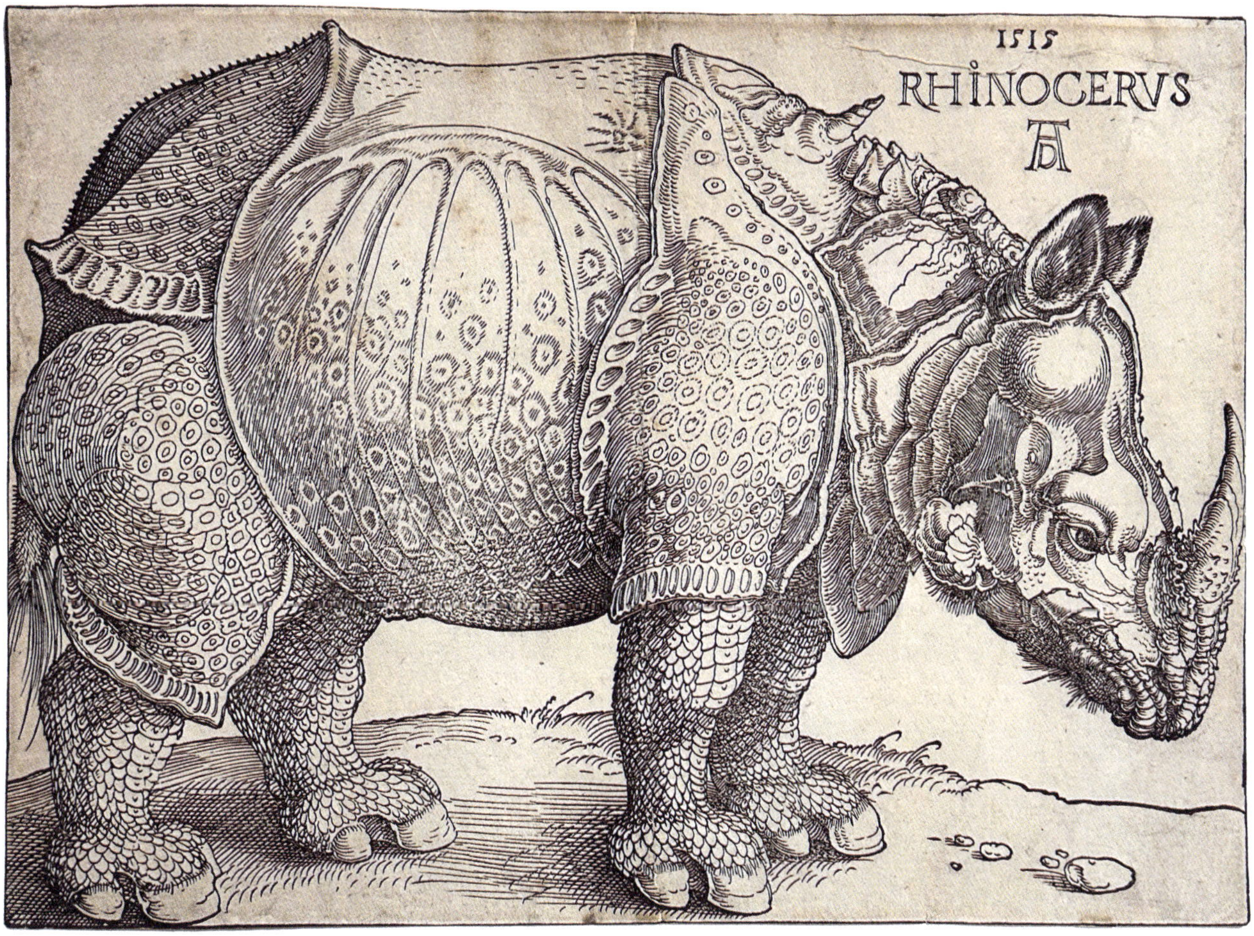

Albrecht Dürer, *The Rhinoceros*, 1515, engraved wood, 21 × 29.4 cm, galerie Martinez D.

WHAT IS BIOMIMICRY?

The practice of drawing inspiration from nature to innovate has its roots in prehistory and continues to evolve today.

During the Renaissance, engineers studied natural forms, convinced that mimicking them could provide technical solutions to the challenges they faced.

Leonardo da Vinci was among the most astute observers of nature. To design his flying machines, he studied the flight of birds and explored the use of canes to lighten the frameworks of his ornithopters.

Today, animal movements – flying, walking, crawling, or swimming – inspire insect-like robots, bird and dragonfly drones, gecko robots, and automated fish.

The need to replicate animals' highly developed senses, as foreseen by Leonardo, is paving the way for mimicking how they perceive their environments.

Sharkskin provides a model for creating revolutionary swimwear materials. Mimicking the honeycombs of a beehive makes it possible to build strong cardboard boxes and helicopter blades.

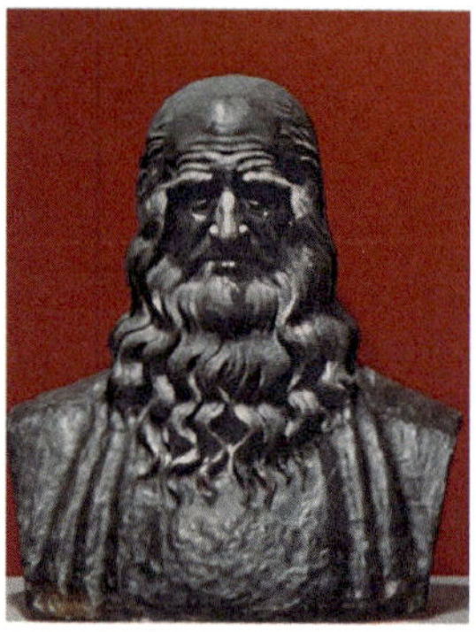

Emilio Quadrelli,
Bust of Leonardo da Vinci,
1919,

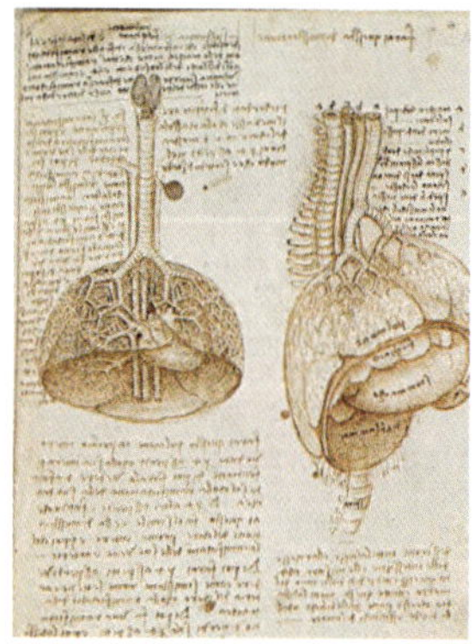

Leonardo da Vinci,
The Lungs
1508

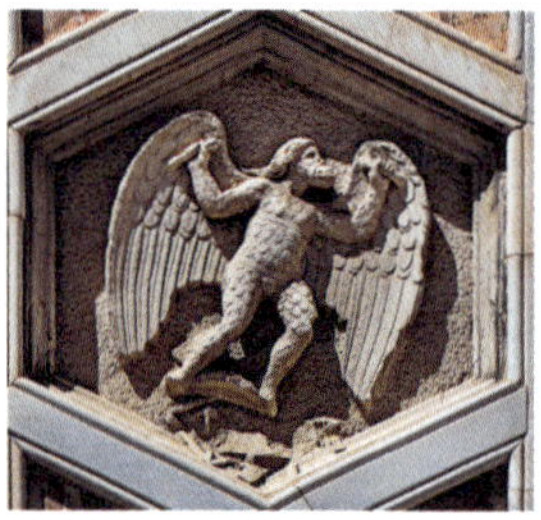

Andrea Pisano,
The Myth of Daedalus and Icarus,
,13th century,

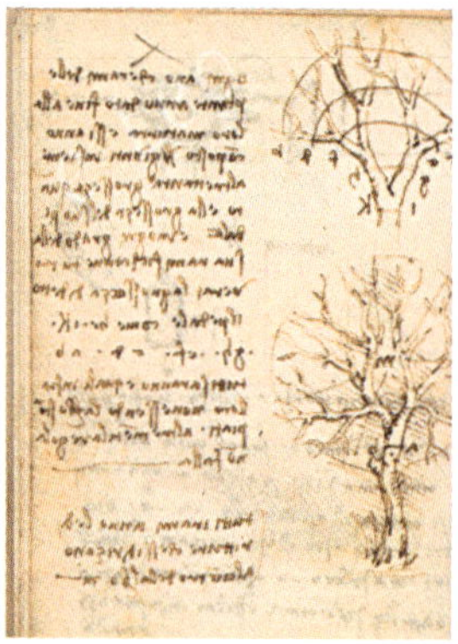

Leonardo da Vinci,
Manuscript M,
c. 1495-1500

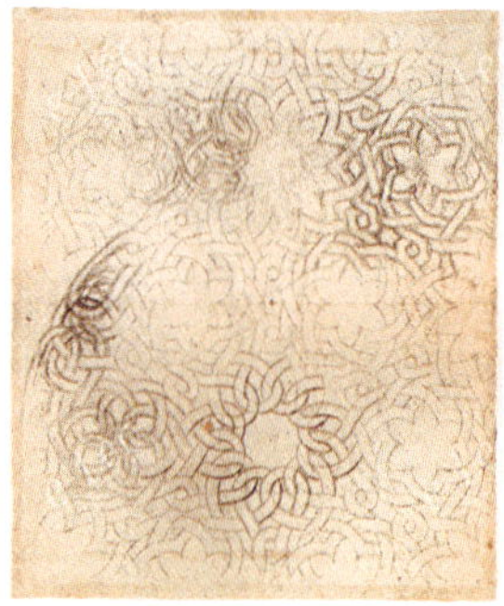

Leonardo da Vinci,
Codex Atlanticus,
1497

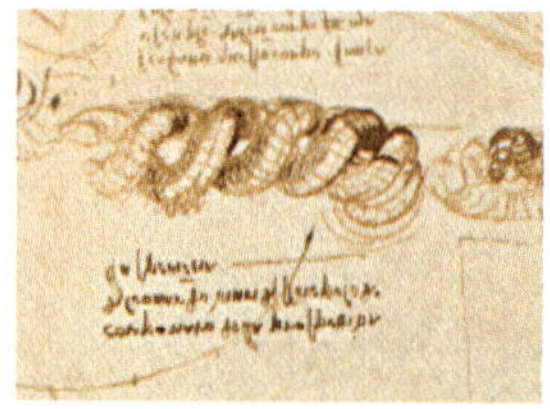

Leonardo da Vinci,
Codex Atlanticus,
1490

Antiquity -3300 - 476

Man's desire to take inspiration from nature and the living world is reflected in the Greek myth of Icarus, who realized his dream of flying like a bird by attaching artificial wings to his body, only to die from hubris after flying too high, his wings burned by the sun.

Renaissance 1400-1600

The mimicking of living organisms was already common among scientists and craftsmen of the Renaissance. Leonardo da Vinci's work in these areas brings to mind a number of modern inventions, from flying machines to the bulbous bows of large ships..

1490-1504

Between about 1490 and 1504, Leonardo da Vinci dreamed of making it possible for humans to fly like birds, insects, or even gliding plant seeds. He observed, sketched and designed several flying machines, including an aerial screw, a parachute, and an ornithopter.
He was inspired by natural forms, such as the spiral of a snake coiling around a stick, and the branched forms of trees, veins, bronchial tubes and rivers.

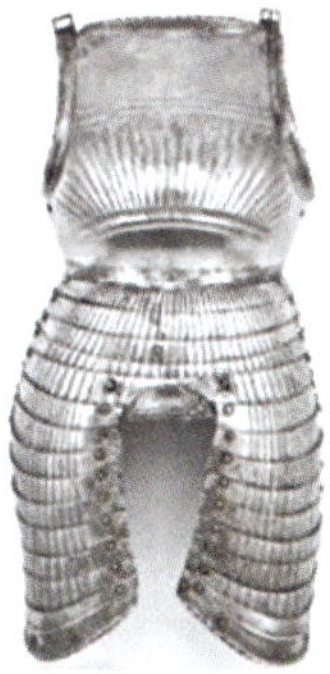

Demi-harnois,
1510–15

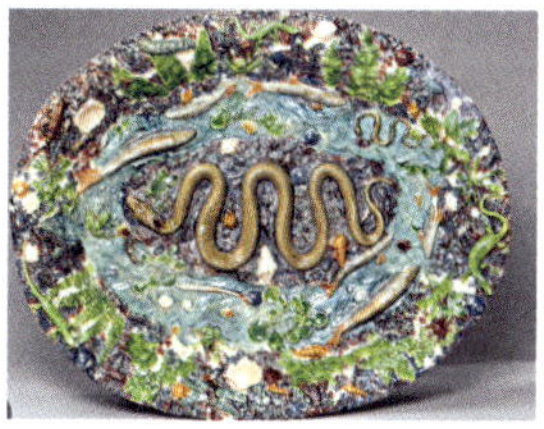

Bernard Palissy,
Rustic platter,
16th century

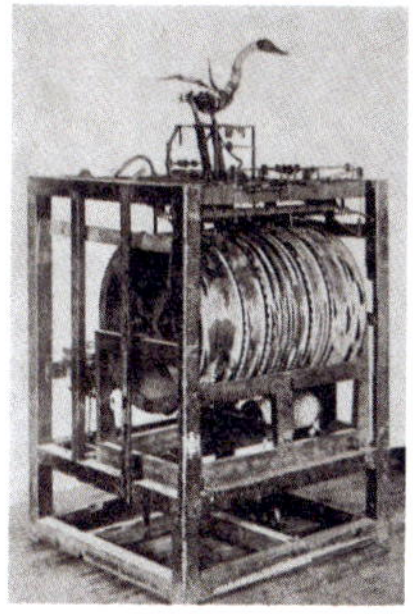

Photo of Vaucanson's mechanical duck mechanism, before 1880

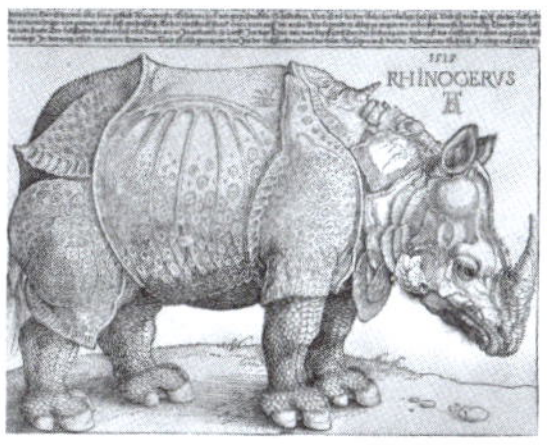

Albrecht Dürer,
The Rhinoceros,
1515

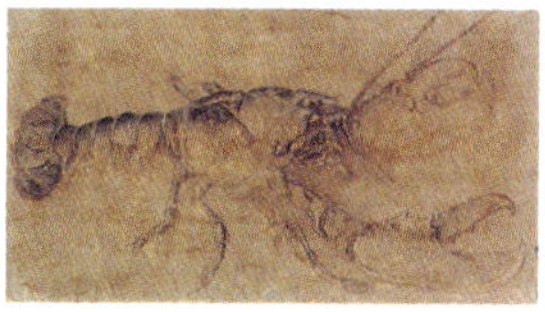

Albrecht Dürer,
The Lobster,
1495

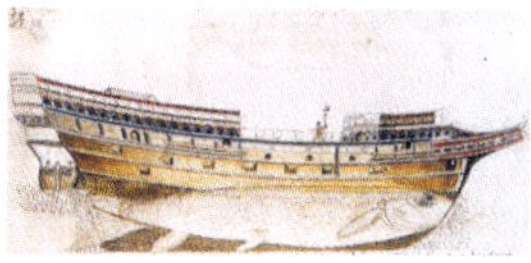

Matthew Baker,
Fragments,
c. 1585

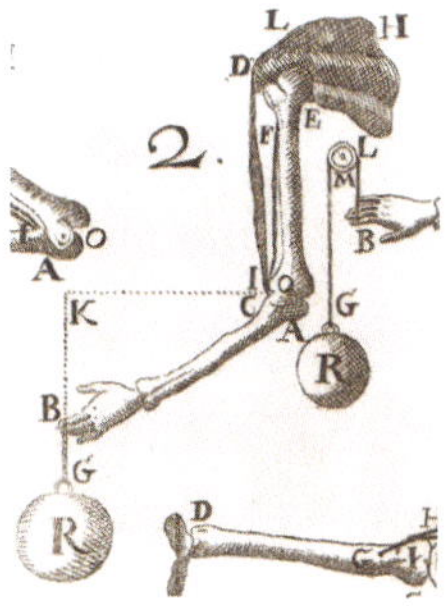

Giovanni Alphonsi Borelli,
De motu animalium,
1680

1520

In 1520, German suits of armour featured fluting inspired by scallop shells or rhinoceros hide. The leg and shoulder protections, made of articulated metal plates, drew inspiration from the shells of crustaceans. This fluting strengthens the breastplates while reducing the metal's thickness.

In the 16th century, artists like Bernard Palissy and Wenzel Jannitzer created moulds of snakes, lizards, crustaceans and fish which they reproduced in ceramic. Palissy's dishes cause a sensation at the table of Catherine de' Medici.

1580

In 1580, English naval engineer Mathew Baker designed a ship's hull shaped like a giant fish to optimise hydrodynamics. His biomimetic approach, drawing on the fluidity and efficiency of a fish's body in water, aimed to reduce hull resistance and increase speed.

Modern Period 1600–1789

1646

In 1646, in a letter addressed to the Marquis of Newcastle, René Descartes compared animals to machines. This concept of the animal-machine was taken up around 1680 by the Italian Giovanni Alfonso Borelli, a pioneer of iatromechanics, a medical approach based on the mechanics of the human body. His work *De motu animalium* (1681) refers to the drawings of Leonardo da Vinci.

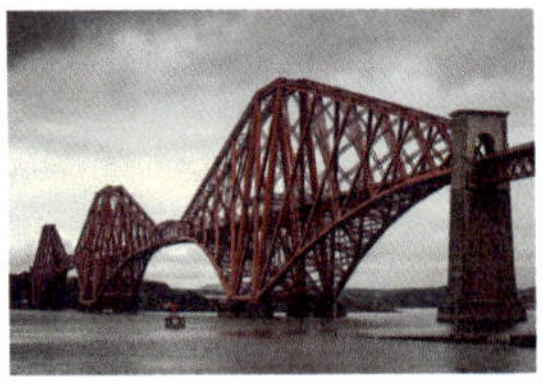

Firth of Fourth Bridge, 1882

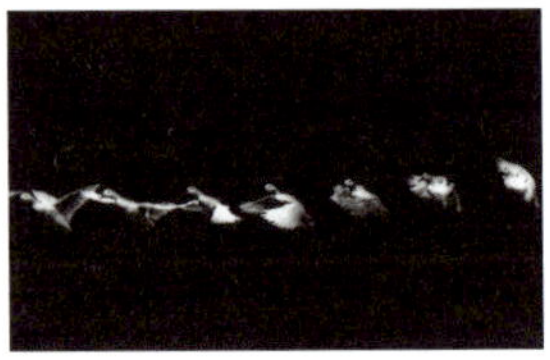

Étienne-Jules Marey,
Bird in flight photographed with 'Marey's rifle'

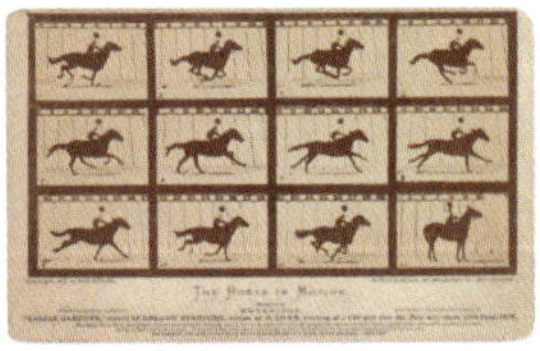

Eadweard Muybridge,
Animal Locomotion,
1887

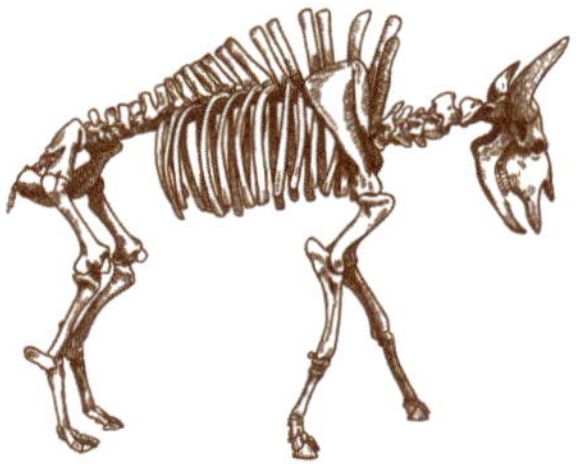

Bison bone structure

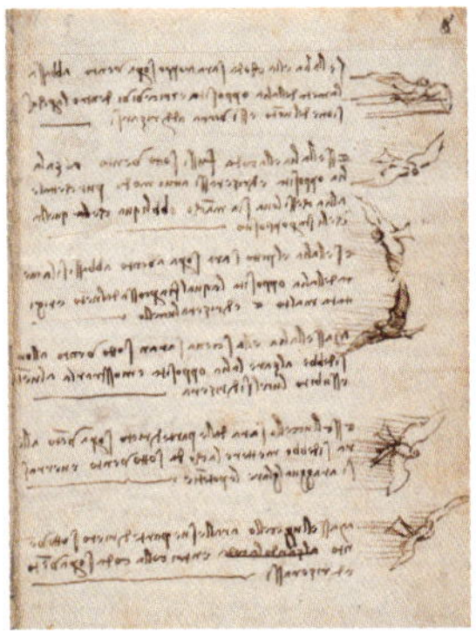

Leonardo da Vinci,
Studies of flying birds,
c. 1505-1506

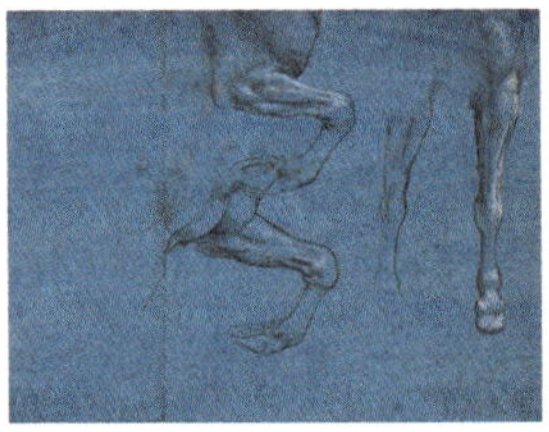

Leonardo da Vinci,
Study of the forelegs of a horse
1490-1492

Contemporary Era 1790-today

De 1808 à 1874

In 1808, George Cayley, a British physicist and engineer, drew inspiration from the flight of birds, particularly the heron, to design his flying machines. By observing the mechanics of flight, he grasped the principles of lift, drag, and propulsion. He was among the first to distinguish the forces of flight and to design a stable, steerable aircraft. He is regarded as the father of aeronautics.

In 1860, German engineer Karl Culmann demonstrated that the isostatic curves of cranes mirror the structure of human bones, which optimally distribute forces to bear loads. This principle was adopted by Gustave Eiffel in the design of his famous tower, which blends strength and lightness.

In 1873, in the same vein, the cantilever bridge drew inspiration from the bone structure of bison. Its design relies on the optimal distribution of forces, inspired by that observed in the spine and limbs of the bison.

In 1874, Étienne-Jules Marey, a physician and author of *La Machine animale (Animal Mechanism)*, studied terrestrial and aerial locomotion using animated photography. He captured sequences of animal movement, notably the pelican's, to analyse the mechanics of flight. His innovative work, based on sequential images, contributed to understanding movement and influenced biomechanics and aeronautics.

1887

In 1887, Eadweard Muybridge, the inventor of the Zoopraxiscope, a machine that animates photographs, published his work *Animal Locomotion*. His breakdown of movement recalls Leonardo da Vinci's lost treatise on human movements.

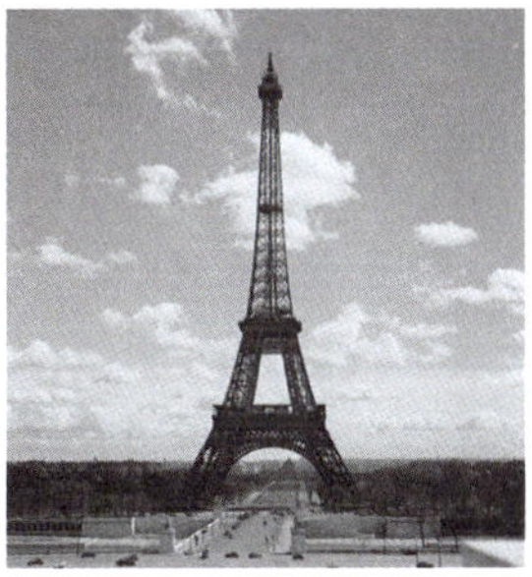

The Eiffel Tower,
1889

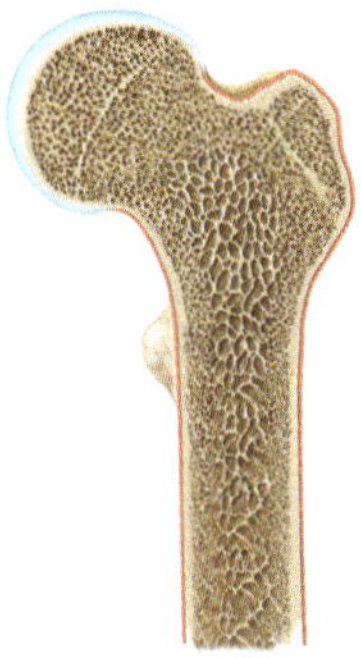

Cross-section of femoral head

1889

In 1889, the Eiffel Tower, built for the 1889 Universal Exposition, mimicked the structure of a human femur.

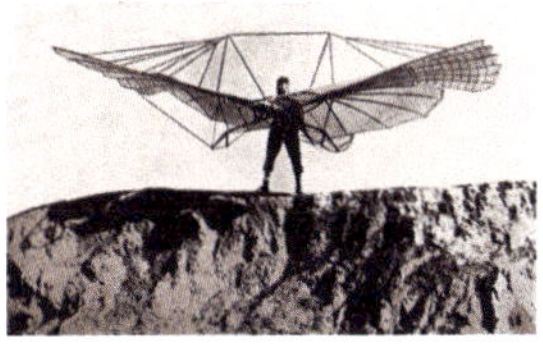

Otto Lilienthal et son planeur,
1894

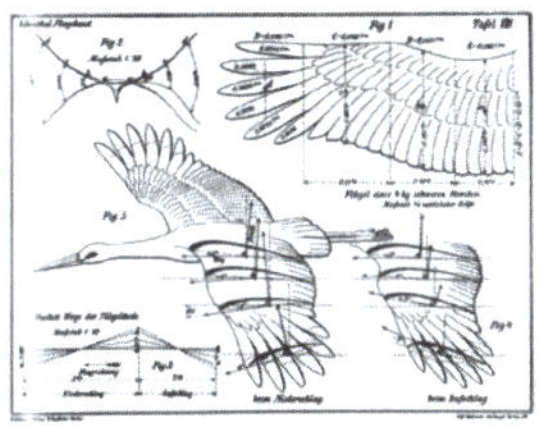

Otto Lilienthal,
flight of a white stork,
1889

In 1889, Otto Lilienthal, the German aviator known as the *flying man*, conducted pioneering research on bird flight, particularly storks, to understand the principles of flight. He studied how they use their wings to control direction and stability in flight.

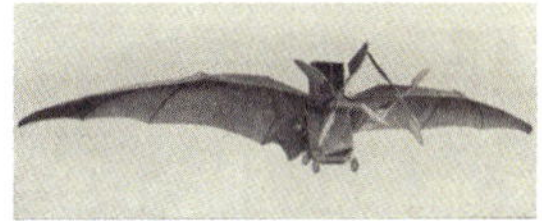

Ader's *Plane*,
1910

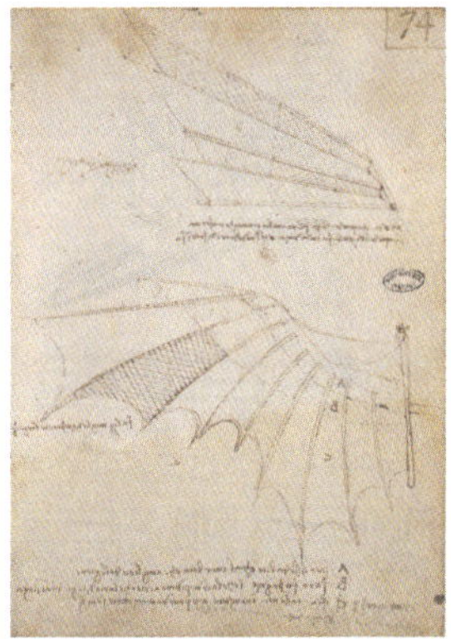

Leonardo da Vinci,
Flying Wing,
c. 1487-1489

1890

In 1890, Clément Ader, a French engineer and inventor, designed a powered flying machine – the *Éole* – inspired by bat wings. This invention used a steam engine to operate its flexible wings, mimicking the natural movement of bats. Although his trials did not achieve controlled flight, Ader played a key role in aviation history in testing the concept of a mechanically propelled aircraft.

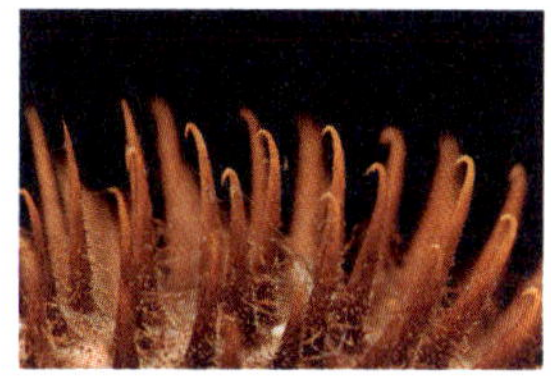

Velcro-inspired burdock dots

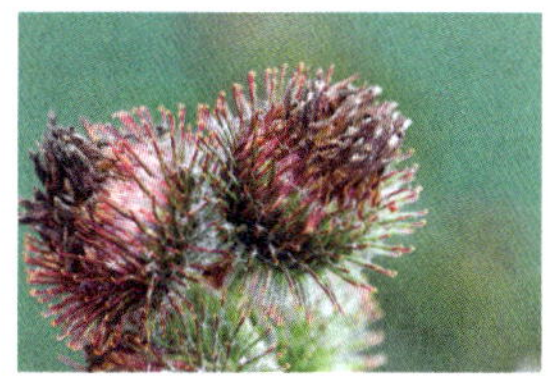

Burdock flower

1952

In 1952, the Swiss engineer George de Mestral patented an innovative fastening system he named Velcro. His invention was inspired during a walk, when he observed that burdock seeds easily attached themselves to his clothing. Fascinated by this natural phenomenon, he decided to replicate this fastening mechanism by creating a fabric with hooks and loops, paving the way for a new closure technology.

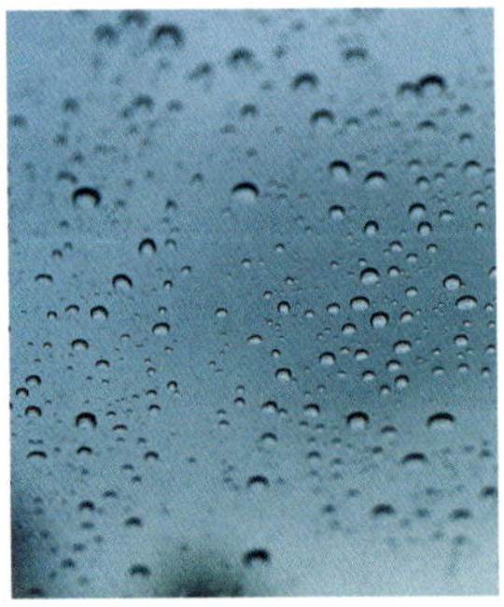

Water drops on hydrophobic glass

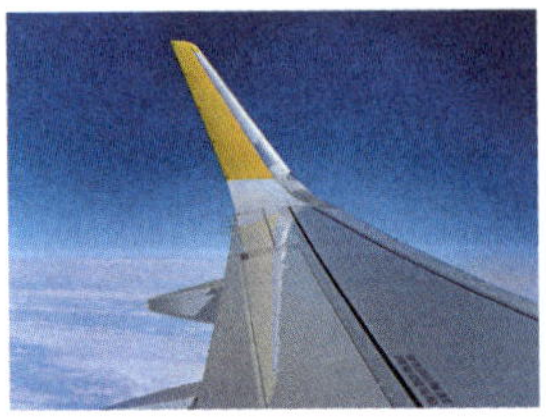

Winglet of an A380 aircraft,, 2017

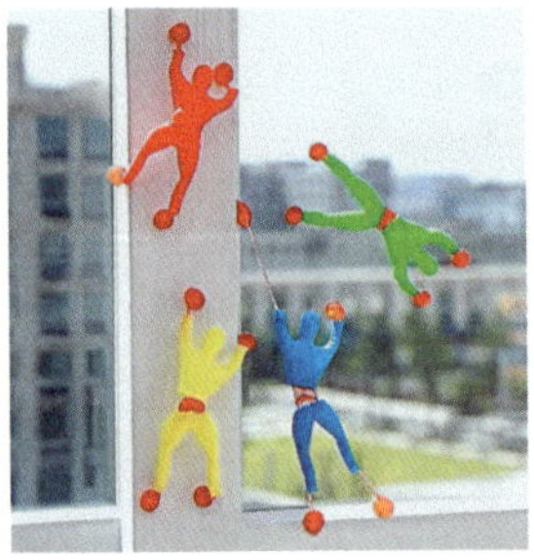

Sticky toy

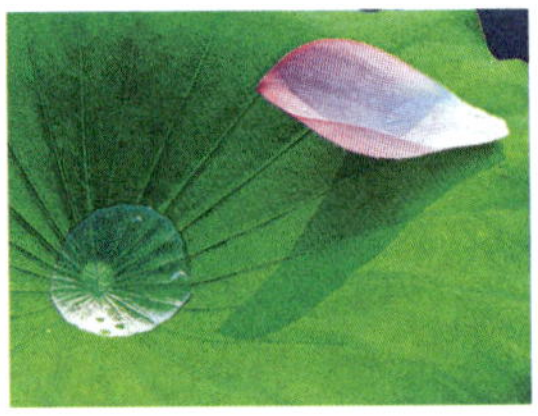

Lotus leaf

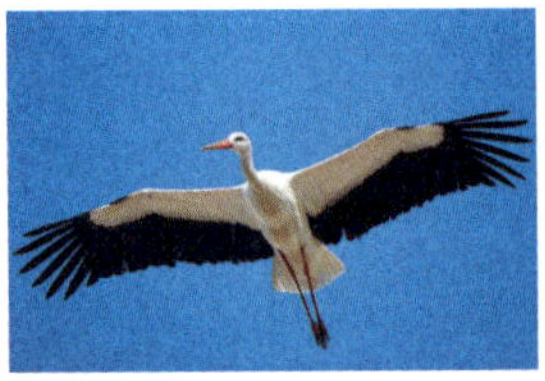

Stork

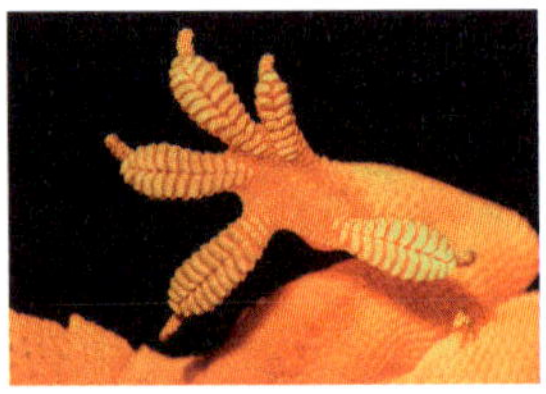

Gecko paw

Contemporary Era 1790-today

1969

In 1969, the term *biomimetics* was coined by biophysicist Otto Schmitt to describe the transfer of biological processes to technology. The concept was popularised in the 1990s by Janine Benyus, an American scientist. She defines biomimicry as "the conscious emulation of life's genius", emphasising that innovation can draw directly on solutions that nature has developed through evolution. In the 20th century, biomimicry encompassed materials, structures, movements and senses.

1977

In the mid-1970s, German engineer Wilhelm Barthlott discovered the self-cleaning properties of lotus leaves. They repel water and impurities thanks to their unique microscopic structure. From this observation, he envisaged coatings and textiles capable of self-cleaning.

In 1977, American engineer Richard Whitcomb, working for NASA, invented winglets, devices placed at the tips of aircraft wings. Inspired by his observation of birds of prey, these winglets enhance aerodynamic efficiency by reducing drag and fuel consumption. This innovation has since been adopted in many aircraft, including those of Airbus.

1984-1997

In 1984, Otto Schmitt published *Biomimetic Designs for the Advancements of Chronobiological Science and Technology*. This work explores biomimetic designs aimed at advancing chronobiological science and technology.

In 1997, Janine Benyus published *Biomimicry: Innovation Inspired by Nature*, which popularised the concept of biomimicry.

2005

In 2005, researchers discovered that the microscopic hairs on gecko's feet enable them to cling to smooth surfaces, such as glass, thanks to the Van der Waals effect. This discovery has paved the way for technological applications, notably residue-free adhesive materials.

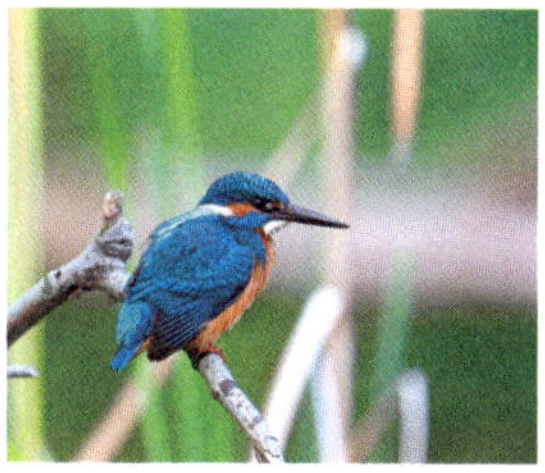

European kingfisher

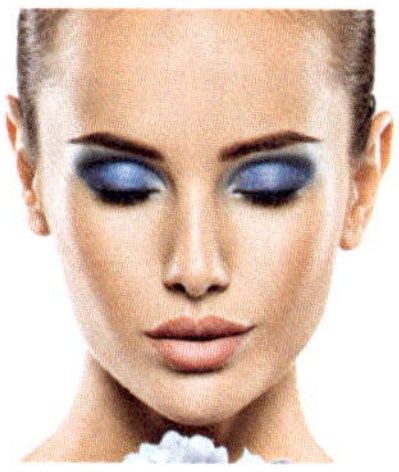

Blue pigment make-up

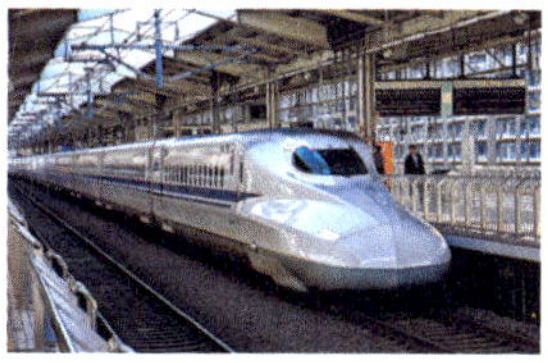

Shinkansen train, 2013

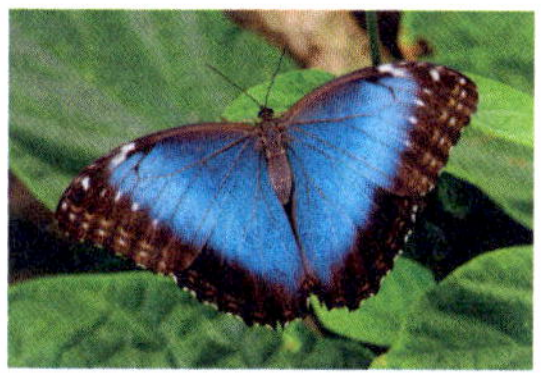

Morpho butterfly

2011

In 2011, the French Association for Standardisation (AFNOR) formalised definitions for *bio-inspiration*, *biomimicry* and *bionics* to clarify their use in scientific and industrial fields. Biomimicry refers to imitating biological processes to create technical innovations, while bio-inspiration involves applying natural principles in design. Bionics, in contrast, focuses on studying biological systems to develop technologies aimed at solving human problems.

2013

In 2013, design of the Japanese Shinkansen train drew inspiration from the kingfisher, a bird known for its ability to dive quickly into water without creating a splash. Engineers studied its streamlined beak to design a more aerodynamic nose cone to reduce air resistance and improve fuel efficiency. This innovative design has enabled the Shinkansen to reduce noise and energy consumption, while increasing speed and comfort.

2015

In 2015, Morpho butterflies became famous for their vibrant blue colour. This hue is not caused by a blue pigment but by the interaction between light rays and the nanostructures covering the tiny scales on their wings. Understanding this phenomenon has inspired innovations in cosmetics. It is now possible to obtain longer-lasting, more environmentally-friendly colours that do not require the use of artificial pigments.

2016

In 2016, foils – underwater wings inspired by whale and dolphin flippers – revolutionised the boating world by enabling various types of craft to sail at extraordinary speeds. By reducing drag and increasing efficiency, foils lift boats above the water's surface, allowing for smoother, faster sailing. Whether used by sailing boats, hydrofoils, catamarans or motorboats, foils have redefined standards of speed and efficiency in the nautical world.

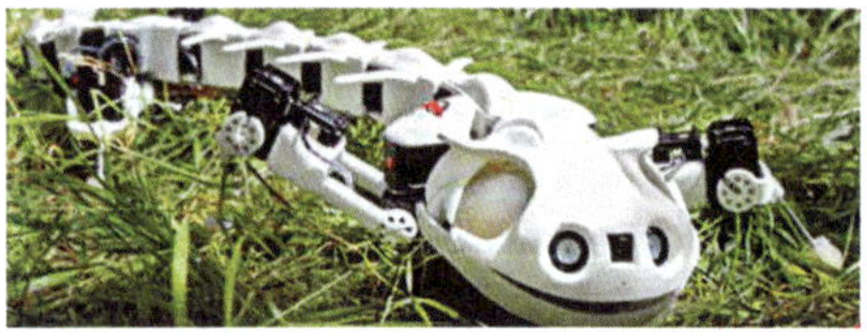

Salamander robot,
2016

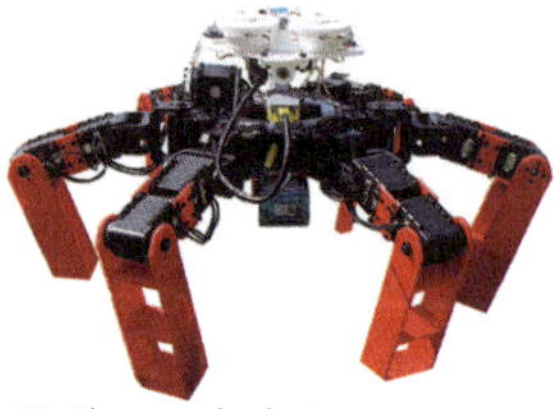

AntBot hexapod robot,
2019

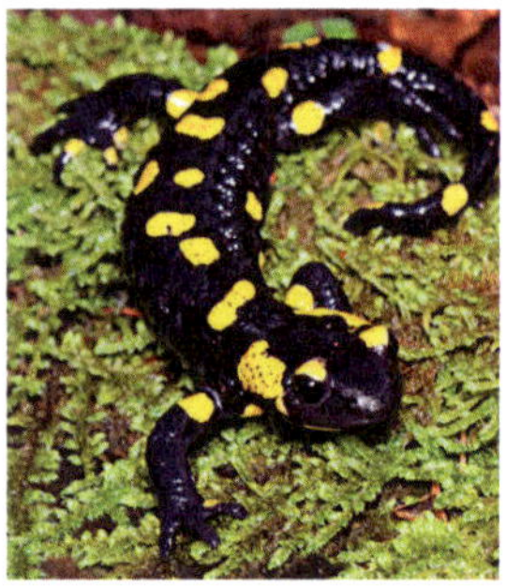

Spotted Salamander

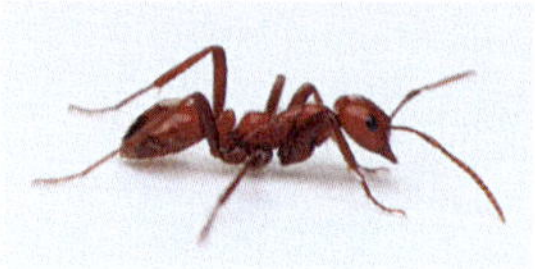

Polyergus lucidus ant

Contemporary Era 1790-today

Researchers at the University of Lausanne, Switzerland, developed a robot inspired by the salamander in order to study spinal-cord function and better understand locomotion in vertebrates. Equipped with multiple motors and sensors, the robot mimics the animal's movements, enabling analysis of how nerve signals are transmitted through the spinal cord during locomotion. This biomimetic project aims to improve treatments for spinal-cord disorders and neurological injuries.

2019

In 2019, Airbus applied the properties of sharkskin, previously used in swimsuit design, to its aircraft. Sharkskin's unique texture, composed of tiny scales called denticles, reduces aerodynamic drag and improves energy efficiency. By integrating this biomimetic technology into its aircrafts' fuselage skin, Airbus reduces fuel consumption and CO_2 emissions while boosting speed and stability.

2020

In 2020, the French National Centre for Scientific Research (CNRS) designed the first legged robot to navigate without GPS. AntBot, inspired by desert *Cataglyphis* ants, is equipped with sensors and a navigation mechanism similar to that used by these ants when returning to their nest after foraging. AntBot can count its steps to orient itself and measure the distance it travels.

Biomimetic polymers – synthetic materials that mimic the structure, properties or behaviours of natural materials found in living organisms – are also attracting researchers' interest, particularly in the field of water purification.

Blue growth represents a major challenge for the future, driving innovations such as unmanned vehicles capable of navigating in water or tackling microplastic pollution. Examples include the manta ray inspired vehicle from the Polytechnic University of Milan presented in section 4 of the exhibition, the octopus robot from the Sant'Anna School of Advanced Studies in Pisa, and the dragonfly larvae inspired designs from the Institute for Research on Insect Biology at the University of Tours.

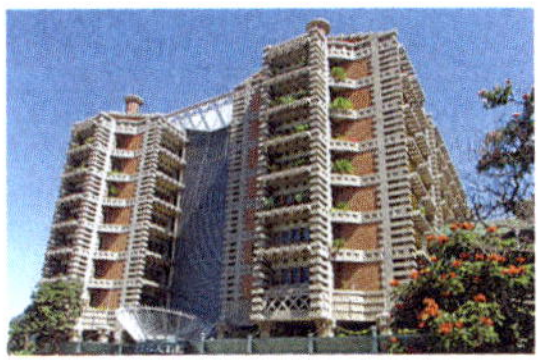

Mike Pearce, Eastgate Center, 1993

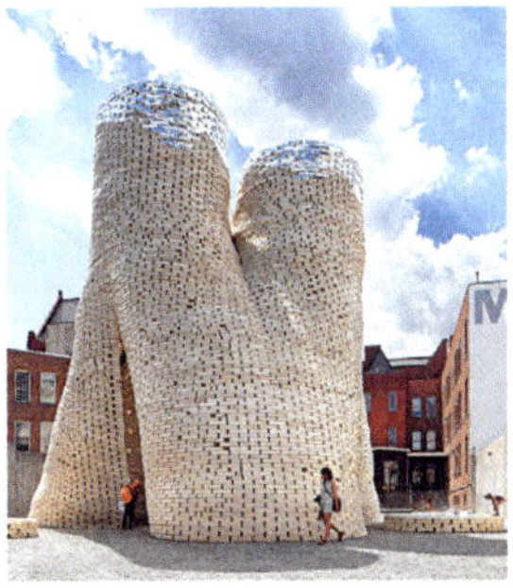

The Living, Tour Hy-Fi, 2014

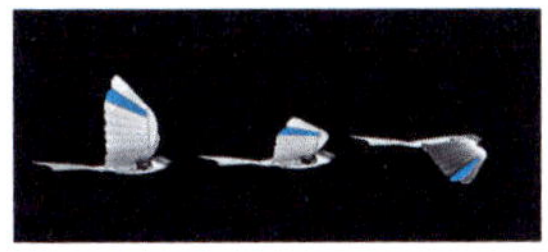

BionicSwifts robots flapping their wings

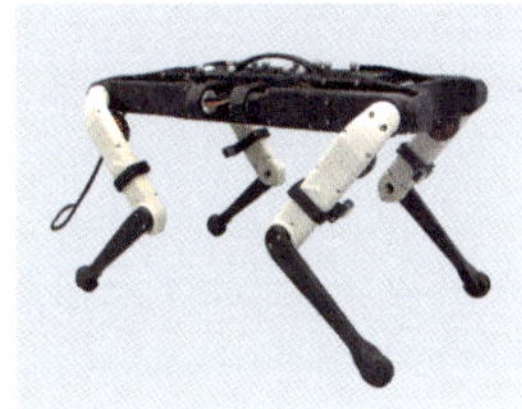

Solo12 quadruped robot, 2020

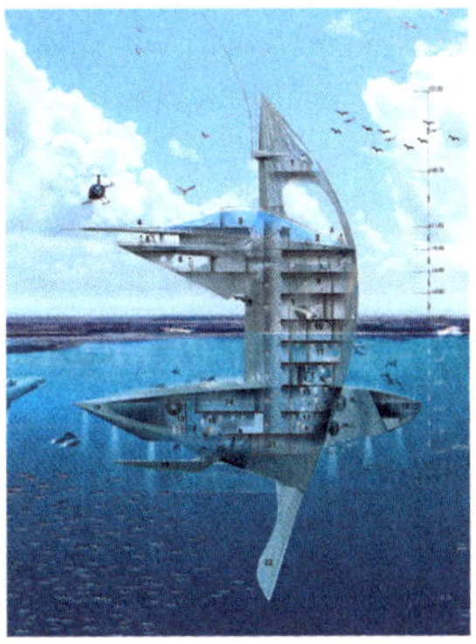

Sectional view of the SeaOrbiter

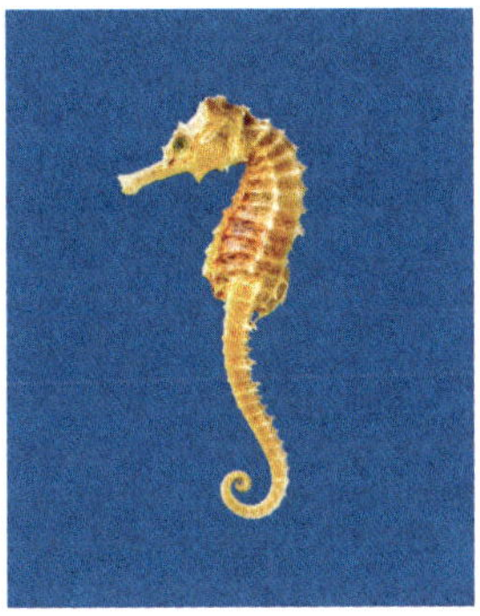

Dried seahorse skeleton

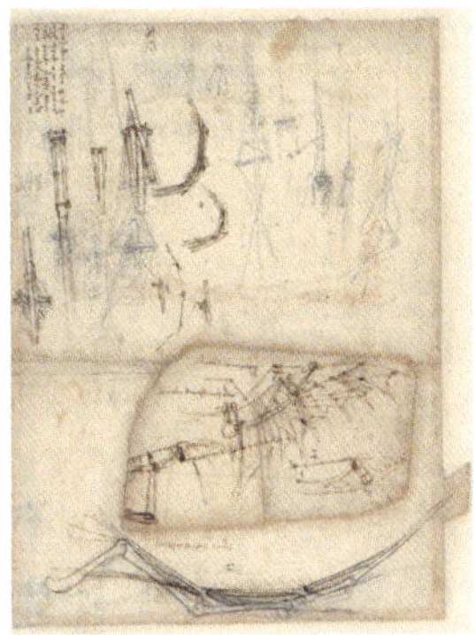

Leonardo da Vinci, *Codex Atlanticus*, 1478-1518

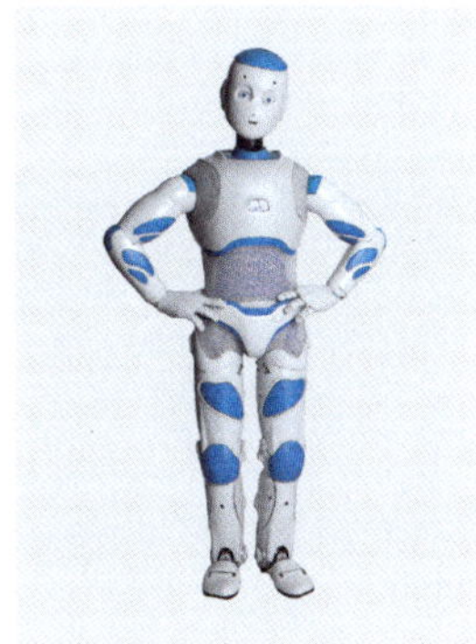

Humanoid robot Romeo, 2016

Bio-inspired architectural projects, which first appeared in the 2010s, are becoming increasingly common. Notable examples include the Eastgate Centre in Zimbabwe, which draws on termite mounds to eliminate the need for air conditioning, the HYfi Tower in New York, constructed from biodegradable bricks made from mushrooms, and the Skolkovo Innovation Centre in Moscow, which emulates the thermoregulation system of emperor penguins. In Singapore, Ali Miserez is developing a project that uses chicken feathers from the food industry to generate energy for buildings while also removing carbon dioxide.

Nanometric structures of certain biological elements, such as those found in butterfly wings and the feathers of peacocks and jays, used to exploit light, offer novel applications in cosmetics and architecture.

Since 2020, Boston Dynamics has continued to innovate in biomimicry. Spot, a quadruped robot inspired by animal locomotion, was deployed by the New York City Police Department for reconnaissance missions in 2023. Stretch, inspired by the flexibility of human arms, is used for autonomous package handling by companies like DHL.

2021

In 2021, Festo, a German company specialising in automation and robotics, launched the BionicSwift, a robotic bird inspired by the swift, improving energy efficiency and performance compared to its predecessor, the SmartBird. Weighing 42 grams, it features ultra-light wings with overlapping segments that mimic bird feathers.

2025

In 2025, biomimicry and artificial intelligence are being used to enhance multiple technologies. For instance, robots inspired by insects and birds, such as those developed by Boston Dynamics, employ AI algorithms to mimic natural behaviours and perform complex tasks, such as autonomous navigation or object manipulation. In medicine, biomimetic AI analyses biological data to develop personalised treatments, emulating the process of human tissue regeneration. Additionally, AI systems are drawing on the neural networks of the brain to improve machine learning and adaptability, making robots more autonomous and efficient.

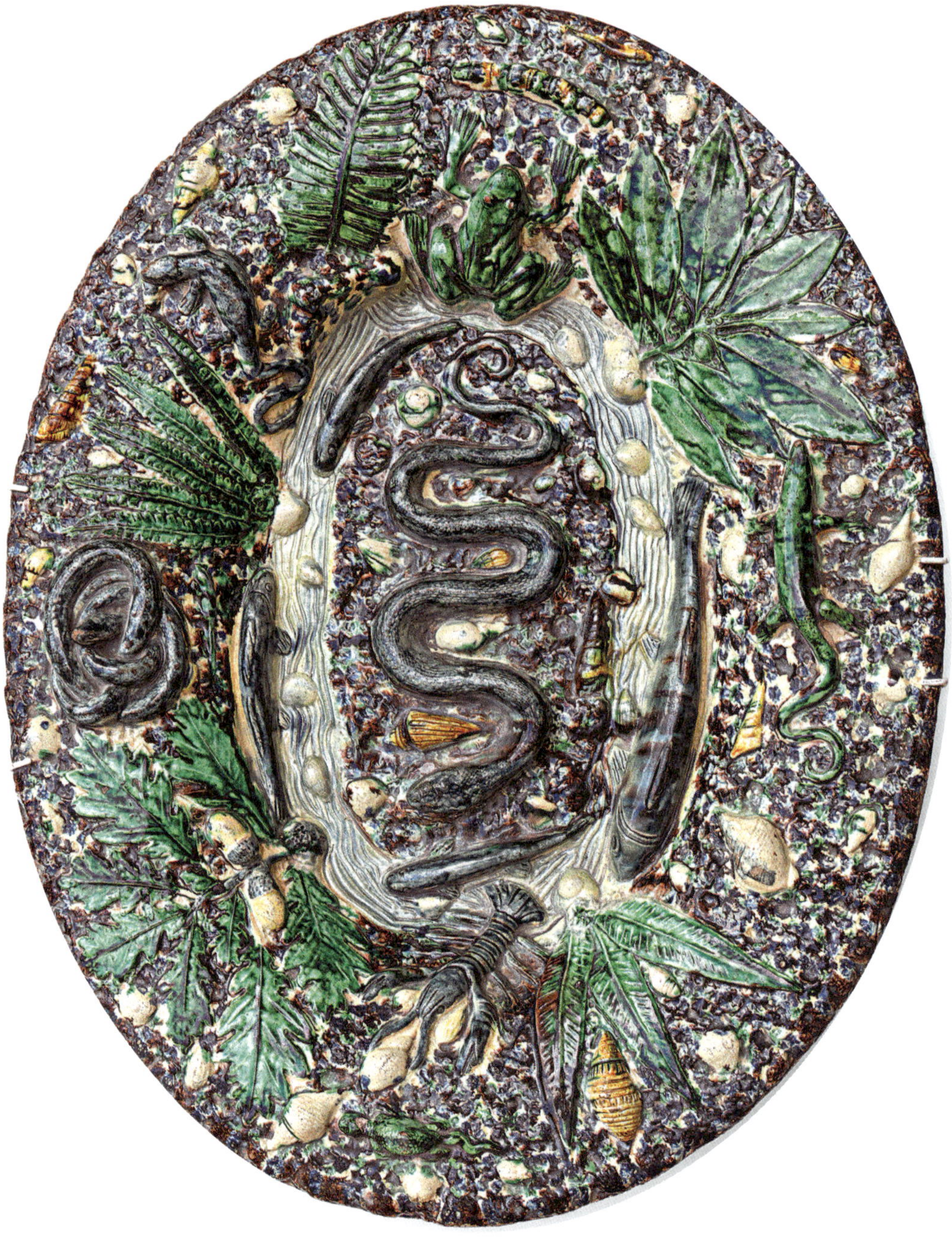

Bernard Palissy, *Rustic platter*,
16th century, ceramic,
château du Clos Lucé

LIST OF LOANED WORKS

Section 1: What is biomimicry?

Emilio Quadrelli
Bust of Leonardo da Vinci
1919
Sculpture in patinated bronze
Amboise, château du Clos Lucé

Albrecht Dürer
Le Rhinocéros
1515
21 × 29.4 cm
Galerie Martinez D.

Breastplate, poacher and tassettes
Italy, circa 1510-1515
Iron, leather, brass
155 × 51.5 × 35 cm
Paris, musée de l'Armée, inv. 611 PO

Flange
Nuremberg, circa 1550-1560
Iron, leather, brass
Paris, musée de l'Armée, inv. 538/2 PO

Bernard Palissy
Rustic platter
16th century
Ceramic
Amboise, château du Clos Lucé

Salamander robot
2016
150 cm
Ecole polytechnique fédérale de Lausanne

AntBot robot
2019
35 × 40 cm
Institut des sciences du mouvement Étienne Jules-Marey, Aix-Marseille Université

Giovanni Alfonso Borelli
De Motu Animalium
1710
Book published by Petrum Vander
Amboise, château du Clos Lucé

Section 2: Human biomechanics, the invention of robotics

Michel Campana, Jean-Louis Pironio
Animated armour
2025
Reproduction based on drawings by Leonardo da Vinci

Jean-Louis Pironio
Internal mechanism of the animated armour
2025
Reproduction based on drawings by Leonardo da Vinci

Romeo robot
2012
1.40m, 37 actuated degrees of freedom
Softbank Robotics, Toulouse, LAAS-CNRS

PoHod15
2018
Institut des sciences du mouvement Étienne Jules-Marey, Aix-Marseille Université, Centre national de la recherche scientifique (CNRS)

Solo 12 quadruped robot
2023
40 cm high, 12 actuated degrees of freedom
Toulouse, LAAS-CNRS

Michel Campana
Lion robot
2014
Reproduction based on the testimonies of the ambassadors who saw it
Poitiers

Jean-Louis Pironio
Mechanism imitating the functioning of the lung
2023
Reproduction based on a drawing by Leonardo da Vinci
36 × 25 × 32 cm
Rombas

Jean-Louis Pironio
Camera Obscura
2023
Reproduction based on a drawing by Leonardo da Vinci
Rombas

Leonardo da Vinci
Diagram of how the eye works
1491
Paris, Institut de France, Manuscript D, f. 10v (facsimile)

Section 3: Plants and insects

The Book of Hours that belonged to Anne de Bretagne
Illustrated by Jean Bourdichon
Tours, 1500
Amboise, château du Clos Lucé, f. 60r (facsimile)

Artes Mechanicae
Flying sphere
2019
Reproduction based on a drawing by Leonardo da Vinci
Wood, rope, canvas
90 × 90 × 90 cm
Italy, Montevarchi

Artes Mechanicae
Aerial screw
2018
Reproduction based on a drawing by Leonardo da Vinci
Wood, rope, canvas and iron
90 × 90 × 75 cm
Italy, Montevarchi

Leonardo da Vinci
Aerial screw
c. 1490-1495
32.5 × 24 cm
Paris, Institut de France, Manuscript B, f. 83v (facsimile)

École polytechnique fédérale de Lausanne, Fraunhofer Institut de Jena, Université de Tübingen, Centre national de la recherche scientifique (CNRS) and, Aix-Marseille Université
CurvACE
2013
Artificial fly eye
Between 1 and 2 cm
Institut des sciences du mouvement Étienne Jules-Marey, Aix-Marseille Université

Artes Mechanicae
Dragonfly
2018
Reproduction based on a drawing by Leonardo da Vinci
Wood, rope, canvas and iron
90 × 90 × 130 cm
Italy, Montevarchi

Leonardo da Vinci
Flying saucer
1490
Paris, Manuscript B, Institut de France, f. 80r (facsimile)

WowWee
Dragonfly drone
2007
Romorantin, musée de Sologne

Naturalized dragonfly
Romorantin, musée de Sologne

François Delaroziere, Cie La Machine
The Giant Spider
1/10 scale model
Steel and limewood

François Delaroziere
Drawing of the Giant Spider
Study drawing
Pencil on paper
42 x 58 cm

Gyroid networks
Tours, Institut de recherche sur la biologie de l'insecte

Microprocessors
Tours, Institut de recherche sur la biologie de l'insecte

Morpho butterfly
Private collection, Pierre Iselin

Section 4: Sea creatures

Leonardo da Vinci
Comparison between the rudder of a ship and the wings of a bird
c. 1517-1519
Paris, Institut de France, Manuscript E, f. 53r (facsimile)

Leonardo da Vinci
Comparison between the rudder of a ship and the wings of a bird
c. 1517-1519
Paris, Institut de France, Manuscript E, f. 52v (facsimile)

Jean-Louis Pironio
Swimming glove
2019
Reproduction based on a drawing by Leonardo da Vinci
Leather
75 × 44 cm
Rombas

IBM
Bulbous bow
Model
48 × 19.5 × 94 cm
Amboise, château du Clos Lucé

Leonardo da Vinci
Bio-inspired hull models
Circa 1510
Paris, Institut de France, Manuscript G, f. 50v (facsimile)

Jacques Rougerie
Monobipalm
1998
100 × 23 × 26 cm
Paris, Fondation Jacques Rougerie

Smit London Rotterdam
Cable ship with bulbous bow
Model
48 × 19.5 × 94 cm
Paris, musée de la Marine

Jacques Rougerie
SeaOrbiter
2000
Model
78 × 50 cm
Paris, Fondation Jacques Rougerie

Jacques Rougerie
La Cité des Mériens
2009
Photographic reproduction
Paris, Fondation Jacques Rougerie

Jacques Rougerie
Pulmo
1974
Photographic reproduction
Paris, Fondation Jacques Rougerie

Jacques Rougerie
Abyssal Explorer
2016
Photographic reproduction
Paris, Fondation Jacques Rougerie

Jacques Rougerie
Aquasolar
2015
Photographic reproduction
Paris, Fondation Jacques Rougerie

Iris Van Herpen
Dress *Idolomantis*
"Roots of Rebirth" collection
Spring-Summer 2021
Amsterdam, Netherlands

Iris Van Herpen
Dress *Frozen Falls*
"Syntopia" collection
Autumn-Winter 2018
Amsterdam, Netherlands

Manta ray
2024
100 × 60 cm
Milan, École polytechnique

Guillaume Rondelet
La premiere [-seconde] partie de l'histoire entière des poissons
1558
Printed book
Tours, Centre d'études supérieures de la renaissance, SR 52A-16

Étienne Rayssac, Maître d'art
Le Condottière
Bust based on a drawing by Leonardo da Vinci, in the British Museum, London
Bronze, black patina on brown background
65 × 60 × 38 cm
Amboise, château du Clos Lucé

Leonardo da Vinci
The fish swim
1499
Paris, Institut de France, Manuscript M, f. 67r (facsimile)

Section 5: Birds and flying machines

Milvus milvus (Linnaeus, 1758)
Paris, Muséum national d'Histoire naturelle, MNHN-ZO-2014-341

Pierre Belon
L'Histoire de la nature des oyseaux
1555
Printed book in Paris
Tours, bibliothèque municipale, Rés. 7509

Leonardo da Vinci
Table of contents of a draft treatise on birds
c. 1503-1507
Paris, Institut de France, Manuscript K, f. 3r (facsimile)

Artes Mechanicae
Ornithoptera
2018
Reproduction based on a drawing by Leonardo da Vinci
600 × 250 × 150 m
Italy, Montevarchi

Nyctalus noctula (Schreber, 1774)
Paris, Muséum national d'Histoire naturelle, MNHN-ZM-MO-1991-1441

Artes Mechanicae
Wing with opercules
2018
Reproduction based on a drawing by Leonardo da Vinci
250 × 120 × 60 cm
Italy, Montevarchi

Quad-morphing drone
2018
40 × 25 × 15 cm
Institut des sciences du mouvement Étienne-Jules Marey, Aix-Marseille Université, with the Centre national de la recherche scientifique (CNRS)

Leonardo da Vinci
Studies on mechanical flight and observations on the movement of water
Circa 1490
Milano, Biblioteca Ambrosiana, *Codex Atlanticus*, f. 846v

François Delaroziere, Cie La Machine
The Heron Château
1/10 scale model
Steel, limewood
2.15 m × 1.8 m

François Delaroziere
Study for a heron's wing
Pencil on paper
50 × 65 cm

Leonardo da Vinci
Codex on the flight of birds
1505
Turin, Biblioteca Reale (facsimile)

Pliny the Elder
Historiae naturalis
1537
Printed book
Amboise, château du Clos Lucé

Janine M. Benyus
Biomimétisme, quand la nature inspire les innovations durables
1997
Book published by Rue de l'échiquier

François Delaroziere
Drawing of The Heron Tree
General study drawing
Pencil on paper
50 × 65 cm

François Delaroziere
Detailed study of the root system of the Heron Tree
Pencil on paper
50 × 65 cm

François Delaroziere
Detailed study of the branches of the Heron Tree
Pencil on paper
50 × 65 cm

François Delaroziere
Magnificent Riflebird (the Male)
Pencil on paper
50 × 65 cm

François Delaroziere
Study for the little owl
Pencil on paper
50 × 65 cm
La Roche-sur-Yon, "Les Animaux de la place"

François Delaroziere
Study of the great horned owl
Pencil on paper
31.3 × 39.2 cm
La Roche-sur-Yon, "Les Animaux de la place"

PHOTO CREDITS AND COPYRIGHTS

© Alessandro Caproni: p. 32, p. 156
© Allan Cash Picture Library/Alamy Banque D'Images: p. 155
© Andrii-Oliinyk: p. 154
© Anna Ostapova/Alamy Stock Photo: p. 118 (right)
© Biblioteca Apostolica Vaticana: p. 47
© Bibliothèque de l'Institut de France: p. 13, p. 18, p. 57, p. 70, p. 72, p. 117, p. 152, p. 155
© Bibliothèque nationale de France: p. 153
© British Library, London, UK, From the British Library archive/Bridgeman Images: p. 54, p. 55
© Château du Clos Lucé/Léonard de Serres: p. 152, p. 153, p. 160
© Christopher Drek: p. 131 (up, left)
© Christoffer Fägerström et Kohichiro Yoshida: p. 129
© Cie La Machine/François Delaroziere/Photo: Emmanuel Bourgeau: p. 144
© Cie La Machine/François Delaroziere/Photo: Jordi Bover: p. 136, pp. 146-147, p. 148
© Cie La Machine/François Delaroziere/Photo: Pauline David: pp. 140-141
© Coffeechcolate: p. 118 (left)
© Créations Jacques Rougerie: p. 82, p. 85, p. 86, p. 89, p. 93, p. 94, p. 159
© David Chapman/Alamy Banque D'Images: p. 155
© De Luan/Alamy Banque D'Images: p. 155
© Deyrolle: p. 120
© Didier Descouens: p. 94 (up, left)
© Didier Zylberyng/Alamy Banque D'Images: p. 17, p. 157
© Dirk Rueter/Alamy Banque D'Images: p. 16, p. 157
© Dominic Robinson/Alamy Banque D'Images: p. 156
© Duncan Usher/Alamy Banque D'Images: p. 156
© École polytechnique de Milan: p. 100, p. 101, p. 102 (up)
© Éric Sander: p. 10
© Felix Grimminger: p. 63, p. 159
© Festo: p. 159
© Floreano Dario, École polytechnique fédérale de Lausanne (EPFL), Laboratory of Intelligent Systems (LIS): p. 122
© François Baelen/Ocean Image Bank: p. 98
© François Delaroziere: p. 139, p. 145
© Galerie Martinez D.: p. 149, p. 153
© GodefroyParis: p. 15
© Granger/Bridgeman Images: p. 154
© Gribkov: p. 128
© Helen Sessions/Alamy Stock Photo: p. 126

ÉDITIONS SKIRA PARIS
14, rue Serpente
75006 Paris
www.skira-arte.com

Publishing manager
Nathalie Prat-Couadau

Project manager
Roxanne Rebours

Editorial managers
Juliette Chambon
Maria Notó Mora

Commercial and Editorial project manager
Irène Rodriguez

Editorial assistant
Marion Duterque (intern)

Graphic design
Luigi Fiore

Layout
Florence Cailly

Translation
Martin Lewis (French)

Copyediting and proofreading
Timothy Stroud

Colour separation
Litho Art

ISBN 978-2-37074-276-6

This book has been printed on FSC-certified paper, and all stages of its manufacture have complied with this certification, which supports the environmentally appropriate, socially beneficial and economically viable management of the world's forests, using materials from well-managed forests, recycled materials and other controlled sources. www.fsc.org

Printed in May 2025 by Graphius, Ghent, Belgium.
Legal deposit June 2025.

FSC www.fsc.org
MIXTE
Papier | Pour une gestion forestière responsable
FSC® C014767